The Culture of Korean Industry

The Culture
of Korean Industry

An Ethnography of Poongsan Corporation

Choong Soon Kim

The University of Arizona Press
Tucson & London

97   96   95   94   93   92   6   5   4   3   2   1

Library of Congress Cataloging-in-Publication Data

Kim, Choong Soon, 1938–
    The culture of Korean industry : an ethnography of Poongsan
Corporation / Choong Soon Kim.
        p.   cm.
    Includes bibliographical references and index.
    ISBN 0-8165-1309-0 (cloth : alk. paper)
    1. P'ungsan Kŭmsok Kongŏp Chusik Hoesa (Korea)   2. Metal trade—
Korea (South)—Case studies.   3. Business anthropology—Korea
(South)—Case studies.   4. Industrial management—Korea (South)—
Case studies.   5. Economic development—Religious aspects—
Confucianism—Case studies.   6. Capitalism—Korea (South)—
Religious aspects—Confucianism.   7. Korea (South)—Economic
conditions.   8. Korea (South)—Social conditions.   I. Title.
HD9506.K64P865   1992
338.4'7671'095195—dc20   92-4859
                                                            CIP

British Library Cataloguing-in-Publication Data
A catalogue record for this book is available from the British Library.

For Hak-rok, with gratitude

Contents

List of Illustrations   ix
List of Tables   xi
Preface   xiii

Introduction   3
1. The Founder of Poongsan and His Managerial Worldview   30
2. The Characteristics of Poongsan Employees   67
3. Reward, Compensation, and Promotion   99
4. Career Planning   117
5. Social Interaction Among Employees   148
6. Labor Relations   171
7. The Culture of Korean Industry   199
   Epilogue   218

References   223
Index   239

Illustrations

Korea and neighboring countries   9

Figure 1.1   An overview of the village of Hahoe   33

Figure 1.2   Yŏngmokak, Ryu Sŏae memorial   34

Figure 1.3   Inside the Poongsan plant   40

Figure 1.4   Poongsan chairman with workers
and anthropologist   46

Figure 1.5   The locations of Poongsan's four plants   47

Figure 1.6   Organizational chart of Poongsan   48

Figure 2.1   Connection-hiring patterns   94

Figure 4.1   An overview of the Pyŏngsan Sŏwŏn   124

Figure 4.2   Mandaeru pavilion   128

Figure 4.3   Poongsan chairman at his ancestor's shrine   129

Figure 6.1   The structure of the Bupyung
union local chapter   182

Figure 6.2   Damage to a managerial office at the
Angang plant   187

Figure 6.3   Mass rally of the Angang plant strikers   188

Tables

Table 1.1   Volume of sales by Poongsan, 1970–1988   49

Table 1.2   Affiliated companies among Korean *chaebŏl* groups, 1984   53

Table 2.1   Education attained by workers   73

Table 2.2   Korean labor statistics, 1968–1987   84

Table 2.3   Poongsan employees hired through *kongch'ae*, 1976–1988   90

Table 2.4   Employment at the Bupyung plant   93

Table 2.5   Employment of Bupyung plant employees by length of service   95

Table 2.6   Employment of university graduates, 1976–1988   97

Table 3.1   Wage increase of Poongsan employees, 1987–1991   100

Table 3.2   Wage structure of Bupyung plant employees, 1988   102

Table 3.3   Wages at Bupyung plant, 1988   104

Table 3.4   Starting wage by level of education, 1988   106

Table 3.5   Starting wage by job title, 1988   107

Table 3.6   Wages of male and female workers by education,
            1988   108
Table 5.1   Informal organizations of
            Bupyung plant employees   159
Table 5.2   Associations of Bupyung plant employees   166
Table 6.1   Characteristics of key union organizers
            of strikes   190

Preface

My interest in studying industry and industrial workers predates my involvement in the field of business and industrial anthropology. In the early 1960s, as a graduate student of law under the direction of Hahm Pyong Choon, I studied labor law and trade unions in the Korean cigarette and tobacco industry (Hahm, Yang, and Kim 1964). This was before Korean industrialization took its great stride forward, and the Korean economic miracle had not yet impinged on Western public consciousness.

A decade later in 1974, without knowing much about Korea's economic progress or its rapid industrialization, I was conducting a socioeconomic and demographic study of an American Indian tribe in east-central Mississippi, hoping to attract the attention of industrialists to harness the Choctaw labor force (Spencer, Peterson, and Kim 1975). Professor-turned-diplomat Hahm Pyong Choon, then the Korean ambassador to the United States, phoned me at my office at the Choctaw tribal government headquarters to induce me to become involved in an anthropological project on Korean industrialization and industrial relations.

Despite the ambassador's hard sales pitch, however, I was unable to become obsessed with Korean industrialization to the extent that he had. I had been away from Korea while Korean industrialization was taking its great leap forward. I was not well informed. In the meantime, my Choctaw project evolved into another project, and I dwelt on it. In so doing, I confined myself to the United States for seven more years.

I was still unable to comprehend Korean progress until I witnessed the scene myself in 1981, when I returned to Korea for the first time since leaving for graduate school in 1965. Experiencing so suddenly the results of years of economic development and industrialization, I felt a case of "future shock." The entire country seemed to vibrate with economic progress. When I had left Korea, its per capita GNP was only 105 U.S. dollars: in 1991 it was slightly over 5,500 U.S. dollars.

Korean economic growth and industrialization may mean many different things to different Koreans. To most Koreans of my generation and older, who had experienced a marginal living under Japanese colonial rule (1910–45) and during the devastating Korean War (1950–53), it has special meanings—a sense of pride, self-fulfillment, and great relief. In fact, I remember that near the end of World War II, as the colonial subjects of Japanese rule, most Korean school children were unable to wear decent shoes because materials for shoes had been confiscated by the Japanese for war supplies. Ironically, in 1986, Korea was the world's largest exporter of shoes (1.1 billion U.S. dollars) and leather wear (69 million U.S. dollars). During the Korean War, most Koreans were unable to eat three meals a day. Even a bowl of rice could hardly be found. By October 1988, however, nearly 2 million tons of surplus rice bought from farmers were stored in government warehouses, and in 1989, the government bought an additional 2.4 million tons of rice, which exceeded the storage capacity by over 800,000 tons.

Korea's economic accomplishment since the Korean War is indeed astonishing. From 1953, when the Korean War ended, to 1987, when this project started, the GNP increased to 84 times the 1953 level, and per capita GNP grew to 42 times the 1953 level; the volume of trade expanded to 200 times its earlier size, and the total government budget swelled to 1,672 times the 1953 budget. The total number of business and industrial firms jumped from 3,600 employing 240,000 workers in 1953 to 110,000 hiring 4.79 million workers (*Dong-A Ilbo*, 25 June 1988:6).

In 1987, when I saw a Korean-made Hyundai Excel parked in our university parking lot, I dashed to it and touched the exterior of the car. It was an emotional moment for me to see that a Korean-made automobile had come to a small, remote town in Tennessee. Perhaps the younger generation of Koreans, who have not had the firsthand experience of poverty, starvation, and massive destruction caused by war, may find it difficult to sense the sentiment of an older Korean. Not only I but also many other scholars at home (in Korea) and abroad have been interested to know what has inspired Korea's impressive record of growth and development.

To answer this question, in the late 1970s a group of American and Korean scholars began publishing their findings on Korea's formidable economic success. They employed many adjectives and metaphors to lionize the outstanding Korean performance, such as "a new Japan," "Asia's next giant," and "a miracle," to name just a few. Among these studies, the most notable ones are the work under the joint program of the Korean Development Institute (KDI) and the Harvard Institute for International Development (Jones and Sakong 1980; Kim and Roemer 1979; Krueger 1979; Mason et al. 1980) and the work of World Bank scholars (Hasan 1976; Hasan and Rao 1979; Wade and Kim 1978; Westphal 1978). The list is growing yearly and is now getting crowded.

Most existing literature has focused on highly aggregated and abstracted economic analysis—capital accumulation, government policy, international trade flows. The story of a concrete nexus of social relations in a particular industrial setting that allows Korean industry to function is yet untold. As Hamilton and Orru (1989) have warned us, aggregate economic data on and descriptions of many firms are often misleading and uninterpretable. An overzealous effort to generalize Korean industrial success toward model building or theory making that can be applicable to other late industrializing societies might override local realities. Some social scientists have begun to question the merit of constructing theories designed to have universal applicability (Baker 1981; Booth 1984; Keyes 1983).

Also, the existing literature tends to treat Korean economic progress as if it were ahistorical. In witnessing the manifest growth in the 1960s and after, most literature on Korean economic progress and industrialization tends to focus on that period. Without any doubt, the most remarkable progress did take place after the 1960s. However, historians can tell us that the national movement for Korean economic development, as well as nascent capitalism, began in the late nineteenth century (Eckert 1991, 1990:117; Eckert et al. 1990: 388). The movement to raise the general level of national consciousness, education, and economic development was inaugurated in the early 1920s, under the colonial rule, by nationalists, particularly by the "cultural nationalists," to borrow Robinson's label (Robinson 1988; Eckert et al. 1990:254–326). In those years, entrepreneurs and manufacturers were viewed as patriots. Such a perception still lingers in the minds of many Koreans.

The recent Korean economic take-off appears to be deeply indebted to unique Korean historical experiences. It is doubtful that any typology or model of Korean industrialization, whatever it might be, can be applicable to other late industrializing countries without considering the unique historical events in Korean history. In his classic work on Japanese industry, Cole (1971:11) remains equally incredulous about the possible application of Japanese experiences to developing countries, because "the historical period during which Japan industrialized had unique characteristics which can never be repeated for the benefit of presently industrializing countries." Furthermore, in an effort to uphold scientific inquiries, the existing scholarship tends to overlook the feelings of the people—entrepreneurs, workers, managers, and government technocrats—who actually carried out the endeavor. Perhaps foreign scholars, as outsiders, might be unable to grasp the genuine feelings of natives toward their economic accomplishment in terms of their own native categories. Often, the literature, especially the work of foreign scholars in English-language editions, romanticizes too much about Korean achievement to be real. Native scholars often make an extra effort not to relate the inner feelings of the natives who contributed to the process to avoid subjective biases because of their being natives. As a result, final reports deal with statistics and policies, not with people.

Whatever the final scholarly analysis might have been, in a national survey conducted on 23 September 1987 by *Joongang Ilbo* (cited in von Glinow and Chung 1989:34), Koreans rated the top five factors that contributed to Korea's economic success as having been made by the efforts of people, not policy. Among them were the cooperation of all the Korean people (46.8 percent), hardworking wage earners (18.5 percent), the leadership of the president of Korea (11.4 percent), the efforts of businessmen (7.7 percent), and the efforts of government officers (5.4 percent). In this regard, Lewis (1966:270) is perceptive and correct when he says that "the government can persuade, threaten, or induce; but in the last analysis it is the people who achieve."

Hence, free from the existing theoretical models, being less concerned with statistics, I attempt to write this book about the people who are managing and working in a Korean metal manufacturing industry and their rules of industrial relations. This book delineates a holistic picture of Korea's largest nonsteel metal manufacturer, Poongsan Corporation. Anthropologists prefer to use pseudonyms in their publications for the names and places they studied. In this particular study, however, it is futile to do so, given the size and public visibility of the corporation being studied. Nevertheless, except for the chairman, those whose accounts are included in this book are not identified by their actual names.

I attribute the strength of my identity to my being an insider as well as an outsider who has lived in the West for the last twenty-seven years. Thus far, Western scholars have tended to emphasize the positive aspects of traditional values and practices for Korean industrialization, while their native counterparts have stressed the positive aspects of the Western rational model. Hence, those works have a value comparable to the sound, as Zen philosophers say, of one hand clapping. Utilizing my bicultural experiences of living in both the Korean and American cultures, I hope to provide the "other hand" so vital to producing a distinct sound.

In undertaking this project, I am indebted to many people and organizations. Without the earlier inducement of Ambassador Hahm Pyong Choon, I would not have returned to Korea to study Korean industry and industrialization. Without the assistance of Wilfrid C. Bailey, I would not have had an opportunity to study pulpwood industrial workers in the American South (Kim 1972, 1977; Kim and Bailey 1971). This experience enhanced my ability to gain a comparative perspective.

I would also like to express my appreciation to Francis L. K. Hsu, Roger L. Janelli, Thomas P. Rohlen, and Hendrick Serrie for encouraging me to undertake this project. Carter J. Eckert helped me in identifying some references. My gratitude extends to my colleagues in

Korea, Lee Kwang-kyu, Kim Taik-kyu, Frederick F. Carriere, and Cho Haejoang, for their hospitality and assistance.

I gratefully acknowledge the support provided by grants from the 1988–89 Fulbright Program, the Wenner-Gren Foundation for Anthropological Research, the Institute for Far Eastern Studies of Kyungnam University, the Committee on Korean Studies of the Association for Asian Studies, and the University of Tennessee at Martin.

My greatest debt of gratitude is owed to the people of Poongsan Corporation, including Ryu Chan-u, Ryu Min-ha, Ryu Han-ik, Kim Won-chul, Kim Yong-whan, Woo Sung-ha, Ryu Mun-han, Lee Chul-sun, and many middle managers as well as rank-and-file workers. Without their understanding, cooperation, and patience, this study would have been very difficult, if not impossible. In contributing their valuable time they have been not only tolerant but friendly. By answering my insipid questions, they steered me on the right path, which eventually led to this finished product. I am particularly grateful to those rank-and-file workers who invited me to their homes and even offered me meals. The unconditional trust they exhibited made my difficult job of inquisition simpler.

Whatever the weaknesses of this book, rest assured they would have been far greater without Roger T. Fisher, Larry C. Ingram, Judy L. Maynard, and Clayburn Peeples, who took their time to read the early version of the manuscript and offered many invaluable suggestions. Maynard also assisted me in the tedious computer work needed to analyze the survey data. I owe many thanks to Phyllis A. Keller, who typed all the tables and reproduced many draft versions of the manuscript.

The University of Arizona Press was essential in its enthusiastic support, expeditious evaluation, and meticulous editing. My appreciation extends to the anonymous readers consulted by the press for their constructive criticisms that have improved this book. The theme of this book has been refined with the comments and suggestions made by the participants at various meetings: the Department of Anthropology, University of Southern California, 23 March 1988; the International Conference on the Dynamics of U.S.–South Korea Trade Relations at Yale University, 10–12 November 1988; the annual meeting of the Association of Korean Cultural Anthropology, April 1989; the 11th Kyungpook National University International Seminar, 25–27 May 1989, Taegu, Korea; and the Conference on

Developing Business Relationships with Korea at The Carter Presidential Center of Emory University, Atlanta, Georgia, 25 May 1990.

I owe special gratitude to my wife, Sang Boon, who as usual had to carry a heavy burden while I was away from home for fieldwork and then again while I was writing this book. My two sons, John and Drew, filled the roughest spots in reading the first draft of this manuscript and provided many valuable comments and suggestions.

My deepest debt of gratitude is owed to the many unnamed Poongsan workers whose accounts are included in this book. For their hospitality and cooperation, without which this book could not have been written, I am forever grateful.

CSK
Scenic Hills, Tennessee

The Culture of Korean Industry

Introduction

During the preliminary fieldwork, I had succeeded in obtaining permission to do my fieldwork at Poongsan, had witnessed scenes of hardworking Koreans, and had collected much interesting information. Nevertheless, I was deeply distressed by the fact that I was unable to grasp the inner motivation for the drive and dedication of today's Koreans. I was even fearful about the final outcome of my study, that I might fail to understand the native category of motivational force beneath the surface. If I were merely going to present aggregate statistics on Korean economy and industrialization by arranging and rearranging existing statistics, my book would not contain any new information. I told my colleagues in Seoul that I might not publish anything out of this study, and I even thought seriously about abandoning the project. A casual conversation with a Seoul taxi driver, however, kept me from doing so.

Late one drizzly afternoon, on 26 August 1987, I stood politely in line (I assumed it was a line) to catch a cab. Suddenly I discovered that the line formed on the right rather than from the rear. As a timid soul living in a small, rural town in Tennessee for more than two decades, I was pushed aside several times even by women. Finally, in desperation I mustered my courage in order to keep my appointment with the chairman of Poongsan, pushed forward, and was able to hail a taxi. The driver instinctively knew that I was not a Seoulite because of my inability to compete with the others, including ladies. He told me this:

> To survive in Korea, you have to hustle all the time. If you don't push ahead, you do not remain the same, but you are pushed behind. You have to compete well. . . . If any elderly person stood in the place where you were, I don't believe the person could ever catch a cab. Respect for elders, coming from the Confucian custom, is not as strong as it used to be. . . . All these mad scrambles and the "squirrel race" [same nuance as "rat race" in English usage] are Koreans' efforts to release the *han* caused by the chronic poverty for generations and the indignities suffered under Japanese colonial rule.

Han, a Korean euphemism, is an abbreviation of *han't'an,* meaning "deploring," "catalytic bitterness and anger" (Eckert et al. 1990:408), or "unrequited resentments" (Kendall 1985:202). Y. Kim (1981) attempts to characterize Koreans by examining the usages of the term *han* in historical, social, religious, and literary documents.

Western visitors to Korea, if they have carried on casual conversations with taxi drivers in Seoul in the Korean language, can understand such comments. Seoul cabdrivers are free-lance philosophers, sociologists, and frequent political critics. Often they are militant in their tone, especially when they know their passengers do not live in Korea and are not associated with government agencies. They are excellent sources of information and news, since they daily have to face more than twelve hours, often sixteen, of driving through congested and sometimes narrow streets, carrying all kinds of people, listening to all sorts of conversations.

The driver's comment shed a new light on my fieldwork. I became aware of the importance of the native categories of perception about Korean progress. His comment touched on three key propositions of my research and spurred me to trace their sources. First, an overemphasis on the function of "harmony" (*inhwa* in Korean), which originated from Confucian thought (Hofstede and Bond 1988:8; Tu 1976:xi), cannot hide the presence of severe competitions prevailing in contemporary Korean society, including rules for industrial relations. Despite the stress on harmony, there are competitions between enterprises, between departments within an enterprise, and between individuals within a given department. A perceptive observation by native Japanese scholar Sumiya regards outsiders' misconceived notion of harmony versus competitiveness, which is equally applicable to Koreans. Sumiya (1991:142) says,

> Often Japan is perceived as a society that denies competitive relationships and instead honors "harmony." Japanese society is actually quite competitive, however. One can easily see the competition in the examinations for admission to the universities. High school students put all their efforts into studying for the college entrance examinations. The expression "examination hell" is well known. Competition between companies is also intense. Therefore, Japanese economic society is not merely a society of harmony.

Second, the function of Confucianism and its impact on the Korean way of life, including rules for industrial relations, needs to be reexamined. Despite the existence of a lengthy publication list regarding the positive aspects of Confucianism in East Asian industrialization, the direct impact of Confucianism on Korean industrialization is difficult to demonstrate empirically. Some historians even contend that traditional Korean values, especially those of self-cultivation, education, and social harmony, which are claimed to be part of Confucian values, "were already present in varying degrees in Korean culture long before Neo-Confucianism became the country's ruling ideology in the Chosŏn dynasty" (Eckert et al. 1990:409). In fact, Confucianism may mean different things to different Koreans. At times it has even been challenged by some Koreans, especially by students and young industrial workers during their labor strife. Preoccupation with Confucianism may create many blind spots regarding other influences.

Third, the *han* may provide a clue to tracing a possible source of Koreans' historical drive and determination for hard work. The effects of prevailing poverty, loss of sovereignty through foreign invasion, and underdevelopment of science and technology remained as the Koreans' *han* for generations. During my interview with the Poongsan chairman, I learned that his primary motivation for his entrepreneurship confirmed the "folk hypothesis" of the taxi driver. The prevalent poverty that had surrounded the entrepreneur in his childhood remained as his *han*, and his drive to become a successful businessman served as a way of releasing his accumulated *han*. A Japanese futurist, Sha Seiki, has also pointed out that Korea's history of adversity motivates Koreans to work harder to succeed (see Steers,

Shin, and Ungson 1989:135). Perhaps the ethic of hard work and the determination of Koreans to achieve their economic development germinated in their history long before the 1960s.

Prospect

The recent development of the Korean economy has drawn the attention of Western media, scholars, and intellectuals. It is indeed a tale of miracle for such a resource-poor country, still bearing the scars of a devastating war, to have become an economic powerhouse in such a short period of time. "It took the United States 100 years to move from an agrarian state to an industrialized economy, and it took Japan seventy years to make a similar adjustment, but it took Korea less than thirty years" (Steers, Shin, and Ungson 1989:136).

Many explanations for the rapid Korean success are plausible; some, for example, credit the well-educated and disciplined work force; others, a government with a well-defined industrial plan and policy willingly followed by business and industry (Adelman 1969; Hasan 1976; Hasan and Rao 1979; Jones and Sakong 1980; Kim and Roemer 1979; Krueger 1979; Mason et al. 1980; Wade and Kim 1978; Westphal 1978). Still others cite the assistance of U.S. aid and foreign investment (Ho 1978:117; Koo 1987; Steinberg 1989).

Some sources have traced the infrastructure of Korean industrialization to Japanese influence during the colonial era (Cumings 1984: 20, 1987; Mason et al. 1980:75). Other scholars like to give credit to the vigorous risk-taking activities of entrepreneurs (Kim 1986; Lim 1981:66–67), while still others believe that such success has been accomplished by the exploitation of workers (Choi 1983). Some take into consideration all of the above as contributing factors (K. Chung 1989). It appears that everything anybody can say about the rapid Korean economic development and industrialization is indeed true.

The concept of the "privilege of backwardness," used by Trotsky (n.d.:4–5), Gerschenkron (1962, 1968), and evolutionary-oriented anthropologists such as Sahlins and Service (1960:93–122), has also been viewed as an explanation. Some scholars remain skeptical, however, about the role of backwardness: "Even so, many underdeveloped nations in Latin America and Africa today exhibit these same features yet remain locked in poverty with little sustained economic growth" (Steers, Shin, and Ungson 1989:13). The "privilege," according to these theories, is to learn and borrow available technology from the advanced countries rather quickly and inexpensively. As a late industrializer, Korea has taken advantage of advanced industrial technology from Japan and the West.

Along this line of thought, Amsden (1989) has characterized Korean industrialization as "late industrialization" because of its practice of learning (or borrowing) foreign technology from industrialized countries rather than developing its own invention or innovation. She asserts that Korean industrialization is a classic model of late industrialization containing all the elements of late industrializers. She quite convincingly illustrates her argument with the case of the Pohang Iron and Steel Company, Ltd. (POSCO). The initial installation of POSCO, founded by the Korean government in 1968, which became one of the most price-competitive steel makers in the world, employing over 23,700 workers, was indeed accomplished almost entirely on a turnkey basis through Japanese technology.

Yet, even in learning or borrowing, the different degrees of learning ability as apprentices have to be taken into account. In the case of POSCO, although over 500 engineers and front-line supervisors had received overseas training prior to the start-up, "when operations commenced in 1973, local engineers reached desired normal iron production level within eight days, an unprecedented record in the history of the industry" (L. Kim 1989:125). It appears that not all learners are able to digest the technology that they wish to adopt with the same intensity.

Preoccupation with Korea's late industrialization by learning rather than by either invention or innovation might hinder a researcher in seeking the inventive side of Koreans. Yet, as Steers, Shin, and Ungson explain (1989:129), "In the year 1234 Koreans developed the first movable metal type for printing, 200 years before the Germans 'invented' it. In 1442 Koreans developed the pluvuometer, or rain gauge, 200 years before the Italians 'invented' it and employed farming methods unknown in the West. And in 1592, in response to a Japanese invasion, Koreans developed and built the world's first iron-clad ships, again 200 years before they were 'invented' by the Americans."

If one defines innovation as the refinement of existing cultural traits, e.g., industrial products, then in the process of Korean industrialization many indigenous innovations occurred, coupled with the limited technologies that the Koreans developed by themselves. In fact, most Korean industrial plants, except a few giants such as POSCO, upgrade both products and production process through "reverse engineering," that is, taking apart and reassembling the available foreign products. I learned that the early stage of Poongsan technology had in large part evolved from the method of reverse engineering. In 1987, however, the technology of Poongsan became advanced enough to produce leadframes for semiconductors. It was a clear example of innovation. Incidentally, West Germany's Stolberger Metallwerke bought a license to use Poongsan's technology by paying 60 U.S. dollars per ton in royalties. L. Kim (1989:126) also witnessed that through indigenous innovation, a small and simple steel pipe manufacturing line evolved into a world-ranking manufacturer of steel pipe machinery.

To search for a theoretical model for Korean industrialization that can be applicable to every late industrializing country can be difficult, if not impossible. A review of recent Korean history reveals the magnitude of its complexity and distinctive qualities not found in other countries.

Historical Particularism as a Possible Explanation

By briefly reviewing the modern history of Korea, I will highlight the major historical events that inspired Korea's drive toward and dedication to economic growth and industrialization.

The history of Korea can be told in stories of adversities because of its geopolitical situation. Since Korea is located in the middle of the Far East, it has had to confront large and often hostile neighbors. The long northern border of the Korean peninsula is linked with the vast expanse of Manchuria, an area almost forty-three times Korea's size. Comparison of Korea with the Russo-Siberian land mass, with which it shares an eleven-mile border, is almost beyond comprehension. Across the Sea of Japan sits the island nation of Japan, almost 70 percent larger than Korea. As a consequence, the peninsula has always been vulnerable to attacks from neighboring states.

In addition to invasion and domination by Chinese dynasties beginning in 598 and in 612 by Sui forces and continuing over the

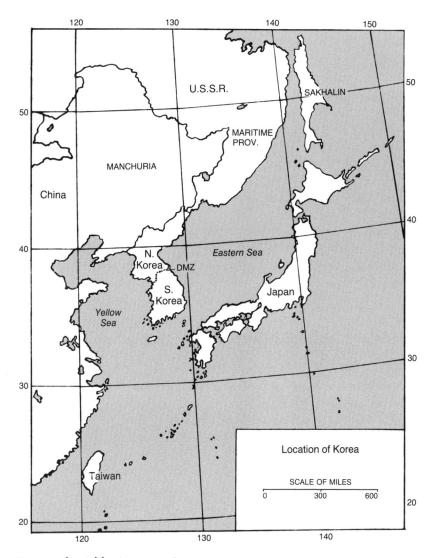

Korea and neighboring countries.

centuries, there have been continual intrusions from nomadic northern tribes such as the Yen, Khitan, Jurchen, and Mongol. The rise and fall of Chinese dynasties has had a profound impact on the security of the country.

Although Japanese pirates were troublesome, particularly during the thirteenth and fourteenth centuries, the Japanese attacks on the Yi dynasty (1392–1910) of Korea from 1590 to 1597 under the leadership of Toyotomi Hideyoshi were devastating. Hideyoshi's invasion of Korea resulted in massive numbers of casualties and captives, including Confucian scholars. The Poongsan chairman's twelfth-generation ancestor was directly involved in this war and suffered from it, which will be related in chapter 1.

Despite these persistent foreign threats, invasions, and intrusions, Korea had been united since the seventh century and had maintained its identity and continuity. As Henderson (1968:13) has pointed out, "smallness of dimension, homogeneity, and exceptional historical continuity marks Korea."

Beginning in the early nineteenth century, Koreans had to deal with yet another threat from the West, including the United States. In direct response to Western intrusion, Yi Ha-ung (1821–1898) of the Yi dynasty of Korea, better known in Korean history as the Taewŏn'gun, adopted a policy of isolationism. (The image of the hermit kingdom was developed as a result of this policy.) In the mid nineteenth century, however, competing foreigners clashed on Korean soil, and this led to the Russo-Japanese War of 1904–1905. Victory in this conflict provided Japan with a firm base for sole control of the Korean peninsula, which it annexed in 1910 and maintained as a colony until 1945. This affected every Korean and virtually every Korean's way of life.

The peninsula was first divided in 1945 along the 38th parallel by the foreign-imposed Cold War. After the Soviet Union accepted the proposal from the United States to divide the liberated Korean peninsula along the 38th parallel, Soviet forces entered the area north of that line almost a full month before U.S. forces arrived. They then suspended travel and communications between north and south. The late-arriving U.S. forces took up their stations in South Korea and established a military government, the United States Army Military Government in Korea (USAMGIK) (Cumings 1981).

Daily life for Koreans immediately became difficult because of the imbalance in the Korean economy brought about by the Soviet blockade. The transfer of products from northern industries and southern farms virtually ceased (Lee 1984:376), even though limited contact between the north and south was maintained for a short period. Even this limited contact was suspended as soon as the general election to form a new government in the south was held in May

1948. Following the election, Syngman Rhee became president of Korea, and the USAMGIK rule came to an end.

Although the entire population suffered during the period of Japanese colonization and then from the division of the country after World War II, Koreans were to face an experience far worse—the worst suffering of their long history—a fratricidal war. The Korean War between North and South Korea began in 1950 and lasted three years. In 1953 the dividing line between the two countries was modified and maintained by the establishment of the Demilitarized Zone (DMZ).

The impact of this war was devastating. Human casualties were enormous, their stories poignant (Kim 1988a). The destruction of property was equally devastating. "Non-military war damage to buildings and structures, equipment, furniture, and other movable assets was estimated at 41.2 billion *wŏn* at July 1953 market prices, U.S. $3.1 billion at the implicit exchange rate for the war years. However, compared to the much higher, recently revised Bank of Korea estimate of GNP for 1953, non-military war damage was equivalent to only 86 percent of 1953 GNP" (Kim and Roemer 1979:30–31). "It is estimated that, during the war, some 45 percent of industrial units nationwide suffered 'substantial' damage. In Seoul, over 80 percent of industry, public utilities and transport, three-quarters of the offices and more than half the dwellings were in ruins" (Mason et al. 1980:248–49).

In the meantime, there began a gradual deepening drift toward authoritarian rule under Syngman Rhee, occasioned by the Korean War and the sagging economy that followed like a shadow. In April 1960, students with the support of other citizens overthrew the Rhee government. The short-lived Chang Myŏn regime that came to power immediately following the Student Revolution of April 1960 managed the national economy until overthrown by a military coup in May 1961.

After about three years of rule by the military government, former military strongman Park Chung Hee emerged from a general election held in early 1964. Park held power until he was assassinated by the head of the Korean Central Intelligence Agency (KCIA) on 26 October 1979.

After the death of Park, it looked as if the Koreans would finally have their long-awaited democratic rule with a civilian government.

Acting president Choi Kyu Ha granted rights to formerly restricted and banned politicians. But potential civilian leaders were struggling and quarreling with one another over the presidency. In May 1980, military leaders took power again, led by General Chun Doo Hwan. In that same year, Chun was elected president, a new party supporting him gained a majority in the National Assembly, and a new constitution was adopted.

At the end of Chun's seven-year rule, in response to furious antigovernment demonstrations by students, workers, and intellectuals, the ruling party presidential candidate, ex-general Roh Tae Woo, handpicked as a successor by Chun, announced his democratic reform package on 29 June 1987. This became known as the June 29 Proclamation (or Declaration). By adopting a new constitution thereafter, Roh was elected as president in December 1987 and took the office of the presidency in February 1988.

Previously, Park had ignited the sparks of Korea's economic modernization, adopting an economic growth strategy. His basic goal was to create an economic base for industrialization and self-sustained growth. The first five-year economic plan was designed to attain an annual growth rate of 7.1 percent between 1962 and 1966, but this target was exceeded by the high growth rate beginning in 1963. Successive five-year plans, the second (1967–1971), third (1972–1976), fourth (1977–1981), and fifth (1982–1986), contained specific goals and directions, but one consistent, basic policy has been export-oriented industrialization and growth. This fundamental policy goal remained unchanged even when Park's government changed over to the Chun government. In fact, when he came to power, "Chun Doo Hwan called on the population to prepare for a 'second take-off'" (Woronoff 1983:35). In retrospect, Korea's geopolitical situation forced Koreans to endure their historical ordeal. Paradoxically, however, such hardships as they experienced encouraged Koreans to retain their identity, homogeneity, and continuity to overcome the challenges confronting them. While they were struggling to sustain life itself, they gained the wisdom to cope with their situation, and at times they were able to turn their worst situations into their best. The following are a few of those instances, I believe, which are directly or indirectly related to Korea's recent economic development and industrialization.

Borrowing Chinese cultural traits, especially Confucianism.

Beginning at the dawn of Korean civilization and continuing to the time of the Korean War, Korea was affected by a Chinese presence. Through those contacts, Koreans learned and borrowed cultural traits, particularly Confucian philosophy and the Chinese written language. Koreans used the Chinese characters until they invented their own language in 1446. Even at the present, to a great extent Koreans have opted to use Chinese characters alongside their own language, as do the Japanese.

Confucianism, which originated in China (551–479 B.C.), was introduced to Korea during the Three Kingdom period (37 B.C.–A.D. 935). It had become an integrated part of Korean culture by the fourteenth century and since the sixteenth century has almost completely dominated the thought and philosophy of Korea (Yang and Henderson 1958). In a sense, Koreans seem more Confucian than the Chinese have been in their devotion to Confucianism, particularly with Neo-Confucianism (Janelli and Janelli 1982:177; Osgood 1951: 332; Peterson 1974:28; Reischauer and Fairbank 1960:426). Tu (1984: 10) has indicated that "Confucianism, for example, featured prominently in Korea, especially in the Yi dynasty. Indeed, from roughly the end of the 14th century to as recently as the 20th century, Korean culture has been greatly shaped by Confucian thought."

Confucianism emphasizes traditional social relations, teaches hierarchical order, and contains five basic principles in human social relations, of which the parental authority of father over son is the most valued. The highest virtue is filial piety (see Choi 1979; Hsu 1970:78; Kim 1988b:127–28). Specifically, Confucianism emphasizes and values highly (1) education and training; (2) emphasis on the group, such as family, organization, and state, over the individual, as distinguished from individual-centered Western values; (3) the family as the most important unit for economic activities; (4) five basic principles in human social relations for a harmonious social relationship; and (5) a positive rather than a pessimistic view on living as taught by certain religions such as Hinduism.

Scholarship studying the influence of Confucianism on economic development has not yet been fully evaluated. Some scholars, championed by Weber (1951), view Confucianism as a hindrance to eco-

nomic development. Specifically, Y. Chung (1989:152) is critical of
the role of Confucianism in Korean economic development: "Confucian teachings rejected training in economics for the pursuit of
wealth and held business people in low esteem. The ruling elite,
yang-ban [*yangban*, or nobility], did not allow themselves to participate in profit-making enterprises." Bae (1987:79) has observed a similar view among Hyundai workers that Korean government and industry were taking advantage of Confucianism to exploit industrial
workers.

Nevertheless, even among the critics, some indirect influence of
Confucianism on Korean economic development cannot be overlooked, especially its influence on education (Kim and Kim 1989:
208; Steers, Shin, and Ungson 1989:130). Even some critics of Confucianism such as Y. Chung (1989:160) acknowledge some indirect
benefit of Confucianism: "The Confucian emphasis on learning and
competitive examination as a means of social achievement has long
motivated the Koreans to pursue scholarly and educational endeavors, which are crucial to the acquisition and diffusion of knowledge—skills indispensable to development." Perkins's (1986:7) comment that Japan, Korea, Hong Kong, Taiwan, and Singapore "were
influenced by Confucian values, used Chinese characters, and ate
with chopsticks" may not be a frivolous observation.

Yet, the most astute explanation of the role of Confucianism in
East Asian economic growth has been given by Tu. Tu (1984:90) distinguishes two faces of Confucianism, one being politicized Confucianism, the other being the Confucian ethic, and illustrates the
differences between them:

> Politicized Confucianism is the power of the state over society; poli-
> tics over economics; and bureaucratization over individual initiative.
> This type of Confucianism, as a political ideology, needs to be
> thoroughly critiqued before a country can be made dynamic. The
> other is the Confucian personal ethic which values self-discipline,
> going beyond egoism to become actively involved in the collective
> good, education, personal involvement, the work ethic and com-
> munal effort.

Tu believes the ethical face of Confucianism is functional for
economic success. In fact, unexpectedly, the Confucian ethic has
contributed to the rise of modern capitalism in East Asia. "This is
analogous to the influence of what Max Weber has described as the

Puritan ethic in the rise of traditional Western capitalism" (Tu 1984:142). Eckert (1990:410) has expressed a similar view that the effect of Confucianism on East Asian economic growth, including Korea, was a case of "unintended consequences, similar to that of Calvinism on early Western capitalists."

Since Confucianism has become so profoundly integrated into the Korean value systems, even the critics, if they are East Asians, have been influenced by Confucianism to a certain extent. Regardless of their positive impact on Korean industrialization and economic growth, Confucian values have been and are still to a great extent pervasive in Korean industrial relations, including Poongsan. Examples include a system of male dominance (chapter 2), a paternalistic reward structure with extra fringe benefits (chapter 3), Confucian academy training (chapter 4), the New Factory Movement, the Labor-Management Council, and formal authoritarian relations (chapters 5, 6), which have grown out of the Confucian family concept.

Colonization as a source of *han* and cultural nationalism.

The increased presence and domination of foreign economic and political penetration in the late 1800s in the Yi dynasty of Korea gave rise to Korean nationalism. The eventual Japanese annexation of Korea beginning in 1910 heightened the emotional trauma of Koreans due to the loss of their dignity and pride, to death, and to dispersal by political imprisonment for activities in the anti-Japanese movement.

When the Japanese were engaged in World War II, 364,186 Koreans were drafted and sent to the war zone, and some 150,000 were killed or missing. Over 724,915 Koreans were conscripted to military installations, and many women ranging from twelve to forty years of age were sent to the war zone to work in brothels for Japanese soldiers. The Japanese authorities even picked up pregnant women to meet their allocated quotas despite having been given instructions to draft only single women between the ages of eighteen and twenty-nine (Kim 1988a:24). These incidents further enhanced the strength and intensity of Korean nationalism.

Korean nationalists, regardless of their origins and factions (Robinson 1988:14–47), acknowledged that if Korea had been able to harness economic wealth, education, military power, and national patriotism, Korea might have been able to avoid the Japanese colonization. This remained as *han* for Koreans. As Eckert (1990:408) has indicated, indeed, "all these feelings—the continued strong sense of national unity and destiny and the catalytic bitterness and anger (*han* in Korean) of the colonial experience—have been consciously and effectively harnessed in the service of economic growth by South Korea's development state." The *han* remained as a motivational source for Korea's recent economic development and dedication to hard work in an attempt to prevent history from repeating itself.

In their efforts to regain Korea's independence, each Korean nationalist chose to pursue his or her (there were some female nationalists) own means. Some fled overseas as the colonial repression became intensified, especially in the first decade from 1910 to 1919, while others were imprisoned; but the majority remained in Korea.

Among them, one group of nationalists adopted a gradualist approach in obtaining Korea's independence from Japan. Robinson (1988; also see Eckert et al. 1990:289–96) called this nationalists' movement "cultural nationalism." Having experienced the brutal retaliations by Japanese as a repercussion of the anti-Japanese demonstrations—especially following the March First Movement (Samil Undong), which began on 1 March 1919—in the early 1920s cultural nationalists adopted the strategy of realists.

The March First Movement was indeed the largest and the most organized anti-Japanese nationalist movement, mobilizing leaders from every religious group in Korea (see Lee 1984:258). Mass demonstrations followed afterward. Japanese brutality and violent clashes between Japanese police, with the help of military reinforcements, and Korean demonstrators created enormous casualties. "Estimates of casualties range from the official Japanese count of 553 killed, 1,409 injured, and 12,522 arrested between March and December to a Korean nationalist estimate of over 7,500 deaths, roughly 15,000 injured, and some 45,000 arrested" (Eckert et al. 1990:279).

Knowing that direct confrontation with the Japanese was a self-defeating proposition, cultural nationalists urged each other to "raise the general level of national consciousness, literacy, and economic development in Korean society in order to develop a mass base" (Eckert et al. 1990:289; elaborated in Robinson 1988). Their effort gradually laid the foundation for future independence.

Despite the criticism by radical nationalists of cultural nationalism because of its gradualism, elitism, and acceptance of the colonial status quo (Robinson 1988:107–36), cultural nationalists launched a variety of projects and movements. The most notable examples are the national university movement for elite education and national economic development. "Their plan was to mobilize national sentiment in support of Korean industry and handicrafts, thus to encourage self-sufficiency and the development of national capital in competition with Japanese capitalism" (Eckert et al. 1990:291). Patriotic appeals for economic development by cultural nationalists were revived after the Protectorate period in the early 1900s and provided a guiding metaphor for economic betterment, including the economic growth in the 1960s.

Aside from the Koreans' emotional disdain for the Japanese stemming from colonization, some scholars claim that the Japanese did remake the face of old Korea by laying railways, building parts, and installing modern factories, especially in the north, for obvious reasons. According to Cumings (1984:20), economic growth during the colonial period was substantial. Despite the colonial bureaucracy's authoritarian, exploitive, and repressive approach, agricultural output rose significantly in the 1920s, and industrialization developed in the 1930s. The growth rate in the Korean economy often outstripped that of Japan. The annual economic growth rate for Korea from 1911 to 1938 was 3.5 percent, compared to a rate of 3.4 percent for Japan. But whatever good the Japanese had done, they had exploited Koreans for their own purposes.

Perceptions of native Koreans on the role of the Japanese in Korean industrialization are decidedly negative. The installation of modern industry was concentrated in North Korea and can hardly be said to have influenced recent South Korean industrialization. Furthermore, most of those installations were destroyed or too damaged during the Korean War to affect recent development.

Whatever the aggregate statistics show about Korean economy during the colonial period, most surviving Koreans, including myself, who weathered those hard times vividly remember that life was not as any outsider can assume it must have been. I recall that spring after spring until new crops were available, Koreans had to depend for food upon the roots of edible wild plants and the husks of pine trees, which often caused constipation. Eating *ch'ogŭn'mokp'i* (literally meaning the consumption of such a wild variety of food) originated from that experience. For Koreans who were there, their experiences and poverty remained as *han,* and their hard work for economic improvement is not any miracle.

Education was another hunger for Koreans during the Japanese colonial era. During colonial rule, by Japanese intention, there was very limited opportunity for Koreans to pursue any formal education. Except for a privileged few, the average Korean could not even dream about college. Even those who could afford to do so ended up going to Japan to complete their education. "Indeed, by limiting access to college and university education in the colony, the Japanese encouraged an exodus of bright Koreans to Japan" (Eckert et al. 1990:264). According to one study, "only five percent of Korean students passed beyond the primary level, and although there was a tremendous expansion of student numbers over time, in 1945 only about twenty percent of the population had received some schooling, while the general rate of literacy was still below fifty percent" (Eckert et al. 1990:263). Those statistics are in stark contrast with the most recent figures: for instance, "secondary school enrollment increased more than 28.5 times between 1945 ([when] the colonial rule ended) and 1986, while enrollment in colleges and universities increased almost 150 times during the same period" (L. Kim 1989:117; see also Song 1988:233). But many first-generation Korean entrepreneurs were unable to pursue their elite education by attending colleges and universities, including the chairmen of Poongsan and Hyundai as well as many others. It remained as *han* for them, too.

Trusting the strong link between economic power and political autonomy, President Park presented his vision of national wealth and power through economic development and appealed to the patriotism of the Korean masses. An additional factor was that "it was made known by the United States aid authorities that United States' aid would be gradually reduced and terminated in the foreseeable future" (Kim and Roemer 1979:44). Park himself had suffered through the life of *ch'ogǔn'mokp'i* in his childhood and youth. He had been a capable student, yet unable to pursue his college path. He knew what poverty can do to a person. He himself had much *han.* Korean entrepreneurs and workers alike responded to Park's call for economic development and industrialization.

Park stated that his ideas for national wealth and political autonomy were influenced by revolutionaries Sun Yat Sen, Kenal Pasha Nasser, and Meiji rulers (see Amsden 1989:14). It seems to me that

his tenet of the linkage between economic power and political autonomy was taken from the early cultural nationalism aimed at economic self-determination. His concept of the New Village Movement
(Saemaŭl Undong), especially, resembled that of the village self-rule
(nongch'on chach'i) of Yi Kwangsu (1892–1950?), a cultural nationalist, which was outlined in Yi's most controversial articles (Robinson
1988:140).

Park was not the only leader to plan Korean modernization and
economic growth. In fact, King Kojong (1864–1907) of the Yi dynasty
(Robinson 1988:19), Syngman Rhee (1955), and even short-lived
Chang Myŏn (1960–1961) tried to improve the Korean economy. It
was actually the Chang government that developed the initial five-
year economic development plan, but the Park cabinet approved the
plan when Park took power by a military coup (Jones and Sakong
1980:46). The only difference between Park and the rest is that Park
was successful in mobilizing the masses of Koreans with authority
and confidence. He successfully appealed to Koreans: "In the past
few years, the government and people awoke from sleep and strove.
. . . We have acquired the self-confidence that, we, too, can successfully compete with others in the international export race" (Amsden
1989:305–6). "We can do" became a household phrase. Perhaps the
Korean social condition was ready to take off in economic growth:
the timing must have been right (Eckert et al. 1990:406–12).

For these reasons, many Korean entrepreneurs believed that their
entrepreneurial activities were patriotic, and workers' contributions
were viewed in terms of nation building. Poongsan was no exception,
particularly with Poongsan's munitions plant, which was a manifestation of the chairman's patriotic desire for a self-sufficient supply of
ammunition for the Korean armed forces. The Poongsan chairman's
entrepreneurial philosophy of sanŏp'boguk (meaning that one serves
one's country by running a useful and successful business, so that
the country can benefit from one's business success) seemed to fit
squarely within cultural nationalism.

The experience of the fratricidal war.

The Korean War devastated the entire Korean population and literally
ruined the peninsula. As has been stated, it created one of the worst
human tragedies ever, in addition to enormous property destruction.

Paradoxical though it may sound, the near-total destruction of existing industry, often small and obsolete facilities inherited from the Japanese, allowed Koreans to build newer, larger, and most modern ones without limitation from the existing facilities. Almost all Korean industrial plants, ranging from the top-ranking steel plant to the gigantic shipyards, are in newly built industrial sites (Amsden 1989:293).

Specifically, during and after the war, some entrepreneurs, most obviously Chǒng of Hyundai, actively participated in "repairing bridges, paving roads, and building army barracks, simple dams, and reservoirs, using 'appropriate technology' specified by the Corps of Army Engineers" (Amsden 1989:266). The skills and technologies acquired by Hyundai during the Korean War, for instance, allowed that company to win the bids of construction projects throughout the world, including bridge construction in Alaska. Diversifying his business interest in heavy industry and the auto industry, Chǒng, with just a grade-school education, became the twelfth-richest person in the world (Fortune, Sept. 1991:52–114).

The founding of Poongsan to produce copper and copper alloy products is bound up with the outcomes and by-products of the remnants of the Korean War. After the war there arose many small-scale factories that collected spent artillery shells, rolled and processed them, and manufactured copper-related products. Poongsan evolved from it, and at an early stage of Poongsan, workers acquired minimal skills from those primitive operations.

The Vietnam War gave the Korean economy a boost when Korea dispatched about 300,000 troops to Vietnam between 1965 and 1973. In spite of all the human casualties, in 1966 the war accounted for 40 percent of Korea's crucial foreign-exchange receipts. Many Korean business firms, including two of the largest business groups, Hanjin and Hyundai, received a tremendous economic boost from the war. Their construction experiences later paved the way to construction in the Middle East.

Besides the above historical events, Eckert (1990:388–418) has listed other serious events that contributed to Korea's recent economic growth and industrialization. Eckert's complete list is not reviewed here; however, a few words have to be mentioned regarding a potential advantage of the location of Korea, since the negative aspects of its geography have been discussed extensively.

As Korea's recent economic growth has shifted toward the level cultural nationalists once hoped for, there is promise for Korea's attempt to capitalize on its adversarial relationship and to become friendly with former enemies in the future. Koreans began to recognize the potential to import ample resources such as coal, oil, natural gas, and timber at a rather inexpensive price from their northern neighbors, China and the Soviet Union, while they exported manufactured goods to them. Koreans already have made significant progress in this regard. "Korea enjoyed $1.1 billion of trade with China in 1987. . . . In 1986 the trade between the Soviet Union and Korea was $140 million" (von Glinow and Chung 1989:32). Korea, among the Asian countries, is situated closest to the two economic giants, Japan and the United States. This is convenient for trade and commerce. Seoul, the capital of Korea, can easily serve as the dispersal point for other major Asian cities: Tokyo, Beijing, Osaka, Hong Kong, Singapore, and Shanghai. By air, only a few hours separate Seoul from these cities. Seoul also has the great potential to serve as a center for commerce, transportation, and an international money market for the Pacific Rim countries.

Considering all of the above aspects, it appears that recent Korean economic growth and rapid industrialization were stimulated and conditioned by numerous internal, external, social, political, and cultural factors that are deeply grounded in Korean history and culture. To search for a theoretical model for the explanation of Korea's economic growth and industrialization that can be applicable to other countries can be frustrating. Instead of searching for such a theoretical model, I follow the tradition of "historical particularism"—the school of anthropological orientation led by Franz Boas (1858–1942) that emphasizes the purpose of mindful data, free from prejudice and distrustful of all schemes. I primarily attempt to describe a single Korean metal manufacturing industry, Poongsan.

An Industrial Ethnography

As an industrial ethnography—an anthropological case study of whole industrial cultures found in a single industry (Baba 1986:5–7; Holzberg and Giovannini 1981)—this study delineates a holistic picture of Poongsan. In this ethnographic work, I only claim to have thoroughly examined the culture and organization of one Korean industry, but the description is so detailed that many existing theoretical schemes might be applied, if anyone wishes.

Descriptions are constructed from inductive findings, including the entrepreneur's background and his philosophy in relation to recent Korean industrialization; the employment system, including recruitment, training, rewards, and promotion; and interpersonal relations. I also examine the extent to which traditional culture, including Confucianism, pervades a Korean industrial organization, including the role of kinship in the industrial setting.

This book is basically an ethnography of Poongsan. Nonetheless, as Peacock (1986:83) concedes, "ethnography is always more than describing. . . . [It] is also a way of generalizing." Likewise, in describing Poongsan, I have made some limited generalizations within the limit that they not override local realities.

Specifically, by summarizing the organizational culture of Poongsan, I try to examine whether the conceptions of tradition and modernity are mutually exclusive and exhaustive or inclusive and syncretistic. If they are coexistent and dualistic, this may help to substantiate and explain the contradictory forms of Korean behavior that Brandt (1971:28) has observed. It is hoped that this ethnography is detailed enough to provide some data for assessing general myths about Korean industry: the myth that the culture of Korean industry is merely a version of that which is traditional for the Orient with special emphasis on Confucian ethics; the myth that docility among Korean industrial workers is endemic to the culture; and the myth that the industrialization via technology that is common to industrializing societies will drive out traditional Korean culture and produce in Korea a mirror image of other industrial societies, known as convergence theory (Kerr et al. 1960) or contingency theory (Chung and Lee 1989:164).

Convergence theorists explain that the technology common to industrializing societies generates increasingly uniform patterns of bureaucracy and rationality and growing individualism. The result is that industrial societies become more alike than different, and unique national identities play an increasingly restricted role in determining behavioral patterns. Evaluation of the validity of the convergence theory is not the primary purpose of this study. However, by identifying the pervading traditional cultural traits manifest in the industrial culture of Poongsan, I attempt to examine the applicability of the convergence theory to Korean industrialization as some sociologists have advocated (Bae 1987; Bae and Form 1986; Form and Bae 1988; Shepard, Kim, and Houghland 1979). This study should provide some data for assessing the validity of the theory in a rapidly changing Korean society.

My choice of Poongsan for a case study was neither random nor accidental. Since the anthropological case study, being contextual in nature, has to approximate the holistic and integrative dimension of an industry instead of focusing on any specific aspect, I tried to select an industry that could facilitate my anthropological inquiries. My focus is more on the culture of this company than on its profits. Nevertheless, the fact that Poongsan ranks with the top thirty enterprises in Korea offers several advantages for this study (see Jung 1987: 214).

First, the metal industry is indispensable to the success of Korean industrialization, and it is desirable to select such a basic industry over a trade firm. Poongsan produces copper, copper alloy products, and military and sport ammunition. Second, Poongsan is large enough to have a sufficient number of blue-collar and white-collar workers so that comparisons between the two groups can be made. Poongsan employs 9,430 workers in four plants. Third, the chairman of the board and founder of the corporation, his executives, and many employees are members of well-established clans in Korea from the Yi dynasty. They are affined with the founder of the corporation by either consanguineous or marital relations, or both. This allowed me to study Korean kinship and its role in modern industrial settings. Fourth, in terms of political economy, Poongsan was founded in the midst of the Korean industrialization and has grown as it has benefited from the government's five-year economic plans. This circumstance provides an opportunity to examine the close relationship between governmental economic planning and the entrepreneurship of Korean businessmen who take advantage of government policy. Finally and most importantly, Poongsan has been receptive to my study.

Fieldwork was done on three occasions: three summer months each in 1987 and 1988 and six months from December 1988 to June 1989, totaling twelve months. Additionally, in the summer of 1990,

as I completed the first draft of this book, I had an opportunity to
check some of my field data while I was assisting in a filming at
Poongsan by Pacific Century. In the summer of 1991, I was a guest
speaker at Poongsan's annual training for its middle managers. I
was then not only an observer but also an active participant in the
training.

While I was engaged in the research, major changes took place in
Korea. When I began, there was no organized labor union at Poongsan, but one was born after the Korean government dramatically announced its sweeping democratic reform package in June 1987, the
June 29 Proclamation. This proclamation was made by a government
on the brink of collapse because of massive antigovernment demonstrations. The announcement included the lessening of labor control. Had my fieldwork not been conducted from the summer of 1987
to the summer of 1989, I would not have had the opportunity to
observe the most furious labor unrest in recent Korean history.
Clearly, one should heed the advice of accomplished fieldworkers:
the longer one stays in the field, the more reliable information one
can acquire.

A lengthy observation of one industry has allowed me to acquire
an in-depth understanding, thus enhancing the validity and reliability of my information by observing repetitive activities and by developing good rapport with those whom I have contacted. The disadvan-
tage of such an in-depth but narrow focus lies both in the inability
to generalize the findings to all of Korean industry and in the impos-
sibility of replication by other researchers. I have chosen validity
and reliability over the ability to generalize.

Regarding the identity of the fieldworker, I have taken much advantage of my dual identity: I am in a sense an insider who was born,
raised, and partly educated in Korea for twenty-seven years, and I am
also an outsider who has been absent from Korea for a prolonged
period of time—living, working, and doing fieldwork in the West for
the past twenty-seven years (Kim 1977). The bias inherent in the
approach of the inside (or native) anthropologist can be reduced, if
not eliminated, by living and studying other cultures before studying
one's own and by deliberately distancing oneself from the natives
both physically and psychologically (Ohnuki-Tierney 1984a, 1984b:
13). I have acquired reflexivity resulting from my life and work in
alien cultures (Kim 1987, 1988a:4–14, 1990).

Indeed, fieldwork in my own native society has the advantage of allowing me to develop more insight into the culture because of my familiarity with it and to arrive at abstractions from the native's point of view. Greenhouse (1985:261) cautions that "our sense of familiarity 'at home' can itself be deceptive" (see also Kim 1987: 943–45, 1990:196–201). I do not have to learn the Korean language or understand a different way of life, and I may have little difficulty in developing rapport. Emic hypotheses can be more easily developed by someone like me than by outsiders. As Maruyama (1969) points out, "Inculture persons are full of hypotheses of their own. There are inculture-relevant hypotheses, and [these] are often of the sort that cannot be dreamed up by outsiders." Most of all, without an introduction of my study by mutual friends and relatives to the chairman of Poongsan, I doubt that I would have been granted permission to study the industry. In fact, Jackall (1988:13) relates that in obtaining permission for his study on corporate managers, he had to cope with refusals by thirty-six corporations. Considering such hardship, I have been fortunate.

Also, my understanding of Confucianism acquired during my early enculturation has facilitated my understanding of Poongsan's *sŏwŏn* training. My manners, language usage, and kinship ties with villagers have given me access to details about the customs of the village and to very sensitive corporate information. My kin have responded to my questions frankly, without fear of possible reprisals from management. In my earlier work on dispersed families, I also had found that without the assistance of relatives and friends it would have been difficult to gather sensitive information. Our relationship not only minimized their possible suspicion of me but also reduced the likelihood of their misinforming me (Kim 1988a:8–9). This is not to say that Koreans do not lie to their relatives and friends, but it does mean that the possibility of deception is easier to rule out through cross-checking. As one scholar notes, "In general informants seem most likely to give deceptive information in three situations: (1) when information is sought from which a person's failure in role performance can be inferred, (2) when information is sought which might reveal deviations from valued cultural norms, and (3) when the information sought is a maker of social rank" (Sorensen 1985:10).

Being a native has not always proved to be an advantage, however, and has not necessarily made me more perceptive than Western anthropologists. Because I am a native, people expected me to conform to their norms. In contrast, a foreign fieldworker might be assumed to be ignorant of local customs. The insider anthropologist enjoys no such advantage, and it is understandable that many experienced researchers have found fieldwork at home surprisingly difficult (Powdermaker 1966:13; Sayles 1978; Strathern 1983). Furthermore, because of my identity as an overseas resident and because the institution with which I am affiliated is overseas, I have been treated as a marginal person, neither a complete insider nor a complete outsider. Whereas the Sinai student fieldworker described by Strathern (1983:8) "could not be turned away because he had a basic right to be there," as a transplanted American myself, I had no such right. My feeling of marginality reminds me of the experience of Hamabata as a third-generation Japanese-American while doing his fieldwork in Japan. Hamabata (1990:6) was puzzled by his marginality: "Was I inside or out? ... When I thought I was in, I was actually out, but when I acknowledged the fact that I was out, I was let in."

The main source of my marginality "at home" has been the change in Korean culture during my prolonged absence and a concurrent change in my own expectations. My knowledge of Korean culture was limited to the Korea of the early 1960s, and I was unable to adjust completely to the change. In fact, the recent anthropological works on Korean society and culture by Western anthropologists such as Brandt (1971), Janelli (1982), Kendall (1985, 1988), and Sorensen (1988) appear to be more perceptive than mine might have been, and those anthropologists are seemingly more familiar with contemporary Korean society and culture than I am.

My identity as a university professor has often dissuaded Koreans from accepting my participation in physical work: "How can a professor do that? Why don't you send your assistant?" Even if I wanted to be involved in many activities myself with the rank-and-file workers, most of the time I have not been invited on the grounds that it would not be appropriate for a professor. A young assistant to the president of the labor union's local chapter once asked me why I had to come to the plant myself all the time on such hot days, and he told me that when a Korean university research team was conducting a survey, no senior professors were present. Since very little anthropological work on Korean industry has been done, and Korean industry has seldom faced such an inquiry from anthropologists, I have spent much of my time explaining what anthropology is all about, industrial anthropology—anthropological research focusing on the industrial domain (Baba 1986:1)—in particular. Virtually no native anthropologists have ever studied Korean industry. Brandt's (1980) case studies of small and medium enterprises, Spencer's (1988) ethnography on Korean female workers, and Hattori's (1986, 1989) work on the large Korean enterprises are a few apparent exceptions. All of these scholars are, however, foreign anthropologists. Even at the present, I trust that a good many Poongsan employees who have been associated with me during this study believe that I am a professor of business or management.

Despite all these impediments to fieldwork at home, it may be that my primary contribution lies in serving as a distanced native, to minimize a possible bias.

Organization of the Book

The focus of this book is on Poongsan, which was founded in 1968, in the second year of Korea's second five-year economic development plan (1967–1971), led by forty-five-year-old Ryu Chan-u. Since then, following the evolutionary path of Korean industrialization, Poongsan has grown into a world-ranking manufacturer of copper and copper alloy products, employing 9,430 workers in 1988. During the twenty years from 1968 to 1988, the number of employees increased 119 times, assets 169 times, and capital 3,273 times. In 1988 the total assets of the company were more than 782 million U.S. dollars and capital totaled 105 million U.S. dollars. Sales for 135,000 metric tons of copper and copper alloy products, sports and military ammunition, and coin blanks reached more than 593 million U.S. dollars in the same year. Export sales accounted for slightly more than 33 percent of the total sales. In 1988 the chairman was reported to be the eighth-highest personal income taxpayer in Korea (*Hankook Ilbo*, 6 Oct. 1989:7).

One may wonder what factors have contributed to such phenomenal growth in such a short period of time. Has the company a unique managerial strategy based on the strength of traditional Korean culture with Confucian ethics? Was it possible to accomplish such a success by the vigorous risk-taking activities of the founder of the company? Did the company hire extraordinary employees who are different from the other Korean manufacturing workers?

I attempt to answer these questions by describing the ethnography of Poongsan in the following order. A detailed description of Ryu is important because, as is the case with most large Korean business enterprises, Ryu is the founder and owner of the company (although the company went public recently, he owns a majority of the stock), and he shaped the philosophy, direction, and style of the company. Ryu's influence in Poongsan's decision making is greater than that of the chairman of the board in Western firms. Thus, in chapter 1, Ryu and his managerial worldview, including his business ethic and morality, are described. In chapter 2, descriptions about Poongsan employees are provided: how they were recruited and employed, and who they are. They, after all, are the ones who carry out Ryu's objectives and accomplish the company's goals. In an effort to describe the major pillars supporting the complex of industrial relations rules, chapter 3 describes the reward system, including wages, other compensation, and promotion, and chapter 4 delineates the career planning of Poongsan employees, including training, security, and retirement. For the description of the social interaction and social relations that characterize this firm, chapter 5 analyzes social interaction among Poongsan employees, and chapter 6 discusses labor and management relations. Two final chapters summarize the culture of Korean industry as evidenced by Poongsan: chapter 7 provides a summary of Korean industrial culture in terms of the coexistence of tradition and modernity, a view that is based on the ethnographic information of the previous chapters; and finally, in the epilogue, concluding remarks on Korea's new challenges resulting from the "penalty of taking the lead" are discussed.

Because I wish to make this book accessible to a rather diverse audience, from professionals in various disciplines to lay persons who are interested in understanding the impact of traditional and modern cultures in the industrialization of the Pacific Rim region and Korea in particular, I have tried to keep disciplinary terminology to a minimum.

The official name of South Korea is the Republic of Korea (ROK) and that of North Korea is the Democratic People's Republic of Korea (DPRK). Throughout this book the informal designation of the ROK as Korea is adopted for easier reading. The DPRK is specified as North

Korea to avoid any possible confusion. In adopting these terms, I do not mean to undermine or discredit the integrity of either regime.

In this book, Korean terms including the names of persons and localities are romanized according to the McCune-Reischauer system. However, the exceptions are the few Korean names, including the name of the corporation, its plants and localities, and personal names, which have established different romanizations for themselves. For instance, by the McCune-Reischauer system, Poongsan should be romanized as P'ungsan, Dongrae as Tongnae, and Bupyung as Pup'ŏng. Also, following the customary practice of Korean and Japanese usage, contrary to American usage, I give the family names of people first in the text without placing a comma before their personal names when they are native Koreans, except Syngman Rhee.

1

The Founder of Poongsan and His Managerial Worldview

When I first visited the chairman of Poongsan, Ryu Chan-u (Yu Ch'an-u), it was one hot and muggy summer day of 1987 in his corporate headquarters' office. I found him informally attired because of a malfunctioning air-conditioning system. He had taken off his coat, had loosened his necktie, and was wearing slippers. But as soon as I walked in, he hurriedly dressed up as a Confucian gentleman should to greet a guest. His manners and etiquette reminded me of the old Confucian tutor who had taught me Confucian classics in my preschool years in a Korean *yangban* (nobility) village (see Brandt 1971: 11–12; Hatada 1969:103; Osgood 1951:44). In our first meeting, Ryu of Poongsan did not impress me as a dynamic entrepreneur as much as he reminded me of a Confucian scholar.

As I was listening to stories of the financial plight and relocation of his family, I saw tears in the eyes of the gray-haired chairman. It was the day he was to spend the first night in his newly built house in his hometown, Hahoe. It was an emotional return eighty-seven years after the unhappy relocation of his family to Tŏkch'ŏn because of their financial predicament and sixty-seven years after the death of his great-grandfather, who had been forced to relocate. A hanging scroll in the porch of his newly built house tells vividly the history of his family's relocation and final return to Hahoe.

The chairman told me, "When we were very poor, my mother was unable to spend a night in any house when she visited this village. No one had welcomed her, and no one wanted to be burdened by having her as a guest." As the leader of nearly ten thousand employees and their family members, he was able to fulfill his family's *han.* Returning to Hahoe remained as his family's imperative *han.* The fulfillment of his family's wish may have been the motivational force behind Ryu's success as an entrepreneur.

Regarding Poongsan's dedication to produce only copper and copper-related products, while other entrepreneurs have diversified their business interests and ventured for a large margin of profits, the chairman of Poongsan commented,

> Without concentrating on one kind of product, it would be difficult to be a world-ranking company. Besides, perhaps more importantly, if I were interested in making money only, I would rather be gambling. As a businessman, of course, you have to generate profits. But, at the same time, I must serve my country by running a useful and successful business, so that the country can benefit from my business success [*sanŏp'boguk*]. Without having a manufacturing industry that produces copper and copper alloy, I could not manufacture ammunitions. I had strong feelings about self-sufficient ammunitions for our military needs. If we had been strong militarily, we could have avoided the Japanese invasions in the sixteenth century led by Hideyoshi. My ancestor [referring to Sŏae] as prime minister during the Hideyoshi invasion felt so badly about Korea's lack of military strength that he wrote a book entitled *Chingbi-rok.* The title of the book literally means "I condemn myself for the past and will be on my guard against future calamity." As you have a copy of the book [I borrowed a copy of the book from my brother-in-law, who is a Ryu member and lives in Hahoe], the book describes how the Yi dynasty of Korea was ill-prepared militarily before the Hideyoshi invasion and advises what Korea must do for the future. It was my ancestor's *han.* I wanted to repay his *han.*

His ancestor's agonizing records written in *Chingbi-rok* seem to serve as a guide and moral justification of the chairman's entrepreneurship in copper production and his involvement in the defense industry. The chairman wants to fulfill the "catalytic bitterness and anger" of his ancestor by producing ammunitions for a self-sufficient

Korean defense. He seems to find the legitimacy of his industrial project by linking to the strengthening of Korea rather than to bourgeois money-making. His justification seems to fit with the theme of the cultural nationalists, as outlined in the previous chapter. Also, his justification later drew the attentions of President Park in expanding his plant.

By and large, like that of many first-generation Korean entrepreneurs, Ryu's entrepreneurial career has been influenced, stimulated, and conditioned by a number of socioeconomic and cultural factors that are deeply grounded in Korean history. An understanding of Ryu's socioeconomic background is essential to understand the culture and organization of Poongsan.

Ryu as a Financially Deprived *Yangban*

Ryu and the village of Hahoe.

The chairman of Poongsan is a member of the Poongsan Ryu clan, which originated in the village of Hahoe. Hahoe has drawn on its reputation as a *yangban* village since 1590, when one of its clan members, Ryu Sŏng-nyong (1543–1620), with the pen name of Sŏae, became prime minister of the Yi dynasty. Ryu is a twelfth-generation descendant of the prime minister.

Hahoe is located in a northeastern county of Kyŏngsangpuk-do (North Kyŏngsang province). The village is encircled by the Nakdong River, which is why it is called Hahoe, literally translated as "water encircling." Ryu clan members began moving into Hahoe near the end of the Koryŏ dynasty (918–1392), around 1355. Ryu clan members who moved into the village started to dominate over other clans such as the Hŏ and Ahn. Most members of those clans left the village, and the Ryu clan has had sole control over the village since the 1600s. Non-Ryu members who have resided in the village have been mostly either farmhands or slaves of the Ryu clan members (T. Kim 1964, 1979). Even after the land reform in 1949, for instance, in 1988 in Hahoe I calculated that 73.5 percent of the population were Ryu clan members, and 87 percent of the village land was owned and controlled by Ryu clan members.

FIGURE I.I   An overview of the village of Hahoe.

Hahoe retains the very special history and culture of the late Koryŏ and Yi dynasties of Korea. In the Yi dynasty, Hahoe was the traditional ritual center of the *yangban* clans of Kyŏngsang province (which includes Kyŏngsangpuk-do and Kyŏngsangnam-do). It still preserves many traditional *yangban* traditions, customs, and rituals. "Discrimination along traditional class lines is still strong; intermarriage between descendants of the Yu [Ryu] aristocrats and commoner residents of the village never occurs, and members of this kinship group retain a monopoly of prestige, wealth, and power" (Brandt 1971:9). The traditional mask dancing (wearing the masks of scholars, monks, maidens, old women, butchers, commoners, and servants) originated in Hahoe. Ryu clan members allowed the commoners and servants to express their feelings and to satirize society freely as they were hidden by the masks (T. Kim 1979:252–60).

After the birth of a new republic in 1948 and the land reform in 1949, Hahoe was not as prosperous as it used to be and was almost

FIGURE I.2   Yŏngmokak, Ryu Sŏae memorial, where the relics of Ryu Sŏng-nyong (Sŏae) are displayed.

forgotten by the public, except the diehard Confucianists. Also, Hahoe is relatively far from major transportation, except for a bus line that runs from the city of Andong, the county seat of Andong county. Hahoe suddenly reemerged to the public in the late 1960s when President Park showed his interest in restoring Yŏngmokak, the Ryu Sŏng-nyong memorial, to exhibit the relics of Ryu Sŏng-nyong for his agonizing over Korea's lack of military strength during the Hideyoshi invasion.

In 1972, Hahoe was designated by the Korean government as a "traditional village." The new status of the village regulates that no Western-style houses may be built in the village, in order to preserve the traditional village scenery and the structure of traditional Korean house.

Since then, Hahoe has become practically a national shrine for Confucianists as well as foreign visitors who want to see the traditional Korean culture. To the critics of Confucianism and traditional Korean culture, Hahoe remains as a faithful remnant of the *sadae* (serving the great) of China, which transmitted Confucianism along with authoritarianism to Korea.

Relocation of the Ryu family.

Some written sources report that Ryu was born in Hahoe, but he was actually born in the village of Tŏkch'ŏn, Ch'ŏngsong-gun, in the extreme northeast edge of Kyŏngsangpuk-do. He was the first son born to a *yangban* in financially reduced circumstances. His great-grandparents had moved from Hahoe to Tŏkch'ŏn before he was born.

Ryu's great-grandfather was a poor Confucian scholar who passed the literary licentiates, or *chinsa*. As a means of recruiting officials, the Yi dynasty of Korea administered qualifying examinations for appointment as civil officers (Lee 1984:180). Anyone who passed the literary licentiates was qualified to take a second-stage examination in Seoul. Ryu's great-grandfather nevertheless did not pursue a civil servant's career any further and never held any official position. However, his scholarship was well respected. Because of his *yangban* origin and promising scholarship, he was able to marry a member of the Shims family in Tŏkch'ŏn, one of the richest families in Kyŏngsangpuk-do.

The financial plight of Ryu's family deteriorated further, as his great-grandfather lived as a scholar without having any regular income or a proper means of livelihood. Family members were no longer able to maintain elite status in Hahoe. They did not even own any arable farm land. At the same time, they were reluctant to be tenant farmers for their own clan landlords: Ryu's great-grandfather's pride as a Confucian scholar did not allow him to do so. Finally, in 1901 Ryu's great-grandfather decided to live off his wife's wealthy estate, and the entire family moved to Tŏkch'ŏn. His in-laws made an arrangement to give humble housing and a plot of land to the Ryu family.

The Ryu family's relocation to Tŏkch'ŏn deviated from the patrilocal rule of residence that requires a newlywed couple to live with or near the parents or the grandparents of the groom. Currently, many young Korean couples establish their own independent residence. Nevertheless, many first-born sons and their brides still tend to live with the groom's parents. "A man should not live with his wife's kin, if he only can have three measures of raw barley"; that is to say, living off the wife's family is so bad that it has to be avoided if at all possible. Ryu told me the story he heard from his parents and other kin, that the relocation of his family was so regrettable, disappointing, and dishonorable that they had to make every effort to return someday to their hometown, Hahoe. It remained as his family's *han,* and Ryu inherited the *han* as his lifelong goal. Eighty-seven years after the unhappy relocation of his family to Tŏkch'ŏn, Ryu was able to build a traditional Korean-style house in Hahoe equipped with all the modern facilities.

In his childhood Ryu attended a traditional Confucian *sŏdang* (a private school for *yangban* youth) for a few years before entering a modern primary school at Ch'ŏngsong; he graduated in 1937. Although the family eked out a scanty livelihood from the small plot of land, the financial situation never improved. To ease the pressing financial worry of his family, Ryu worked in a brewery owned and operated by the Shims family. Ryu recalled, "I did not even have a decent pair of shoes to wear. I was so hungry that I felt I could eat all the rice cooked for *magŏli* [a traditional Korean raw rice liquor]. I was hungry all the time." He continued, "I was rubbing my hands so hard for so long against the screen in the process of brewing rice liquor that I was unable to read my fingerprint."

Although his father was as immersed in Confucian scholarship as his great-grandfather and grandfather had been, his father and two uncles were a little better off financially than their forefathers. Because of this improvement, Ryu was able to attend Taegu Vocational and Technical School, which later evolved into a three-year senior high school, graduating in 1941. Incidentally, two Korean presidents, Chun Doo Hwan and Roh Tae Woo, attended the same high school as Ryu did, although Roh later transferred to another school.

Upon his graduation, Ryu found himself unemployed. There was little business opportunity for anyone without capital; moreover, one needed political connections under the oppression of the Japanese. These were the years when Korea was caught up in the Japanese war effort; in 1939 Japan had proclaimed the National Manpower Mobilization. Under this act Korean laborers and military draftees were involuntarily brought to Japan to fill the labor shortage created by the expansion of the war to Southeast Asia. The mobilized laborers were forced to work in munitions plants and coal mines and to perform various other forms of physical labor to support the war. As Japan escalated its war effort, the National General Mobilization law affected increasing numbers of Koreans. In 1942, following the Japanese attack on Pearl Harbor, Koreans became subject to the Japanese military draft.

To avoid the mobilization, Ryu worked at the Andong county office as a clerk, a position that exempted him from the mobilization; he held onto the position until the end of World War II. The magistrate of the county was a Ryu clan member. By then, his family, including his uncles, had left Tŏkch'ŏn and had returned to Poongsan, a township near Hahoe. One of his uncles, who was entrepreneurial, opened a brewery at Poongsan. Incidentally, Poongsan Corporation was named after the origin of the Ryu clan; it is also the name of the township to which Ryu's family returned from Tŏkch'ŏn. (Korean name groups are divided into scores of clans, each distinguished by a name of prefecture, or *kun*: for example, Poongsan Ryu, Andong Kim, and Ŭisŏng Kim. Poongsan, Andong, and Ŭisŏng are the prefectural names.)

Soon after the liberation of Korea from Japanese colonial rule in 1945, Ryu resigned from the county post and went to Seoul to start his entrepreneurial career. His business career in Seoul from 1945 to 1958 had many ups and downs. He first opened his own small trade firm, which lasted until 1958. Utilizing his training in engineering from the vocational and technical school, Ryu was involved in importing diesel engines. He founded Poongsan Industry in 1956.

The sagging Korean economy and the cutback of U.S. aid from an annual average rate of 88 million U.S. dollars from 1954 to 1957 to only 38 million U.S. dollars from 1958 to 1960 provided something less than optimum conditions for Ryu's business. In 1959, to take advantage of better business opportunities, Ryu went to Japan to continue his trading business from there. His trade became prosperous as he delivered war goods and materials to Vietnam (*Chaegae Journal*, 1 June 1986:195).

Ryu recalls that when he went to Japan in 1959, Korea had not yet established formal diplomatic relationships with Japan. Thus, it was difficult for him to obtain a proper visa to enter Japan, and as a Korean in Japan, it was extremely hard for him to make money. However, with the assistance of his American business associates, Ryu was able to enter Japan and conduct business. The outbreak of war in

Vietnam was the major turning point in the prosperity of his business (*Chugan Maegyŏng*, 12 Feb. 1987:38).

Because he stayed in Japan for ten years, some thought that his legal status in Japan was that of a Korean-Japanese or that he had at least become a permanent resident in Japan. Ryu said, however, that both assumptions were "pure speculation" (*Chugan Maegyŏng*, 12 Feb. 1987:38). The speculation might have been attributed to his lengthy stay and lucrative business in Japan. He remained a Korean citizen, so that in establishing Poongsan, he was able to transfer his capital from Japan to Korea under the Foreign Capital Inducement Act (FCIA). The act was created for the purpose of attracting foreign capital that would promote rapid economic development in Korea by offering various incentives, including tax incentives. Article three of the FCIA specifies that Korean nationals who have been away from home and doing business for ten years or longer overseas are qualified under the act to take advantage of the tax breaks. A comprehensive study of the FCIA is in Kim (1982).

The Growth and Development of Poongsan

The Founding of Poongsan.

The founding of Poongsan to produce copper and copper alloy products is bound up with the outcomes and by-products of the Korean War. After the war there arose many small-scale factories that collected spent artillery shells, rolled and processed them, and manufactured copper-related products. However, those small manufacturing plants were unable to meet the ever-increasing demands of the nation's economy on the eve of the Korean industrialization. A large-scale plant with modern machinery and equipment was much needed. Ryu saw the promise in the opportunity to do such business in Korea.

Another factor attracting Ryu back to Korea was the government's second five-year economic development plan, which emphasized the steel, heavy machinery, and chemical industries (Shin 1986:78). At the same time, in Japan, copper-producing industries were fading away because of the demand of workers for high wages. Many copper-producing plants in Japan went bankrupt during this period. In fact, Japan was looking to the Korean copper industry to supply its need for copper. Ryu was in an ideal position to know the two business worlds. Moreover, he thought that he could purchase Japanese machines and equipment at a reasonable price from the firms that were going bankrupt.

At the time Ryu was looking for a site for his plant in Korea, the Korean government was designating certain locations as industrial complexes to assist small and medium industries. Bupyung (Pup'yŏng), a suburb of Inch'ŏn, was one such site. The location was ideal, not far from the capital city, about an hour's driving distance under normal traffic conditions, and yet within the city limits of the major seaport of Inch'ŏn. Moreover, a four-lane highway between Seoul and the plant at Bupyung was under construction. Ryu managed to acquire the land.

On the site in Hyosŏng-dong, Bupyung, Poongsan started with a few tents, and in December 1968 plant construction began. During construction, people sneaked in at night to steal construction materials, including electronic cables and wires. Supervisors had to stand guard day and night on the construction sites. Ryu stayed on the site to direct the construction himself. Most of the time, work continued through the night hours by torchlight. As there were no restaurants, workers had to continue their work sustained only by a few pieces of dried bread. Often, Ryu's wife cooked for the workers. One worker who participated from the time of the ground breaking until now remembers the early days vividly; he commented, "It was a genuine family atmosphere." The completed plant went into production on 5 January 1970.

The installation of the machinery and equipment was completed with the assistance of two Japanese engineers. According to the memories of workers from those days, the hardest part was acquiring the knowledge to operate those machines. Hardly any of the workers had operational skills; even the Korean workers who had worked in other copper plants had never operated such modern equipment. Some recall that "there was no operational manual. Some bought the Japanese manual books on rolling machines at their own expense. They learned themselves how to operate the machines, mostly by trial and errors." It was not as same as POSCO's startup. Poongsan required many indigenous innovations.

Because of their lack of skill in operating the machines, the plant workers often injured and maimed their hands. As the number of

FIGURE 1.3   Inside the Poongsan plant.

injuries to young high school graduates grew, Ryu's concern mounted. He once asked his wife with tears in his eyes, "Should I quit this business? I cannot watch these injuries helplessly." Nonetheless, eleven workers labored hard to overcome the obstacles, loading and unloading heavy coils manually; there were no loading machines they could use.

Starting in January 1970, Poongsan managed to produce 6,000 tons of copper and copper alloy products annually. Immediately, the firm pursued the opportunity to become the supplier of coin blanks for the Korean mint. In April 1970 Poongsan was designated the coin blank manufacturer for the Mint of Korea, and beginning in July of the same year Poongsan started to produce the blanks. Poongsan has since been the exclusive supplier of all kinds of coin blanks for domestic use; it has also gained a reputation as a reliable supplier in the international coin blank market. In 1973 Poongsan began exporting coin blanks to Taiwan, in 1974 to Thailand, and in 1981 to the Philippines. Poongsan leads the world market in the production of coin blanks. In 1986, 42 million U.S. dollars worth of coin blanks were exported to Southeast Asian countries, Australia, and the United States. Beginning in 1990, the list included Japan. Poongsan also turned out precious metal commemorative medals and coin blanks for the 1986 Asian Games and the 1988 Seoul Summer Olympic Games.

A close tie with the government under the ancestor's shadow.

When, in Presidential Order No. 5224 of July 1970, the government designated the company as one of the nation's five key industries, recognizing Poongsan's potential role as a major defense contractor, Poongsan took a major leap forward. Being designated as one of the five key industries proved to be an enormous advantage.

Recognition such as this is characteristic of the intimate relationship between government and private enterprises in Korean industrialization. Eckert (1986, 1991) and McNamara (1988, 1989, 1990) indicate that the formation of big business groups and the close ties between the state and large private enterprises in Korea had colonial origins during the Japanese occupation. Mason has stated, "If there is a 'Korea, Inc.,' as there is alleged to be a 'Japan, Inc.,' it is the government that is the chairman of the board of the corporation" (Jones and Sakong 1980:xxix).

In its dealings with industry, the Korean government has used industrial licensing, price control, rationing, and the allocation of foreign borrowing under government guarantees (Jones and Sakong 1980; Lim 1981:66–67; Mason et al. 1980). Although Poongsan was obliged to expand the capacity of its plant, it has also been able to enjoy the privilege of financial, banking, taxation, and skill and technological aid from the government. Such forms of assistance have allowed Poongsan to establish its semimonopoly in copper and copper-related products in Korea.

Poongsan has responded to the government's call to expand the plant by increasing its investments, including a loan from Nissho Iwai in Japan, and by upgrading its facilities with modern equipment. As the company grew, with the increasing capital and newly installed equipment, Poongsan needed to improve skills and technology. To this end, in 1971 Poongsan contracted for the assistance of the Korean Institute of Science and Technology (KIST), the think tank for Korean science and technology established in 1965 as a nonprofit independent research organization. This contract for scientific and technological assistance from KIST eventually was responsible for many new products, including the leadframes for semiconductors.

Metal Bulletin Monthly (Oct. 1987:45) reported, "At a time when most other South Korean companies are desperately importing foreign technology, . . . PMC [Poongsan] became one of the few to reduce that flow and sell its technology to the West." West Germany's Stolberger Metallwerke bought a license to use Poongsan's technology for producing copper and copper alloy for leadframes. Poongsan reportedly received 200,000 U.S. dollars in technology fees, followed by 60 U.S. dollars per ton in royalties for ten years. More than the amount of income, it serves as a major morale booster for Poongsan.

By the end of the government's second five-year economic development plan (1967–1971), Poongsan demonstrated to the government that as a major copper producer the company remained more than able to play a major role as a defense contractor to produce military ammunition. Korean-made ammunitions for the Korean military were high on the list of President Park Chung Hee's priorities during the third five-year economic development plan (1972–1976). Actually, three other copper-producing firms were competing for the government's bid for the defense contract, but Ryu of Poongsan managed to win the bid over the others, mainly because of the strong support of President Park.

Many people speculate that President Park's strong support of Ryu was mainly due to a provincial favoritism for Kyŏngsang province, since Park was also from the Kyŏngsang province. In fact, according to M. Kim's (1989) survey, Kyŏngsang favoritism is prominent in high government positions and among the top fifty Korean enterprises: 9 out of 24 cabinet ministers, 6 out of 13 executive board members of the central bank of Korea, 5 out of 9 managerial board members of the Korean monetary and circulation control board, and 23 out of 50 Korean big business owners are of Kyŏngsang origin. And yet the Kyŏngsang population is only 15 percent of the total population. Jones and Sakong's (1980:213) survey indicates that Kyŏngsang origin among Korean elites (entrepreneurs, managers, public managers, public bureaucrats, and politicians) is underrepresented in all elite groups. Nevertheless, they point out that among the forty-six largest entrepreneurs, "Kyŏngsang province is indeed more heavily represented . . . than among the entrepreneurial set as a whole" (Jones and Sakong 1980:217).

When I asked Ryu about his connection with Park, he told me,

> I believe the regional ties helped me a great deal, without any question. In fact, it is not far from here to President Park's home town [the chairman pointed in the direction of president Park's hometown, Sangmori of Kumi, Sŏnsan-gun, from his Hahoe home]. Perhaps the direct distance could be less than twenty-five miles. He must have a feeling of closeness because both of us were from the same region. However, I believe I took more advantage of my ancestor, Sŏae, than of regional favoritism. He trusted me because I am a descendant of Sŏae, whom he respects the most, and he understood why I was particularly interested in the defense industry.

Indeed, Park's interest in and respect for Sŏae, Ryu Sŏng-nyong, and his heroic role as prime minister during the Japanese invasions in the sixteenth century were evident even before he became friends with Ryu of Poongsan. As a professional soldier, Park understood Sŏae's agonizing over Korea's lack of military strength. At President Park's suggestion, Yŏngmokak, the Ryu Sŏng-nyong memorial, was opened on 11 June 1966; its purpose is to protect the relics of Sŏae and to exhibit them to the public. Park was particularly interested in displaying Chingbi-rok. Financial support from the government was instrumental in opening the Sŏae memorial. President Park's interest in Sŏae was manifest in the opening ceremony at Yŏngmokak: the president sent the plaque and his commemorative speech in his own writing. Later, Park's wife actively supported the extension of the memorial hall.

Ryu continued to talk about the development of his friendship with Park:

> I told him that, for the sake of my ancestor and to fulfill his wishes for a strong defense, I would like to play a vital part for the national defense. Since I am producing copper and copper-related products, I can easily direct a munitions plant that would supply all the ammunitions for our military needs. The president was very happy to hear my request and approved it at once, saying, "You are the right person to do it. You can understand better than anybody else how much your ancestor, Sŏae, suffered from the military ill preparedness during the Japanese invasion." I believe the president took my request to become a major supplier of ammunitions for our military as a manifestation of my patriotism. Thereafter, we became very close friends.

A close tie between the Poongsan chairman and President Park has been developed in the shadow of the chairman's ancestor, Sŏae. Development of such a rapport with government figures through family ties and connections is not uncommon in Korea. Who you are, what your family background is, what school you have attended, and where you are from are often considered to be more important in Korea than what you can do.

The existing Bupyung plant alone could not accommodate large-scale defense contract work. In 1972 Poongsan planned to build a plant that could be devoted mainly to producing military ammunitions. A site near the township of Angang, in the southeastern corner of Kyŏngsangpuk-do, was chosen. Although Angang was a sleepy township far from major metropolitan and industrial complexes, the site was considered to be an ideal locale for a munitions plant. Although it was in a less-developed region, it was located conveniently; it allows easy access by railroad and the Seoul-Pusan superhighway, and it lies a short distance from the Eastern Sea and its ocean routes. Moreover, the ammunition magazine of the Korean Armed Forces was nearby. Furthermore, residents of Angang and its vicinity wanted to have such a plant near because of the employment opportunity it would provide. Farming had been the only means of livelihood for generations. President Park himself along with his defense minister visited the site and approved it. A loan of 1.7 million U.S. dollars from Girard Trust Bank in the United States was instrumental in bringing the Angang plant to Poongsan.

In October 1972 the Angang plant started to produce experimental products, even before plant construction was completed in March 1973. On 23 April 1973, the Angang plant was officially designated as a defense contractor by the Korean government. Thereafter, the organization of the corporation became more formal and structured. President Park visited the plant in May 1973, donating a presidential gift as an expression of his gratitude to the company for making the Korean production of ammunition possible.

In the munitions plant there were minor industrial accidents and injuries. A major accident occurred on 14 February 1976. Because of the workers' lack of experience and the facility's lack of appropriate equipment for handling explosives, an explosion occurred in the laboratory for producing antiaircraft ammunition. No one was killed, but Poongsan's financial loss was estimated to be more than one-half million dollars. The accident was certainly a setback. Those workers who were at the explosion site recalled realizing that there was the potential danger of a chain explosion; indeed, Poongsan headquarters ordered the workers to seek shelter for safety. Even though the firemen were reluctant to approach the fire, the plant manager and his workers took over the firemen's equipment and controlled the fire. One participant remembered, "When you talk about loyalty, that was it. I saw it, and I was part of it. No one wanted to avoid the danger. All of them knew that the plant was the means of their livelihood."

As the government moved into the fourth five-year economic development plan (1977–1981), the emphasis was on a policy of growth, development, and an export-led economy. Poongsan responded by opening overseas offices to promote exports and increase overseas sales in Tokyo, New York, London, Los Angeles, Boston, and Hong Kong. Some of these offices have since closed; currently there are only three overseas offices, in Tokyo, Hong Kong, and Los Angeles.

In 1977 Poongsan continued to grow, building a plant in Onsan, Ulju-gun, in the southeastern tip of Kyŏngsangnam-do (South Kyŏngsang province), near Pusan. The new plant would produce basically the same products as the Bupyung plant but with more modernized facilities and equipment. Plant construction began in March 1978. By July 1980 the Onsan plant for the production of brass was completed. Currently, it generates nearly 60 percent of Poongsan's income.

As the Angang and the Onsan plants came into full operation, the volume of exports increased. In 1980, at the seventeenth national commemoration of exports, Poongsan received a governmental award for its exports. The awarding president, however, was not Park, the supporter, advocator, and personal friend of Ryu of Poongsan, but a new president named Chun Doo Hwan. Park then had been assassinated by the head of the KCIA. Although Ryu had lost his strong supporter and personal friend, the new president was not a stranger. Not only was Chun from Kyŏngsangpuk-do, he was a member of the high school alumni association of which Ryu was and still is president. Hence, the two men had known each other. Most of all, Chun's economic policy, like Park's, was focused on export-oriented industrialization and growth (Woronoff 1983:35).

Under the Chun government, on 1 January 1982, Poongsan took over the government's First Arsenal at Dongrae (Tongnae) and integrated it into Poongsan's own Dongrae plant. In January 1982 a new

FIGURE I.4   The Poongsan chairman with workers and the anthropologist
at the Onsan plant.

Dongrae plant, located in the vicinity of Pusan, a major seaport and
the second most populous city in Korea, was opened by Poongsan to
produce ammunition, including sport ammunition. Some facilities,
including rifle lines, moved from the Angang plant to the Dongrae
plant. Poongsan now had four plants, at Bupyung, Angang, Onsan,
and Dongrae, plus the main headquarters office in Seoul (Figure 1.5).
In 1982 the board of the corporation promoted President Ryu to chairman, Vice President Lee Yŏng-sae to president, and Executive Managing Director Ryu Min-ha to vice president. Poongsan later added the
position of vice chairman, but otherwise the basic organizational
structure of the corporation remains the same today (Figure 1.6) as it
was in 1982.

The four Poongsan plants produce various products: the Bupyung
and Onsan plants produce mainly copper and copper alloy lines:
sheet and stripe, pipe and tube, rod, bar and wire, coin blanks, and
welded titanium tube. The Angang and Dongrae plants produce not
only ammunition, including sports ammunition, but also tools,

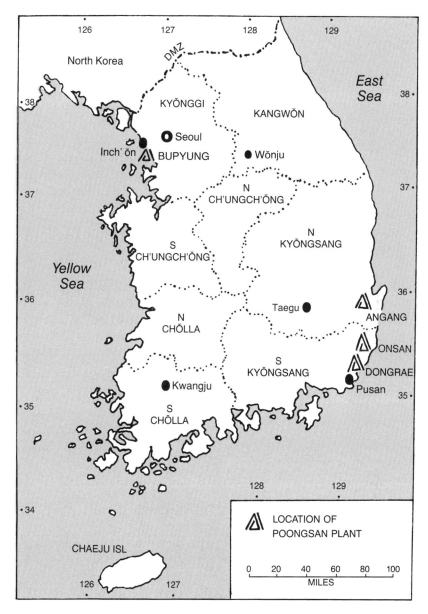

FIGURE 1.5   The locations of Poongsan's four plants.

machines, gauges, precision dies, and leadframes for semiconductors as well. Altogether, these four plants under the Poongsan name manufactured nearly 126,575 metric tons of copper and copper alloy products in 1987 and 130,058 metric tons in 1988. The sales of these products reached more than 375,341 million *wŏn* in 1987 and 406,119 million *wŏn* in 1988, with export sales accounting for slightly more than 33 percent of the total sales in both 1987 and 1988 (table 1.1).

At its twentieth anniversary in 1988, with a remarkable accomplishment of rapid growth and development, Poongsan went public on 13 June, and its stocks were listed in the Korean stock market. In fact, the Korean government has "provided considerable tax incentives to encourage corporations to go public" (World Bank 1989:10). Ryu personally owns 51.24 percent of the stock, 2.9 percent for his two sons, 0.19 percent for his younger brother, and 0.37 percent for his two brothers-in-law (*Yŏngŏp-bogosŏ* 1989:15). It is not

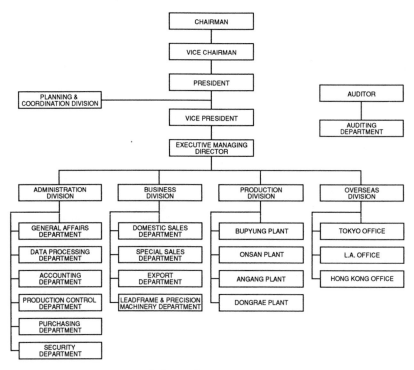

FIGURE 1.6 Organizational chart of Poongsan.

Table 1.1 Volume of Sales by Poongsan, 1970–1988 (in million *wŏn*)

Year	Total	Domestic		Export		Leadframe & Precision Machinery
		Domestic	Gov't Supply	Export	Special Products	
1970	300					
1971	446					
1972	659					
1973	3,401					
1974	13,100	3,300	4,400	5,400		
1975	12,600	3,500	5,700	3,200	200	
1976	27,100	5,400	13,400	7,500	800	
1977	30,157	10,467	15,213	2,751	1,726	
1978	55,577	15,417	33,391	3,296	3,473	
1979	71,322	19,697	39,218	5,195	7,212	
1980	114,526	20,191	44,439	24,742	25,154	
1981	171,696	31,350	51,679	70,326	18,341	
1982	173,728	40,450	50,259	57,762	25,257	
1983	224,111	65,915	47,468	48,974	61,754	
1984	225,858	75,013	55,379	77,910	17,556	
1985	263,172	86,029	77,321	79,462	20,360	
1986	342,069	104,605	101,314	113,165	22,300	685
1987	375,341	133,857	111,728	108,695	17,069	3,992
1988	406,119	163,900	91,535	124,306	17,187	9,191

SOURCE: The author's field data.

unusual for the founders of big Korean enterprises to own the majority of their companies' stocks. *Chosun Ilbo* (15 Mar. 1989:6) reported that 60.3 percent of the founders and the first generation of the top *chaebŏl* (big business conglomerates) leaders own 80 percent of their companies' stocks.

On 27 February 1989, at the first stockholders' meeting since Poongsan had gone public, the stockholders passed a resolution to change the official name of the firm from Poongsan Metal Corporation to Poongsan Corporation.

Despite its rapid growth, Poongsan faced a most difficult challenge from its employees during the labor union unrest that began in August 1988 and continued into the early part of 1989. In fact, the Angang plant was closed for 72 days, from 1 January to 13 March 1989, because of a strike. The firm's loss of production and the workers' loss of wages during the strike were not small. Moreover, the backlog of orders from 1988 was large.

In reviewing the growth path of Poongsan, I have learned that the dynamic entrepreneurship of Ryu has been the key to the firm's success. However, the socioeconomic and political conditions in Korea affected the growth of Poongsan. Strong entrepreneurs might exert a significant influence on the growth of their companies, yet they may nevertheless owe some of their success to their social settings and social conditions. Besides Ryu's own entrepreneurship and the hard work of his employees, certainly the Korean government has played a major role as well. The role of government in Korean business and industrialization is so well documented that a detailed discussion is not needed here. Nevertheless, specific instances of the initial contacts between the entrepreneurs and governmental figures, including the president, are almost untold.

In the case of the Poongsan chairman, the initial contact has been developed in the shadow of the chairman's ancestor and his regional ties with the president. The chairman's connection with the president, who then had an unchallenged power to either make or break any business conglomerate, was developed and enhanced through his kin group affiliation as a descendant of a well-respected Neo-Confucian scholar and the most heroic prime minister in modern Korean history, especially from the view of the president. Also, the chairman's origin from Kyŏngsang province allowed him to take advantage of regional ties with government figures and business associates. Additionally, the chairman's school ties as alumnus with two presidents, former president Chun and current president Roh, allowed him to be closer to them. In Korea, relationships between *sŏnbae*, (senior) and *hubae*, (junior) are analogous to fictional kin relationships between older and younger brothers, and they even address each other using real kinship terms of older and younger brother. It is similar to the *senpai-kohai* (senior-junior) relationships of the Japanese, and both use the same Chinese characters. Although I was unable to document any specific evidence that the chairman took advantage of his being *sŏnbae* to the presidents, it is generally believed that the chairman's school ties with them would not hinder his business activities. If the chairman would seek an appointment with the presidents, they would find a time for him.

H. Lee (1989b:156–57) observed that in the Korean business world, school connections, regional ties, and kinship networks work not only in power group formation at the top levels, but also in the formation of informal relations, and cliques at all levels throughout the Korean organization. He further elaborates on these that

> *Hahk-yun [hakyŏn]* (school tie) is a particularly strong factor in informal relationships, giving common identities and feeling of belonging. Hahk-yun places much attention on the year of graduation, as older employees are in the position of *sun-bae [sŏnbae]* (a senior) and the younger the position of *hoo-bae [hubae]* (a junior). These relationships work as important factors affecting employees' behaviors. Similarly, *ji-yun [chiyŏn,* meaning "regional connection"] gives those from the same region a feeling of common background and compatibility, and it likewise affects the employees' social interactions and personnel decisions.

As one of Poongsan's top executives and Ryu's close business associates pointed out, "To be a successful businessman, you have to have some luck occasionally. Unbelievably, Chairman Ryu has had two presidents, back to back, both of whom were his *hubae* in the same school. I have never seen any man who has had such good luck with presidents as Ryu has had. Don't tell me that this thing can happen to everyone, and can be achieved merely through hard work!" The chairman's wife concurred.

Ryu's Entrepreneurial Philosophy and Morality

My examination of Ryu's background and his twenty years of leading Poongsan allows me to sketch his entrepreneurial philosophy and morality in managing his corporation.

No business diversification.

Ryu seems to find legitimacy in his industrial project by linking it to the strengthening of Korea rather than to bourgeois money-making.

His justification seems to fit with the theme of cultural nationalists, viewing constructive entrepreneurial acts as patriotic. His claim is on the basis of his dedication to producing one kind of product, whereas other Korean conglomerates have built empires to generate larger profits by engaging in every aspect of business, to facilitate information channels for market information, and to reduce risks and uncertainties.

Regarding his opportunity to diversify his business, he commented,

> When my munitions plant at Angang was completed and started to produce ammunitions, President Park, who was pleased by the work and dedication of Poongsan, asked me what other business I wanted to start besides the copper industry. He assured me that he would help in any way he could. I knew I could count on his support for the business, if I had wanted to do so. If I had wanted to make money only, I could have done so, then. But I told him thank you, but no thank you.

The president at the time would have been able to make or break any business conglomerate, had he wished.

Ryu even denies that Poongsan is a *chaebŏl* (a big business conglomerate that is analogous to the Japanese *zaibatsu*). Although the Chinese characters for *chaebŏl* and *zaibatsu* are identical, and the two forms share many common characteristics, scholars who are familiar with both forms find some distinctive differences (Hattori 1989). Yoo and Lee (1987) define a *chaebŏl* as a business group consisting of large companies that are owned and managed by family members or relatives in many diversified business areas. Jones and Sakong (1980:259–60) define it as follows:

> At the center of each group is the *hoejang* or "chairman," who is the dynamic and cohesive force of the group. Most typically, he is an entrepreneur, . . . who founds one enterprise and then leaves its management to a relative (or, more recently, to a trusted associate) as he moves on to a new venture. Majority shares in the various enterprises are held by the *hoejang* and his immediate relatives. . . . Guidance and direction, however, remain highly centralized in the *hoejang*.

Review of several available definitions and characteristic features of *chaebŏls* (S. Lee 1989:182) seems to indicate two major characteristic features, that is, ownership by family and diversified business operation (Kim and Hahn 1989:52).

Ryu's denial of Poongsan as a *chaebŏl* is not an attempt to avoid

Table 1.2 Correlation of Ranch and Number of Affiliated Companies among Korean *Chaebŏl* Groups, 1984

Ranking of Enterprise	No. of Affiliated Companies	Average No. of Affiliated Companies
Top 5	136	27.2
Top 10	213	21.3
Top 20	336	16.8
Top 30	409	13.6
Top 50	542	10.8
108 *Chaebŏl* Companies 788		7.3

SOURCE: Data from Jung's (1987:85) table 4-1.

the negative connotations of being labeled as a *chaebŏl*, although there is a prevailing negative attitude among some Koreans toward *chaebŏls*. "These negative attributions have resulted in large part from the perception that some of the chaebols accumulated their wealth either because of unfair advantage or government connections" (Steers, Shin, and Ungson 1989:35). Ryu's Poongsan is certainly one of Korea's top business enterprises. Ryu uses the title of *hoejang*; his entrepreneurship, his power and authority for decision making in the company, and his ownership of the majority of the stocks all match the definition of a *chaebŏl*. Yet Ryu's Poongsan does not have a key feature of the *chaebŏl* —diversified business operations. Ryu has not yet left his original firm to engage in another business interest or venture. He has stayed with the company and remains dedicated to producing one kind of product.

On the other hand, other *chaebŏl* groups have diversified their business interests. About 20 percent of 113 large firms in Korea actively pursued diversification strategies during the period from 1976 to 1983 (D. Cho 1989:111). Although Korean *chaebŏls* numbered fewer than 10 after the Korean War, by 1975 the number had grown to 46, controlling 398 companies (Lim 1981:46–47). The patterns of affiliation of top-ranking *chaebŏl* groups in Korea are shown in table 1.2.

Poongsan does not follow the typical Korean pattern; it has only three affiliated companies, all dealing with copper products. Even Poongsan's two overseas plants under construction, one in Cedar Rapids, Iowa, and a joint venture with Thailand, are also planned to produce copper products. Also, during the construction boom in the Middle East in the 1970s, most of the large *chaebŏls* rushed into construction. Ryu refused to participate and even sold his existing construction company, the Poongsan Kaebal, to focus on copper-related business.

Ryu's self-restraint on diversification is related to his business ethics and morality. On the one hand, Ryu is very reluctant to involve himself in any business that is not manufacturing, whereas some diversified large *chaebŏl* groups have earned a large share of profits even by investing in the stock market (*Hankook Ilbo*, 12 Oct. 1989:7). Other *chaebŏl* groups even cheated Korean customs to import certain fish, which were prohibited, to generate a large profit margin. In turn, they created a small-scale fishing industry out of their businesses (*Hankook Ilbo*, 6 Nov. 1989:1). In many Koreans' eyes, including those of some conscientious businessmen, these unethical business deals by the big *chaebŏl* groups only prove their irresponsibility. Ryu of Poongsan believes such unethical business deals may partially be related to the unintended consequence of too much diversification of *chaebŏl* groups. It is known to be an "octopus arm" style of expansion, including virtually every kind of business within the group.

Assisted by the so-called *sam-jŏ-ho-hwang* (meaning the economic prosperity that is due to the lower prices in three items: oil, imported raw materials, and interest rates), profits in Korean business and industry for the three years beginning in 1986 were very high. However, instead of expanding the scale of the existing industries and investing in research and development, say workers and the media, some Korean *chaebŏl* groups invested the new and higher profits in real estate speculation. Poongsan, however, does not own any non-business-related real estate. It is an exceptional case among the top thirty Korean firms (*Chosun Ilbo*, 18 May 1989:7; *Dong-A Ilbo*, 19 May 1989:2; *Hankook Ilbo*, 21 Oct. 1989:22; 17 Aug. 1990:9). Poongsan does not even own its own building for its headquarters' offices in Seoul. It is indeed unusual.

Ryu as an "unconscious" Confucian.

Considering Ryu's background and observing his mannerisms in the early stage of my fieldwork, I presumed that his managerial rules were based entirely on Confucian virtues. My assumption was further supported by witnessing his commitment and respect for his ancestors, particularly for Sŏae, his care for the *chonga* (the house of the *chongson*, that is, the main heir of the lineage or clan) in Hahoe, and his efforts to preserve the relics of his ancestors. He also committed himself to assist his clan members in any way he could.

Ryu was instrumental in establishing the nonprofit Sŏae Memorial Foundation in 1976. The major functions of the foundation are (1) to preserve the relics of the ancestors, especially Sŏae; (2) to preserve and repair the historical and cultural remains of the Ryu clan in Hahoe and its vicinity, including ancestral graves, *chonga*, Yŏngmokak, and Pyŏngsan Sŏwŏn (the Confucian academy where Sŏae taught his students); and (3) to publish manuscripts written by Sŏae and to translate Sŏae's published works into the Korean language, because almost all of them were written in Chinese. The foundation also publishes a journal, *Sŏae Yŏngu* (study of Sŏae). Recently, the foundation published a comprehensive bilingual (Korean and English) guidebook on cultural remnants of the Ryu clan and Hahoe.

The foundation accepts token annual dues from all members. However, the endowed funds that finance foundation activities were donated mainly by the Poongsan chairman. Some of Ryu's clan members told me, "Chairman Ryu spends a good bit of his time, energy, and money to preserve the cultural relics of Hahoe and his ancestors, as much as he does to his business." The chairman's wife also told me that to protect the sanctity of the Confucian academy of Pyŏngsan Sŏwŏn, for instance, her husband bought land surrounding the academy and provided the landscaping. "The expenses involved in doing those things are not small," she said. The Poongsan chairman has been elected to serve as chairman of the foundation. The office of the foundation is located in the company's headquarters in Seoul, and the foundation office has access to all the facilities of Poongsan, including its communication network.

The chairman regularly sends money to the *chongson* in Hahoe to cover the expenses involved in ancestor-worship rituals and in entertaining the frequent visitors, ranging from local dignitaries to foreign ambassadors. An average of two foreign visitors per day visit Hahoe. One Hahoe villager told me,

> Without such a strong belief in Confucianism, especially without such filial piety, he would not be so devoted to the ancestral village. Look, he is not the only one among the Sŏae descendants who made a fortune. There are several big businessmen, a bank president, congressman, many professionals, yet their contributions are limited. The Poongsan chairman is the only one who does most of the work for the clan and the village.

Following the tradition of social relationships among those of a kin group organization, the chairman perceives all of his clan members as close kin. Everyone in the same clan, regardless of how remotely one might be related to another, addresses other members by using kinship terms that encompass the entire membership of the clan; members of the same clan are all blood kin, even many generations removed from the common ancestor. Marriage between clan members, no matter how remote the relationship may be, is considered taboo in Korea and is illegal: the marriage license cannot be issued, and the marriage cannot be registered in the local record office (or *hojŏk*). Because of such a sense of kinship, Ryu as Poongsan chairman has hired many members of the Ryu clan, if they were qualified and willing to work.

Sometimes Ryu's concern and respect for Confucianism extends well beyond his own village of Hahoe. For example, after my return from Hahoe, when I pointed out to him the awkwardness of the English translations of the labels of the relics exhibited in Hahoe, his immediate reaction was rather surprising. He commented, "I bet the same is true for the labeling of the relics of T'oegye [Yi Hwang] in Tosan." Yi Hwang (1501–1570), pen name T'oegye, was the foremost Korean Confucianist philosopher of his age; he explicated Neo-Confucianism in Korea. Upon his retirement from his government post, Yi taught Confucian scholars at Tosan Sŏwŏn. Yi's school of thought was carried on by three prominent students, Ryu Sŏng-nyong (1543–1620), Kim Sŏng-il (1538–1593), and Chŏng Ku (1543–1620), later known collectively as the Yŏngnam (Kyŏngsang province) School. The English versions in both exhibits were made by the Andong-gun, the county office.

The Poongsan chairman was concerned about the relics of his ancestor's teacher. Ryu instructed his vice president to examine carefully the English translations for all the exhibit displays because an increasing number of foreign visitors come to both Hahoe and Tosan.

Ryu's Poongsan offers an annual *sŏwŏn* training for eighty middle managers yearly. This training resembles the Japanese spiritual education described by Rohlen (1973, 1974:192–211). It takes place at the Pyŏngsan Sŏwŏn, which belongs to the prominent *yangban* clans in Kyŏngsang province and is located in the vicinity of the chairman's hometown, Hahoe. The origin of the *sŏwŏn* in Korea goes back as early as the Silla period (57 B.C.–A.D. 935), but it was not well established until the Yi dynasty. The *sŏwŏn* where Poongsan's training takes place was established in 1572 and is one of the best known. The *sŏwŏn* was originally a combination of private academies and shrines dedicated to past Confucian worthies. Such academies were established to train young men in Neo-Confucian ideology, manners, and morals. They were also the centers of regional cultural development of the local literati. The milieu surrounding the Confucian academy and the aesthetic beauty of the location are sufficient for the trainees to have a spiritual education. This training is described in some detail in chapter 4.

Like most Koreans of his generation, Ryu's life has been deeply rooted in the Confucian tradition. Confucianism is in his blood. Surprisingly, however, my detailed ethnographic study led me to conclude that my earlier assumption had been too presumptuous. The culture of Poongsan cannot be characterized solely in terms of the traditional Confucian virtues, although some scholars indicate that the East Asian rules of industrial relations are based on the Confucian ethic (Tai 1989). As we will see in the remaining chapters, the culture and organization of Poongsan include both the traditional culture with emphasis on the Confucian virtues and the modern culture with Western rationalism. They coexist in the organizational culture of Poongsan. This argument is synthesized in chapter 7. Some critics see even the *sŏwŏn* training as a manipulation of the Confucian indoctrination. Yet, the contents of the training do not include anything about Confucianism.

Also, Ryu does not openly admit that his managerial principles are based solely on the Confucian ethic. Yet there are many indica-

tions that the Confucian ethic pervaded the Poongsan management.
Perhaps Ryu's managerial philosophy with the Confucian ethic can
best be characterized by Tu's (1984:67) explanation:

> This is not to say that an individual will consciously bring his reli-
> gious beliefs or values to bear on his economic activities. Indeed, he
> may unconsciously translate values in his religious belief system into
> factors that motivate his economic behaviour. It is not as though the
> mind has compartments with religious and economic notions and
> motivations neatly and separately packaged. But as a person naturally
> works out the values that he strongly believes in, they may spill over
> into other areas of his life. It is important to recognize, however, that
> the spillover itself is not necessarily part of the natural working out
> of the belief system; it is often an *unintended consequence* [empha-
> sis added].

If Ryu is consciously unaware of the fact that he is a strong advocate
of the Confucian ethic, he must be a "hidden, unconscious Confucian," to borrow Tu's (1984:87) label.

For Ryu of Poongsan, the Confucian ethic, not the politicized Confucianism, as Tu distinguishes the two, seems to inspire his entrepreneurial activities by mobilizing his internal resources. And, also, it
serves as a kind of moral persuasion. Ryu of Poongsan has maintained
a good reputation ethically and morally. He is not involved in the
"octopus tentacles" (*mun'ŏbal*) of some *chaebŏl* groups, a reference
to their concentrated and expanding power over the Korean economy.
He has been free from the unethical real estate scandal. Like many
other big Korean entrepreneurs, however, Ryu of Poongsan has suffered from criticism for his close association with the Korean government: "Recipients of a cornucopia of special privileges and favors
from the state" (Eckert 1990:145). Such a close tie between government and business has tarnished the business elite's moral standing
(Eckert 1990:146), including Ryu of Poongsan. It gives an impression
that Korean *chaebŏl* groups support authoritarian politics.

In fact, when Chun's term as president was completed and Roh's
Sixth Republic came into power, the Congress, dominated by the
opposition party, opened hearings to investigate the possible unethical activities of the Chun government. One issue was related to
highly questionable fund-raising for the Ilhae Foundation, a govern-
ment-led research foundation, by which leading businessmen were

enticed into donating assigned amounts. Ryu's name was on the list of the donors, which also included Chŏng Chu-yŏng of Hyundai and many others.

During the hearing one congressman asked Ryu about his takeover of the Dongrae Arsenal and whether the government's favoritism toward Poongsan could be attributed to his school ties with Chun. The congressman suspected that Ryu's school association with Chun might have been the reason that Ryu was able to take over the arsenal. Ryu replied that his donation had been forced by the government against his wishes. The congressman cynically asked Ryu whether he had any plans to visit Chun and pay his condolences for the president's seclusion at a Buddhist temple, Paekdam-sa. (The president had gone to the mountainous Kangwŏn province to seek refuge from unending anti-Chun demonstrations by students.) Ryu answered, "If there is anyone who needs consolation, that is I, not the president" (*Hankook Ilbo*, 10 Nov. 1988:21–22; *Chugan Hankook*, 25 Nov. 1988:8).

Ryu's frank and straightforward answers to questions about his contribution to the foundation drew sympathy from both congressmen and the general public. Everyone in Korea knows that during Chun's rule one could not go on with business without "donating" to such a fund. In fact, some large *chaebŏl* groups such as the Kukje-ICC have been punished and pilloried. Yang Chung-mo (Yang Chŏngmo), the founder and former chairman of the Kukje, claims that he was punished by the Chun government for not donating to such a fund as Chun wished. Some Korean businessmen believe that "it is not a donation, but a taxation."

However, the public revelation of the diversion of such large sums of company funds (Ryu's share was reported to be 3 billion *wŏn* for the seven years of Chun's term) for political use, even if it was forced, became a major issue during the labor unrest in 1989 by Ryu's workers. Ryu told me that he certainly had enjoyed the enthusiastic support of President Park during his tenure as president, particularly in the start-up stage of Poongsan, but despite the speculation about his school ties with Chun, he had not received any particular favoritism from the Chun government. In fact, according to the log of Poongsan visitors, Chun visited Poongsan on only one occasion, on 17 February 1981; Park had been a frequent visitor.

Is Ryu Atypical?

Ryu of Poongsan is atypical in his business ethics and morality. He has not involved himself in diversification of his business interest in the manner of "octopus tentacles" and in the unethical real estate scandal, although his close tie with the Korean government has been the same as that of other Korean entrepreneurs. By and large, however, Ryu of Poongsan shares many of the characteristics typical of the other 311 Korean entrepreneurs surveyed by Jones and Sakong (1980:210–57), particularly in his ascribed status.

Ryu's *yangban* origin.

According to Jones and Sakong (1980:228), "very few entrepreneurs have risen from the poor masses represented by tenant farmers and rural and urban laborers." Entrepreneurs' fathers tended to be landowners (47 percent), merchants (19 percent), factory owners (16 percent), civil servants (6 percent), teachers (4 percent), or professionals (7 percent). Though Ryu's father was neither a landowner nor a merchant, he was a *yangban;* he belonged to traditional Korean elite groups socially, culturally, and emotionally.

Ryu's "deprived *yangban*" background suggests an interesting hypothesis regarding the background of the Korean entrepreneurs. Lee states that it is not the *yangban* class that is most likely to produce entrepreneurs, but the *hyangban* class, that is, the class of former *yangban* whose status has deteriorated over several generations of rural residence (see Jones and Sakong 1980:283). Ryu is definitely a descendant of *yangban*, but his deteriorated financial situation nevertheless recalls Lee's conceptualization.

As evidence supporting Lee's hypothesis, among Poongsan Ryu clan members, those who achieved distinction as prominent businessmen had left the village of Hahoe early, mostly during the lives of their fathers and grandfathers, because of the family's deteriorated financial condition, and they had grown up elsewhere, not in Hahoe. Those who had been born and raised in Hahoe and whose families were well-to-do did not exhibit above-average achievements. Most new houses in Hahoe belong to the members of the Ryu clan who grew up outside Hahoe and who long to return to the village. If this is typical, Lee's hypothesis may indeed be applicable to the members of the *yangban* class whose status has fallen.

Regarding birth order, Ryu is the first son, as are the majority of Korean entrepreneurs. The common belief is that first sons might like to avoid entrepreneurial high-risk ventures, but Jones and Sakong's (1980:239–41) survey reveals that 52 percent of Korean entrepreneurs are first sons. Although Ryu's father was the second son, Ryu is not only the first son but is also the eldest male of his generation among all his cousins and brothers. He was highly motivated by the urge to do something to uplift his family.

Ryu's Kyŏngsang origin.

After the military coup d'etat in 1961 by General Park, three Korean presidents were ex-generals and also were from Kyŏngsang province. Only an interim president who followed in office after the death of Park was an exception to this pattern, which has favored entrepreneurs from Kyŏngsang province. Koreans from non-Kyŏngsang provinces, particularly from Chŏlla province, are convinced that there has been and still is a strong regional favoritism at work. Indeed, the current president, Roh, is also from Kyŏngsang province. In a national survey conducted by *Joongang Ilbo* (1 Jan. 1989:8), more than 85.3 percent of the respondents acknowledged that regional competition and conflict, especially between Kyŏngsang and Chŏlla provinces, are severe. In fact, Koreans often use a word, "TK," which is an abbreviation for Taegu and Kyŏngsangpuk-do. "TK" and "Non-TK" are used to dichotomize and label people in the business world and in the arena of politics. Regionalism, and particularly the dominance of Kyŏngsang province, has become a hot political issue in Korea. Ryu's originating in Kyŏngsang province has never been a liability in his business activities. He is one of the Kyŏngsang entrepreneurs who is among the forty-six major entrepreneurs, along with Lee of Samsung, Koo of Lucky-Goldstar, and many others (Jones and Sakong 1980:43).

Jones and Sakong (1980:222) do not see religion as an important variable in Korean entrepreneurs' backgrounds. In fact, "when a Westerner is asked his religion, it takes a conscious act to say 'none'; for a Korean, it takes a conscious dedication to specify anything other than 'none.'" Often, Koreans express no religious preference. According to Jones and Sakong (1980:223), "religion plays an extremely minor role in differentiating the entrepreneurial elite from the population as a whole."

It is debatable whether Confucianism is a religion. Among the Korean religious population (42.6 percent of the 41,975,000 total Korean population in 1988), however, only 2.8 percent claim that they are Confucianists, whereas 48.5 percent claim to be Christians, either Roman Catholic or Protestant (National Bureau of Statistics 1988b: 286). During my fieldwork, Koreans estimated that over a quarter of the entire population are Christians. Estimates of the Christian population in Korea are no longer accurate because of the growth of the Christian population. Ryu belongs to this small minority of Confucianists or "hidden, unconscious" Confucianists, to use Tu's term. Geertz's (1965:149–51; also see Sayigh 1962) hypothesis that religious minorities are potential sources of entrepreneurial supply may be applicable to our case herein. Yet, an accurate account of Confucianists in Korea may be difficult, if not impossible.

As for the educational attainment of Korean entrepreneurs, Jones and Sakong (1980:231–38) concluded that Korean entrepreneurs are well educated (70 percent of their sample had some college education) despite the common belief that entrepreneurs elsewhere are not particularly well educated. Certainly they are better educated than the previous generation, and some have had college educations in reputable institutions, including foreign universities. Considering the Korean obsession with higher education, this pattern is not surprising.

Ryu differs from a majority of the other Korean entrepreneurs in Jones and Sakong's survey. His educational attainment is limited. Nonetheless, he is not exceptional either. Some of Korea's first-generation entrepreneurs and top Korean *chaebŏl* leaders such as Chŏng of Hyundai and Cho of Hanjin have educations that were curtailed at the precollege level.

The Corporate Culture of Poongsan

In terms of the corporate culture, Poongsan can best be understood in comparative terms, by its location on the continuum between two well-known Korean *chaebŏl* groups, Samsung and Hyundai. Koreans refer often to the contrasting corporate cultures of these two giant Korean enterprises. The corporate culture of Samsung is basically conservative. The largest Korean enterprise, it was founded by Lee Pyŏng-ch'ŏl, who was the youngest son of a wealthy landlord of *yangban* origin and who attended a traditional Confucian *sŏdang* and later Waseda University in Japan. The corporate culture, the managerial style, and the manner of Hyundai is the opposite; it is characteristically adventuresome and risk taking. The second or third largest of all Korean enterprises, Hyundai was founded by Chŏng Chu-yŏng, who was the first-born son of an average farmer and who attended a traditional Confucian *sŏdang* but whose formal education was curtailed at the primary school level (Jones and Sakong 1980:349–58).

Hyundai's corporate culture is believed to be progressive, creative, and frugal. Thus, Hyundai employees, often called "Hyundai men," proudly wear working clothes, cut their hair short, and present an image of frugal tenacity. On the other hand, Samsung emphasizes superiority, "number-one-ism." Its dominant image is that of the conservative, clean, and well-mannered businessman. Thus, "Samsung men" wear a coat and tie, maintain clean and combed hair, and look smart and polished (*Economist*, 5 Oct. 1985:32–51; H. Lee 1989a:15–16). Further, according to my observation, while Samsung and its affiliated companies are involved mainly in high-tech industries and white-collar work such as electronics, finance, real estate, mass communications, hotels, and hospitals, Hyundai and its affiliated companies are engaged in heavy industries, including construction, shipbuilding, automobile manufacturing, machinery, cement, ceramics, engineering, repair services, and marine transportation.

Ryu shares some similarities in Confucian *yangban* background with Lee. Also, both are from Kyŏngsang province. However, their economic and educational backgrounds differ significantly. Whereas Lee is the last son of a wealthy landlord who has never experienced poverty and attended a respected university in Japan, Ryu knew poverty in early childhood, and his education was limited to vocational and technical school. In these respects, Ryu's background more closely resembles that of Hyundai's Chŏng. Chŏng even engaged in manual labor in Inch'ŏn. In sum, Ryu's background falls somewhere between Lee's and Chŏng's.

Accordingly, the corporate culture of Poongsan can be described as falling between those of Samsung and Hyundai. The official motto of Poongsan adopted by Ryu when he established the company was *ch'angŭi, silch'ŏn,* and *hwakin* (creativity; performance and execution; and verification and confirmation) and is also a mixture of some Samsung traits and characteristics of Hyundai. *Ch'angŭi* and *silch'ŏn* are traits that Hyundai strives for, and *silch'ŏn* is what Samsung emphasizes. Poongsan shares with Hyundai the traits of simplicity, frugality, and informality yet resembles Samsung in its pursuit of "number-one-ism," the determination to be one of the top manufacturers of copper-related products in the world. My casual observation of my three nephews who are working in these three companies confirms these descriptions.

As I have studied the corporate culture of Poongsan, I have entertained the hypothesis that when the Korean entrepreneurs come from poor economic backgrounds, even if their origins were *yangban* with limited formal educations, they tend to engage in adventuresome risk-taking businesses, and they are likely to engage in manufacturing fields in heavy industry, metal-related work, as is the case with Chŏng of Hyundai. And if the entrepreneurs are from wealthy backgrounds and they have high levels of educational attainment, they tend to be involved in light industry or service-oriented businesses, as demonstrated in the case of Lee of Samsung. It will be interesting to test this hypothesis on more Korean entrepreneurs.

My rather extensive description of Ryu's managerial philosophy might leave the impression that Ryu is unique. Nonetheless, according to my survey of Poongsan's Bupyung plant employees, only two respondents (1.9 percent) thought of Poongsan as atypical. Rather, the great majority thought Poongsan was typical of Korean companies in this respect. Because young industrial workers tend to view traditional Confucian virtues and the family analogy as exploitive and backward, many Korean *chaebŏls* prefer not to be labeled as advocates of Confucianism. The major criticism appears to be to politicized Confucianism, which Tu presents as distinct from the Confucian ethic. It is nevertheless highly doubtful that the managerial worldview of any first-generation Korean *chaebŏl* leaders, including the chairman of Poongsan, can be exempted from the Confucian orientation. Confucian virtues have been deeply embedded in the Korean way of life for a very long time. Furthermore, despite all the changes of recent years, the essential mores governing Korean family and kinship systems, which are based on Confucian virtues, still remain intact. As long as those values persist in Korean society, the authoritarian rule of the *hoejang* of the Korean *chaebŏl* can hardly be challenged.

Hsu (1965, 1971, 1975:208–38, 1983:217–47) entertains an interesting hypothesis to explain the genesis of the authority-centered culture of the family system as it is manifested in the Chinese and Japanese kinship systems. Hsu has identified the kinship attributes of the father-son dominant dyad. These attributes include continuity, inclusiveness, authority, and asexuality, whereas the husband-wife dominant dyad of the American kinship system reveals the opposite attributes: discontinuity, exclusiveness, volition, and sexuality. Serrie (1976, 1986) has explained the behavior of Chinese business management by examining Chinese kinship attributes, using Hsu's hypothesis of psychocultural attributes of kinship. It seems to me that this approach is equally applicable to the behavior of Korean business and industrial management.

The dominant dyad in Korean kinship is indeed the father-son dyad, with its four major attributes (C. Kim 1989). I exclude the sexuality versus asexuality characteristic, which is irrelevant in this discussion. The remaining three attributes are directly applicable to the managerial behavior of Korean *chaebŏl* leaders. Since the first-generation Korean entrepreneurs were raised under the strong influence of the traditional Korean family and kinship system, they are inescapably authoritarian, inclusive, and concerned about the continuity of their business. The extensive involvement of kin members in the business of the Korean *chaebŏl*, as evidenced in the presence of many Ryu clan members in Poongsan, is an example of inclusiveness. Hattori (1986) indicates that in Korean *chaebŏl* groups, a large number of kin members of the founders of the *chaebŏl* typically participate in management. Highly centralized guidance, direction, control, and decision making by the chairman (Jones and Sakong 1980:259–60), again a pattern manifest in Poongsan, is an important characteristic of the Korean *chaebŏl* and an indication of authoritarianism. The inheritance of the business through the sons (or at least the closest family members), a manifestation of the value of continuity, does not directly apply in the case of Poongsan because the first generation is still active. However, scholars and journalists report that in large Korean enterprises most company heads are succeeded by their sons. Recently, Samsung and Hyundai have exemplified this very pattern (*Chugan Hankook*, 14 Feb. 1987:10–13; 10 Dec. 1987:25). Shin's (1986:51) survey indicates that 90 percent of the enterprises in his sample that have completed the transfer of the business to successors or that are in the process of the transfer are passing the business on to family members or to people closely related to the families. Moreover, 65 percent of the successors are eldest sons. The pattern is simply that of the traditional Korean family and kinship system, following the rule of patrilineal descent and the rule of inheritance.

In summary, according to my observations and to the great majority of Poongsan employees who responded to my survey, Poongsan is not an atypical company.

2

The Characteristics of
Poongsan Employees

Poongsan's growth for the twenty years since it was founded in 1968 has been astonishing—the number of employees increased 119 times, assets 169 times, and capital 3,273 times. It epitomizes the growth rate of Korea's economy and industrialization. For such a phenomenal growth, the entrepreneurial leadership of the chairman (and the strong support of the Korean government, especially by President Park) was key. Nevertheless, although the chairman and founder of the company could persuade, direct, or induce his employees to act in accordance with the goals and objectives he set, the employees are the ones who carried out the endeavors. Because of their importance, this chapter describes how the employees were recruited and employed and who they are.

Regarding the philosophical base of the recruitment, a top executive of Poongsan and close associate of the chairman of Poongsan told me, "You know the old Confucian saying, 'If there are good fruits such as peaches and pears on the trees, even though those fruits cannot advertise themselves, people will come in flocks and eventually make a road leading to those fruit trees' [*toribulŏn, hajasŏnghae* in Korean pronunciation using Chinese characters]. As long as the company is good and has a good reputation, people will come to work for it."

Such a philosophy is indeed manifest in the recruiting of good students in Korean colleges and universities. The top-ranking universities in Korea, such as Seoul National, Yonsei, Ehwa, and Korea universities, do not make an effort to recruit good students. They believe that because of their reputation good students will seek admission to those schools without any recruiting effort at all. By comparison, even the most prestigious universities in the United States (in the world as well) make deliberate efforts all the time to recruit the best students.

The executive added,

> Of course, times have changed. Nowadays, for certain positions, we have to make a conscious effort to recruit them, because we are experiencing a shortage of people and are confronted with competition with other firms. In the past, however, it was a sheer buyer's market. Up until a decade ago, we had never experienced a shortage of prospective employees. This does not mean to say that we do not do anything at all. Contrarily, if we see exceptional candidates, we make every effort to recruit them. Sometimes, we use our kin network and friendship ties and any other networks to recruit the exceptional prospective employees. Let me tell you a story. When our company was in expansion in the early 1970s, we recruited an exceptionally talented young engineer who was working for a top Korean *chaebŏl*. We made every effort to recruit him, but he turned down our offer. The only way we knew how was to appeal to his kin tie with our chairman. The engineer and our chairman belong to the same Ryu clan and originated from Hahoe. Although they had never met before, we were persuasive enough to be successful in recruiting him: how meaningful it would be working for a kinsman rather than for someone with whom he does not have any relation at all. I don't believe any Westerner can understand this logic.

Later, the hard-sought young engineer became the major architect for building the most modern, the largest, and the most productive brass mill plant in Onsan. Now he is the chief engineer of the newly constructed copper plant in Cedar Rapids, Iowa. He oversees a project costing 200 million U.S. dollars to construct and install machinery for the establishment of PMX Industries, Inc., a subsidiary of Poongsan. He remembered the recruitment efforts by his clan members. Recently, he recollected and told me at a Korean restaurant in Iowa City,

I don't know what I would be by now, if I had not come to Poongsan. But I recognize that my job now is meaningful, expanding our business from Korea to the United States. Since the glorious days of Sŏae in Korean history, this project is the biggest to be accomplished by one of our clan members. I feel like I am doing something for the honor of our clan and our country. Patriotism may be too big a word for me, but I feel like I am doing something. I hope PMX becomes a successful business enterprise, so that both Koreans and Americans benefit from it.

In this case, it seems to me that the engineer, as the chairman's clan member, does not work simply for a wage but also for the honor of his clan, his ancestors, and his country. Perhaps recruiting from kin members is not necessarily negative as long as one is qualified.

To understand who the rank-and-file workers in Poongsan are, I randomly picked a shop floor worker at the Bupyung plant and asked him about his socioeconomic and demographic characteristics. He happened to be twenty-eight years old, male, married, a high school graduate, had worked for four years, and had joined the labor union. He does not claim any religious preference. He is from a small town in Kyŏngsang province. Like most Korean farmers in the past, his parents were tenant farmers. He understands the values of hard work, the meaning of poverty, and what poverty can do to a person. As an uprooted farmer in his origins and recently transplanted to Seoul, he does not own his own house. He and his wife live in a two-room *chŏnsae* (a system of rent in which the tenant deposits a large sum of money, depending on the market price, and has access to the keys of the house. When the tenant wishes to vacate the premises, the entire sum paid in for deposit is returned to the tenant. In the meantime, the landlord invests the deposited sum to generate interest. It is a unique Korean rental system [Spencer 1988:38–43]). He told me,

> After I completed my military service, I was unable to find any job in my hometown. Since my parents did not own any farmland to farm, I was worrying about my means of livelihood. Luckily, through my relative, I was able to find a job here. I wish I could do better, but I am by and large satisfied with my job. No matter what, my living condition is better than that of my parents. I remember the hard times when I was growing up. Poverty was our unfulfilled *han*.

He appears to be an ordinary Korean; nothing about him seems extraordinary. Also, his commitment to his job is no different from that of American industrial workers. Perhaps Luthans, McCaul, and Dodd (1985) are correct when they say that the level of commitment of Korean workers to their organizations is not higher than that of American workers.

Let me summarize the characteristics of Poongsan employees to see whether the randomly selected worker described above is typical. For this effort, two sources are utilized: precollected company personnel records and a social survey on the Bupyung plant employees. The personnel file for each employee in the company's main office provided me with basic demographic information: the employee's level of education, age, length of service, and origin by province. The facts about marital status, choice of spouse, size of family, filial support for parents, housing, union membership, religious affiliation, previous job, and job of parents had to be obtained from a survey I conducted from 7 to 13 July 1988.

Because employees at the Bupyung plant have essentially the same demographic characteristics as those at the other plants, I selected the Bupyung plant as the site for the survey mainly for the sake of convenience. Since Angang, Onsan, and Dongrae plants are all located more than two hundred miles from Seoul, it would have been impossible for me to make daily observations at those plants. Bupyung, only six miles from Seoul, thus became the site of most of my fieldwork.

The Bupyung plant is located in the heart of an industrial complex. The oldest plant of Poongsan, it manufactures copper and copper alloy products such as sheet and strip, pipe and tube, rod, bar and wire, golden coin blanks and other precious metal commemorative medals, and welded titanium tubes. The plant has seven departments: administrative, security, engineering and maintenance, quality control, production, forging, and research and development. The administrative department has six sections: general affairs, labor, accounting, first material, second material, and electronic data processing. The production department includes production control, casting, rolling, extruding, and the processing section, which employs the largest number of workers. The seven departments and twenty sections at the plant are directed by the plant manager, assisted by the vice plant manager.

The sample used in the survey included 100 males and 4 females, 15 of whom were employed in the office and managerial department,

83 in the production department, 1 as a secretary, 4 as drivers, and 1 as a general laborer. Because the number of females is too small to allow meaningful statistical analysis, no classification by sex is made in my analysis of the responses.

The Demographic Characteristics of All Poongsan Employees

Poongsan's 9,430 employees are located at the plants in Bupyung, Onsan, Angang, and Dongrae, as well as at the main office in Seoul. The Angang plant employs the largest number (4,050); Dongrae, the second largest (2,709); Onsan, the third largest (1,630); and Bupyung the smallest (724). At the main office in Seoul are 317 employees, most of whom are white-collar and managerial.

Poongsan's job categories.

Except for the top executives and temporary consultants, Poongsan employees fall into four groups: office and managerial workers, engineers, technicians, and general laborers. The office and managerial workers are mostly university graduates, although some high school graduates are engaged in white-collar work. The engineers, who are graduates with higher degrees, engage in research, basic planning, and management. The technicians or highly skilled workers are mostly high school graduates, and normally they have received some professional or technical training in addition. They engage in production work, operating machines and equipment. The general laborers engage in manual unskilled labor.

The office and managerial workers range from 5- *kŭp* (rank 5) up to *yisabo* (assistant managing director). There are eight ranks of engineers, ranging from 5-*kŭp* to *yisabo*. There are five ranks of technicians, beginning with 4-*kŭp* and rising to *t'ŭk-kŭp* (special rank) at the top. There is no differentiation by rank among temporary and general laborers.

Most office and managerial positions, including those of the executives, are concentrated in the main office in Seoul, whereas engineers and technicians are found in greater numbers at the plants. Poongsan employees at each plant, including the plant manager and other managerial workers, wear gray uniforms and a hard hat. The rank of each employee is revealed by the color and shape of the mark on his or her hard hat and name tag, which is pinned on the left breast pocket.

No women among the 1,175 female employees of Poongsan hold positions above 3-*kŭp* in the office and managerial field, and none occupies a position above 4-*kŭp* in the category of engineers. The majority of the women (more than 90 percent) at Poongsan are skilled, semi-skilled, and general laborers. Their work is usually simple, repetitious, and mundane. The only area where women outnumber men is in the category of general labor: there are 57 male general laborers but 82 female general laborers.

Socioeconomic characteristics of Poongsan employees.

In terms of education, every Poongsan employee has at least attended and graduated from a six-year primary school, and 20 received graduate degrees. A majority (more than 60 percent) finished high school. Although a higher percentage of women (78.56 percent) than men (58.35 percent) finished high school, a higher percentage of men (8.99 percent) than women (0.77 percent) attended and graduated from four-year universities. Only 9 female employees out of 1,175 graduated with a university degree; 5 of these women are located in the main office in Seoul.

There are no patterns of educational attainment that distinguish any of the four plants. The majority of employees at the plants are high school and middle school graduates; primary school and university graduates are evenly distributed among the plants. Predictably, four-year university graduates make up the majority (71.21 percent) of the employees in the main office in Seoul.

The educational level attained by Poongsan employees is higher than that attained by the average Korean manufacturing worker (table 2.1). A higher proportion of Poongsan's employees have high school, two-year college, and four-year university degrees. The educational attainment of Poongsan's top one hundred managers whose ranks are *pujang* (division head) and above, excluding the chairman and vice chairman, matches the Korean norm. Sixty-seven of them graduated from four-year universities, and only one left school after graduating from middle school (junior high). Three have acquired postgraduate degrees. There is no equivalent data available to com-

Table 2.1 The Average Level of Education Attained by Poongsan Employees and All Korean Manufacturing Workers, 1988 (in percent)

Educational Level	Poongsan			Korea		
	Male	Female	Total	Male	Female	Total
Primary[a]	4.93	9.86	5.45	5.09	14.23	9.51
Middle school[a]	17.49	7.08	16.19	31.31	42.80	36.86
High school[a]	58.34	78.55	60.87	53.44	41.45	47.65
Two-year college[b]	10.24	3.74	9.43	4.28	0.98	2.68
University graduate[c]	8.99	0.77	7.95	5.88	0.54	3.30

SOURCE: The author's field data as of 31 May 1988 and the *Korea Statistical Year Book* (National Bureau of Statistics 1988a:92).
[a] Includes those who dropped out before graduating.
[b] Includes the college and university dropouts.
[c] Includes those with graduate education.

pare the Poongsan managers with those of other Korean firms. However, the Poongsan management is better educated than are Korean entrepreneurs, civil servants, *chaebŏl* leaders, and public managers (Jones and Sakong 1980:232). What is most interesting about the educational backgrounds of the Poongsan management is that no one there has an MBA.

The average age of Poongsan employees is a little more than 28 years old, close to the national average: nearly 55 percent of all Korean manufacturing workers belong to the 21–35 age range; almost 60 percent of the Poongsan employees belong to this age group. Only 14 (0.15 percent) workers are younger than 16 years old, and 84 (0.89 percent) are 56 years old and older. The retirement age of Poongsan employees, except for the executives, is 55. Of the 84 employees who are 56 and older, 68 are temporary employees, including consultants and advisers. The other 16 are top executives who stay on regardless of their age. The age variations among the locations, including the main office, are closely related to the history of the plants. Since the Bupyung plant is the oldest and a good many of its employees have worked there for a number of years, their average age is

higher than those who work in the other plants. The average age of
the Dongrae plant workers is the next highest. Although the Dongrae
plant was the last to be integrated into Poongsan, most of its workers
had worked there when Dongrae was an arsenal and stayed on when
it was merged with Poongsan. The Angang plant workers are, on average, the youngest; slightly more than 70 percent of them are less than
30 years of age. This is mainly due to the fact that the Korean government exempts from active military duty all those who work in the
defense industry, and many young men of draftable age (18 years old
and older) seek employment in the Angang plant to be exempted from
military duty. (Women in Korea are exempted from active military
duty other than as volunteers.) Currently, nearly 15 percent of the
workers at the Angang plant fall in this 17- to 20-year-old age group.

The age distribution of Poongsan's top one hundred managers also
matches the Korean national average. According to Shin's (1986:97)
nationwide survey of top Korean executives, 61.8 percent of the respondents were younger than 50 years old, and 39.2 percent were
older. At Poongsan, 61 percent of the managers are younger than 50.
Most of Poongsan's top management fall between the ages of 41 and
50. One is less than 35 years old; seven have passed the age of 60.

As far as length of service is concerned, since Poongsan's history
is relatively short, only a very limited number of employees, 1.6 percent, have worked for the corporation for more than 15 years. The
largest number of workers have worked for more than 1 year but less
than 5 years. The average Poongsan employee has worked there
slightly more than 4 years. The average length of service for women
is almost half that of males. Women usually retire upon getting married, which explains why the average age of female workers is so
much lower. Again, the average number of years of service for the
Bupyung plant workers is higher, mainly because the plant is the
oldest. More than 60 workers in that plant have worked for Poongsan
since the establishment of the firm in 1968.

In terms of origin, most Poongsan employees (80.28 percent) come
from Kyŏngsang province. The distribution of the employees by origin nonetheless follows the location of the plant. The largest number
of Bupyung plant employees came from Kyŏnggi province, where the
plant is located. The other three plants, Onsan, Angang, and Dongrae, are all located in Kyŏngsang province; predictably, more than
90 percent of the workers are from that province.

A preference for those from Kyŏngsang province appears to exist among the top executives at Poongsan: 54 percent are of Kyŏngsang origin. This pattern is closely related to the firm's manner of hiring and promoting executives. Of 100 executives, 93 were hired through the connections based on kin ties and the recommendations of friends, relatives, and acquaintances. Only 7 of them were hired on the basis of kongch'ae, or an open competitive entrance examination. The intent of kongch'ae is to eliminate personal connections and ties in the hiring process and to consider only personal qualifications and merit. Given that so many of the executives were hired through some sort of connection, it is not surprising that they are from Kyŏngsang province, where the founder of Poongsan came from.

My survey indicates that 77.9 percent of the Bupyung plant employees of Poongsan are married. Only a few of the respondents, 1.9 percent, were either divorced or separated. No longer is divorce unthinkable among contemporary Koreans, including industrial workers. This is indeed a change: "Because Koreans have traditionally viewed marriage as a union between entire families, not just a union between two individuals, divorce is considered the separation of two families" (C. Kim 1988a:51).

This is not to say that divorce does not exist in Korea, but it is uncommon. Only 2 of the 104 Bupyung plant employees I surveyed, for example, were divorced or separated. Divorce is male-centered, influenced by Confucian teachings during the Yi dynasty and by the Ta Ming Lü, the criminal code developed during the Ming dynasty (1368–1644). On the basis of the Ta Ming Lü, Koreans derive the three rules of obedience, which state that a woman must follow her parents in youth, follow her husband in marriage, and follow her sons in old age, and the seven evil causes of divorce, which allow a man to divorce his wife when she is disobedient to his parents, fails to bear a child or children, commits adultery, succumbs to jealousy, contracts a repulsive disease, offends with her loquacity, or steals from the family, usually to help her natal mother. To avoid excessively male-centered divorce, Koreans have developed three provisions forbidding divorce from a wife: if she has no one to depend on if expelled from the husband's household; if she has borne with her husband the three-year mourning period for his deceased parents; or if the man has gone from poverty to wealth since marrying her (Y. Kim 1979:100; Lee 1983:250–51).

A thirty-five-year old divorced Bupyung worker told me that his divorce had nothing to do with the seven evil causes for divorce but was due mainly to incompatibility. Said he, "We couldn't get along well. She complained about my night shift, and everything. My mother wanted us to stay married, though. My mother thought she was good enough. In a sense, I thought so, too. But, she did not want to stay in the marriage. Instead of putting up with all those complaints, I agreed to the divorce. I have a three-year old boy, but my mother keeps him." Divorces like this one are certainly contrary to the traditional male-centered divorce. Moreover, in Korea, because of the strong patrilineal rule, the father has the primary right of custody of a child. He continued, "Now, I am in love with someone who was divorced before. I like her, and she likes me, too. I am going to marry next spring." It appears that divorce is no longer as stigmatized in Korea as it once was. Although this case is still an exceptional one, its existence suggests a major change.

In the past, marriages in Korea were arranged, particularly among the noble class, who used marriage to maintain status. During the Yi dynasty, the system of arranged marriages contributed to class endogamy; most Koreans married within their own class. Two modified forms of arranged marriages have been used. In one, the person selects several candidates and then asks his or her parents to choose from among them. In the other, parents and kin recommend several candidates almost equal in their qualifications for final selection by the person who is going to be married. Arranged marriages are still popular in rural Korean villages, although an increasing number of young, educated, and urban Koreans freely choose their own partners.

Even among the former *yangban* class, the forms of marriage arrangement are undergoing change. As an example, the Ryu clan members in Hahoe in the past most often chose to marry the descendants of the Yŏngnam School led by Yi Hwang, Kim Sŏng-il, and Chŏng Ku, who are located in several villages in north central Kyŏngsangpuk-do (Cho 1984). In 1964 more than 87.7 percent of the Ryu clan married members of the descendants of the Yŏngnam School (T. Kim 1979:119–27), through the network of *yŏn'jul-hon*, the chain-string form of marriage arrangement (Kim 1974). However, for the past ten years, there have been no marriages between Ryu clan and Kim clan members. The Poongsan chairman's own children are married not to the descendants of the Yŏngnam School, but to the offspring of newly established elites.

Recently, I. Chang (1989) has completed an extensive survey of the marriage patterns of the children of the top one hundred Korean *chaebŏl* groups and concluded that almost half of the offspring married other *chaebŏl* groups' children whose rankings were similar to their own; the remainder married the children of prominent politicians, cabinet members and associate cabinet members of the government, military generals, and university professors. A classic example of this type of marriage is the in-law tie between two top Korean *chaebŏl* groups, Samsung and Hyundai. In so doing, the *chaebŏl* offspring have created a neo-elite endogamy to replace the former *yangban* endogamy to protect their privileges. The close ties between politics and big business are thus enhanced.

In sum, free choice is the primary means of acquiring spouses among lower-middle-class or working-class urbanites, whereas arranged marriage is still the dominant form of spousal selection among rural farmers and the newly established urban rich.

Since many Poongsan employees are from rural villages, arranged marriage is predictably the predominant form (55.95 percent among the Bupyung plant workers surveyed, for example), although free choice is not uncommon (22.62 percent of those surveyed). A transitional form, representing the change from arranged marriage to free choice, is also presented (21.43 percent). It is generally believed that a massive migration from rural to urban industrial areas since the mid 1960s has established nuclear family patterns. Having left their parents behind in rural areas, these urban industrial workers are assumed to have small, nuclear families. However, the average family size of Bupyung workers appeared rather large. The majority live in households of between four and six members (59.6 percent).

Urbanization and industrialization in Korea has not necessarily led to the Western pattern of the nuclear family. The traditional family and kinship system has combined with urban migration to create a rather crowded housing problem in the urban slums on the edges of Seoul and Inch'ŏn.

A thirty-two-year-old plant worker who lives in a two-room rented house with his elderly parents, a younger sister, and his wife and two children told me, "Whenever I work on the midnight shift, I just cannot rest and sleep well in the daytime. Not only is my house crowded, but also my street is so noisy that I cannot relax and rest." Certainly, such situations were a consideration for Poongsan management in setting its shift policy. One executive who was involved in setting that policy told me,

> We knew that the weekly shift change, compared with the monthly shift of most Western industrial plants, is less productive because of workers' adjustment problems with the midnight work. But not many of our workers can endure a month-long night shift. They must go without enough rest because of their housing conditions and the crowded environment in their residential sections. Our housing situation is not like that of most Western industrial workers, who usually own their own private housing and thus can rest well.

Many workers' elderly parents were supporting themselves instead of depending solely on the support of their children (31.7 percent). Nevertheless, nearly half (49.0 percent) of the workers' parents were supported by the workers or their siblings, mainly because of the absence of an institutionalized social security system. In Korea, filial piety fills the role of social security.

The Poongsan chairman is not the only person at the firm who adheres to filial piety, which still prevails even among young rank-and-file workers whose values tend toward Western values. Accounts of filial piety are found in many Korean folk tales about the feeding and care of aged parents (Choi 1979:63–176). There are even stories of sons "who fed their own flesh and blood to their ailing parents" (Janelli and Janelli 1982:50). Even now, many Koreans, particularly those in rural villages, consider stories of filial piety more instructive for their children than any other kind of tale (Janelli and Janelli 1982:51).

A forty-five-year-old rank-and-file worker who was originally from Kyŏngsang province near the chairman's hometown and also had *yangban* roots told me, "I cannot do as much as our chairman does for my ancestors because I cannot afford it financially. But my filial piety is not any less than his. I always go to my hometown to offer my ancestral rituals to my ancestors during *ch'usŏk* holidays [the harvest festival on 15 August, by the lunar calendar] and New Year's holidays." Because of the difficulty of purchasing bus and train tickets for those occasions, the company has made special arrangements to purchase advance tickets for its employees for their home visits.

Housing problems for those who are living in Seoul and Inch'ŏn are severe; nearly 41.5 percent (17,588,000) of the entire Korean population (42,380,000) in 1989 was concentrated in Seoul and its vicinity, including Inch'ŏn, where the Bupyung plant is located (*Hankook Ilbo*, 15 Aug. 1990:19). Seoul's huge population has driven housing prices sky-high and created an absolute shortage of housing. Some luxury apartments (2,000 square feet) in a good district in Seoul cost more than a million U.S. dollars, and they are in short supply. On the other hand, 2,000,000 Seoulites live in 5-*p'yŏng* (5 *p'yŏngs* equal 178 square feet) rented barrack-houses, often shared by three households including 15 or 16 members in all. Only an estimated 40 percent of the 950,000 householders in Seoul own their own houses.

The housing shortage is reflected in the ownership patterns I discerned among Bupyung plant employees. According to my survey, a majority (52.0 percent) did not own their own houses, while 40.4 percent had their own houses, and only 6 respondents (5.8 percent) stayed in company housing. Company housing can accommodate only 60 households among 724 Bupyung plant employees. The waiting list for company housing is long because the housing is virtually free and the supply is short. A plan to build additional units to meet the ever-increasing demand has been suspended because of the lack of roads that can allow fire trucks passage.

When I was invited to the house of a respondent who was classified as an owner of his own house in the vicinity of Seoul, I saw how badly it needed major repairs. Even at my height, it was difficult for me to enter his gate without bending my knees. His house was literally a barracks. I was surprised that he owned the house. However, when he told me how high the price of his lot was, despite the deplorable shape of the house, I was surprised again. Real estate prices in Seoul would seem outrageous to the average American.

Religious preference and union membership.

Because of the Korean cultural attributes regarding religious preference, as discussed in chapter 1, my survey may not give an accurate picture of the religious preferences of Bupyung plant employees. Nonetheless, according to the survey, 41.3 percent, the largest single category, listed no religious preference. Buddhists formed the second largest group with 28.8 percent; Christians, both Protestants and Roman Catholics, were 25.0 percent. The figures corroborate the national figure on the Christian population in Korea. Only 4.8 percent claimed that they were Confucianists.

A great majority (77.9 percent) of the respondents were union members, but 15.4 percent were not members, for it is an open union. In addition, 5.8 percent were not eligible because of their job classification as office and managerial employees. Workers' views of the labor union are discussed later.

Military service in Korea is mandatory for men. Thus, a large majority of those surveyed served in the military and were honorably discharged (82.7 percent); 17.3 percent were exempt, including four women.

As for their previous job experience before joining Poongsan, half of those surveyed held jobs in other industries.

The exodus of farmers.

In terms of the origins of employees and their parents, although the Bupyung plant is located between the two metropolitan centers of Korea, Seoul and Inch'ŏn, a majority (52.9 percent) of those surveyed were from farming villages. Their parents also had come from farming villages. This figure indicates the important role of the rural labor force in recent Korean industrialization.

A massive migration from rural to urban industrial areas has occurred since the mid 1960s. In this period, at least 9 million farmers and their families, nearly a quarter of the total population, are estimated to have left their farms and moved to cities. Some informed scholars have expressed their concern that the suppression of the agricultural sector in favor of export-oriented industrialization might bring about fundamental differences between rural and urban ways of life, particularly producing an income gap between the two.

The gap between the average household income of rural farmers and that of urban dwellers is indeed getting wider, thus stimulating a further exodus from farms to cities. In 1981 the farmer's average household income was 96.6 percent that of the urbanites, 89.1 percent in 1986, and 83.8 percent in 1987 (Dong-A Ilbo, 18 Feb. 1989:1). The gap was slightly narrowed in 1988, as farmers' income increased

to 84.1 percent that of the urbanites (*Chosun Ilbo,* 22 Apr. 1989:15).
According to a recent survey made by the Center for Consumer Protection in 1989, 79.3 percent of the respondents acknowledged that
the living standard of farmers had improved greatly since the beginning of industrialization, but 92.8 percent indicated that they were
nonetheless aware of a great income gap between rural and urban
Koreans. Nearly 70 percent of the respondents pointed out that rural
farmers' standard of living was worse than that of the urbanites. Un-
derstandably, 44.5 percent of the respondents wished to move to the
cities (*Dong-A Ilbo,* 10 May 1989:9).

The exodus of farmers to the cities has been a continuing process.
From 1983 to 1987, the number of farm households decreased at a
rate of 1.3 percent annually, and the farm population decreased 4.2
percent annually. In 1988 the rates accelerated significantly: there
was a 2.4 percent reduction of farm households and a 6.4 percent reduction of farm population. In 1988 alone, nearly half a million farm
households left their farms for cities (*Dong-A Ilbo,* 8 Mar. 1989:6).

The young adults ranging from 20 to 29 years of age formed 36
percent of the migrants (*Kyunghyang Shinmun,* 15 July 1988:6). The
farm population is increasingly elderly. The proportion of the agricultural labor force aged 55 and over was 10.9 percent in 1966; in
1978 it had risen to 18.4 percent (Y. Chang 1989:245). Beginning in
1986 the rate of change increased: the proportion of farmers aged 55
and older was 21.0 percent in 1986, 22.5 percent in 1987, and 24.4
percent in 1988 (Ministry of Agriculture and Fisheries 1988:17–21).

Meanwhile, the 20 to 29 age group decreased from 12.7 percent in
1980 to 10.2 percent in 1988 (Ministry of Agriculture and Fisheries
1988:17–21). Interestingly, the female population in rural farm villages, especially in the age group of 20 to 29 years old, is much
smaller than the male population. Although national ratio by sex is
nearly even, according to 1988 figures (National Bureau of Statistics
1988b:59), the sex ratio among those of marriageable age in rural
farming villages shows a great imbalance. Men outnumber women
by more than 11 percent, which suggests the emergence of social
problems. Some farm youths experience difficulty in finding available women who are willing to marry future farmers. One survey
revealed that 83.4 percent of rural women preferred to move to cities
or wanted to marry someone who could relocate to a city after marriage (*Chosun Ilbo,* 12 Feb. 1989:4). In the 1980s, it was estimated

that about 300 rural Korean farm bachelors even attempted to commit suicide because of their inability to acquire spouses (*Chosun Ilbo*, 22 Apr. 1989:14; *Dong-A Ilbo*, 13 May 1989:13).

Indeed, a large percentage of Poongsan employees are former farmers and their offspring. When we include the three other rural Poongsan plants, a total of about 76 percent of the Poongsan employees are from rural villages. Successful entrepreneurs such as the chairman of Poongsan whose roots are in rural villages can exercise an enormous influence and keep in close touch with their original home villages, but many rank-and-file workers make minimal contact with their home villages and have become uprooted.

Whatever the living conditions of these uprooted industrial workers in the crowded cities, and whatever their feelings of deprivation in comparison with the rich capitalists, they feel they are better off than their fellows who remain back home on farms. Even though rural farmers' income and their standard of living has improved with their raising cash crops as described by Y. Chang (1989), the average farm household's debt has also increased. From 1981 to 1987, the income of the average farm household increased 1.8 times while its debt increased 5.5 times: in 1988, average farm household income jumped another 24.4 percent, yet its debt increased 31 percent. The debt of an average farm household was reported to be 3,131,000 wŏn, roughly 39 percent of its annual income (*Chosun Ilbo*, 22 Apr. 1989:15).

During my 1988 and 1989 fieldwork I witnessed hundreds of farmers' protests against the poor farm policy of the government, in the period following the June 29 Proclamation and increasing U.S. pressure to open the Korean market to U.S. farm products. The frequency and intensity of farmers' protests were as furious as labor disputes in the industrial sector of the same period. To borrow Y. Chang's (1989) wording, instead of going to town to sell their products, the peasants go to town equipped with bamboo spears to protest the government's farm policy. In fact, on 13 February 1989, about 10,000 angry farmers from all over Korea came to Yŏido Square, Seoul, where the National Assembly Hall is located, armed with bamboo spears to conduct the most militant protest yet in modern Korean history against the government's farm policy (*Joongang Ilbo*, 15 Feb. 1989:3). They were protesting the low price of red pepper and an irrigation tax imposed on farmers. Their action was a manifestation of their accumulating frustration over the years resulting from the government's discriminatory policy against farmers in favor of urban industry.

Recruitment and Employment

The national picture.

Before the industrialization of the late 1960s, Korean employers enjoyed an abundant labor supply. Nonetheless, beginning in 1968, and particularly in the late 1970s, the number of job openings has exceeded the number of job applicants (table 2.2). In fact, the Korean unemployment rate recently was lower than that of some advanced industrial economies (National Bureau of Statistics 1989:173). As industrialization takes hold, Korean firms recognize that the recruitment of well-qualified candidates is an important item on the agenda.

Despite a possible shortage of qualified workers, the recruitment effort of large Korean enterprises does not seem as aggressive as that of some Japanese firms (Rohlen 1974:67). The reputable firms believe that their reputations as first-class *chaeböls*, as fast-growing and dynamic organizations, automatically attracts applicants of high quality. Their attitude is similar to the fruit-tree analogy described earlier. Regardless of the labor statistics, for reputable firms the Korean job market appears to be a buyer's market.

Nevertheless, the Korean national labor statistics can be misleading. Though there is a growing labor shortage in the blue-collar work force, there is an abundant supply of white-collar workers with four-year university degrees. As the Korean economy slowed in 1989, the scarcity of jobs for university graduates became a serious problem. Although the unemployment figure for Korea as a whole was still 2.3 percent in 1989, the unemployment rate for the university graduates was more than 4.5 percent. The average ratio between the number of applicants and the number of job openings in the top four *chaeböl* groups—Samsung, Lucky-Goldstar, Hyundai, and Daewoo—in 1989 was 8 to 1 (12.50 percent), which was worse than that of 1988 (16.67 percent) (*Hankook Ilbo*, 24 Oct. 1989:13). Among the top fifty Korean *chaeböl* groups, seventeen did not have any openings at all. The total number of openings in those firms was reduced to 6.4 percent, less than that of 1988 (*Hankook Ilbo*, 25 Oct. 1989:13).

Table 2.2 Korean Labor Statistics, 1968–1987

Year	No of Job Openings (per 1,000 persons)	No. of Job Applicants (per 1,000 persons)	No. of Placements (per 1,000 persons)	Job Applicant Rate (%)	Job Opening Rate (%)	Employment Placement Ratio (%)
1968	116	128	93	110.3	90.6	72.7
1969	229	247	171	107.9	92.7	69.2
1970	271	287	210	105.9	94.4	73.2
1971	262	286	196	109.2	91.6	68.5
1972	278	299	219	107.6	93.0	73.2
1973	303	295	242	97.4	102.7	82.0
1974	248	283	207	114.1	87.6	73.1
1975	256	271	212	105.9	94.5	78.2
1976	301	326	258	108.3	92.3	79.1
1977	306	291	246	95.1	105.2	84.5
1978	338	291	252	86.1	116.2	86.5
1979	293	238	201	81.2	123.1	84.5
1980	262	257	206	98.1	101.9	80.2
1981	243	246	199	101.2	98.8	80.9
1982	308	347	246	112.7	88.8	70.9
1983	408	341	286	83.6	119.6	83.9
1984	526	500	419	95.1	105.2	83.8
1985	649	669	572	103.1	97.0	85.4
1986	810	793	670	97.9	102.1	84.5
1987	873	703	523	80.5	124.2	74.4

SOURCE: *Social Indicators in Korea* (National Bureau of Statistics 1988b:139).

To provide information on job openings and to assist their graduates in passing entrance examinations, almost every university offers employment services. Some invite the personnel directors of major firms to their universities to do special seminars, and others offer special lecture series on ways to prepare for the entrance examinations. Some universities publish booklets about the entrance examinations for their students, which often sell out (*Hankook Ilbo,* 20 Sept. 1989:6). Some university graduates take two to three years to prepare for and pass the entrance examinations of some prestigious firms. Others whose majors are liberal arts reenter the universities to obtain a second degree in science or technology (*Hankook Ilbo,* 18 Oct. 1989:5).

However, there are shortages of university graduates trained in the high-tech fields of electronics, computers, and semiconductors. The shortages in these fields are expected to be chronic for the next few years. Until 1994, Korean experts estimate that Korean high-tech industry will need an additional 203,700 highly trained workers in electronics, computers, and semiconductors. This need can hardly be met (*Hankook Ilbo,* 18 Oct. 1989:5), for university graduates who were trained in nontechnical engineering outnumber high-tech engineering graduates. Such a trend may be related to Korean Confucianism, which placed engineering and industry at the bottom of the status hierarchy in Korea for generations. Korea is experiencing what Japan experienced in the late 1960s and early 1970s (Rohlen 1974: 67): job openings for manual labor jobs surpass the supply. For example, while there were 11,679 job openings for the Korean workers who graduated from middle school and lower levels, there were only 2,388 applicants for such jobs. Even for high school graduates, the openings outnumbered the applicants 1.2 times. The most severe shortages occur in construction, textiles, and other manual labor jobs. To ease the labor shortage, several medium-sized manufacturing and textile companies in the Kumi industrial complex in Kyŏngsangpuk-do have formed relationships with schools in the remote countryside, offering scholarships and installing modern instructional equipment so as to recruit graduates. However, upon graduation, a good many of these students seek jobs in big cities. Some firms even offer free high school education, mainly through night programs during off-work hours, as a way of recruiting workers (*Hankook Ilbo,* 18 Oct. 1989:5).

While the shortage of qualified industrial workers among the less-educated people persists, so does the abundance of highly educated workers, particularly those who were trained in nontechnical industrial fields and engineering. Often these people are overqualified for demanding manual labor. The Confucian emphasis on education in the Korean culture may be counterproductive in terms of the cost-effectiveness needed to match the supply of and demand for laborers in Korea. Korean Confucianists traditionally did not have much respect for technical, physical, or manual labor but rather despised them. For the first time in Korean history, there are discussions about filling the manual work force with foreigners.

The labor shortage occurring among blue-collar workers is a more serious problem in small and medium-sized companies because of the workers' preference for large firms. The large firms usually offer better fringe benefit programs. Since Poongsan is one of the top Korean industrial firms, it has not yet experienced a shortage of labor.

The recruitment and employment of prospective Poongsan employees takes place at three levels. For its top management, Poongsan scouts capable persons from other organizations without administering any formal examination. This was a rather common practice in the early stages of Poongsan's development, when it was expanding rapidly. A good many current Poongsan top executives, including its president, vice presidents, executive managing directors, and plant managers, were scouted from other organizations in this manner during the 1970s.

Examinations for future managers and engineers who have graduated from four-year universities takes place at the personnel office of Poongsan (as a form of *kongch'ae*). These examinations are administered once a year in December. Most of those taking the examination have not held any job previously.

In 1989 several large Korean *chaebŏl* groups promoted to president of affiliated companies people who had passed the *kongch'ae* entrance examination (*Chosun Ilbo*, 5 Mar. 1989:7). To date, however, no one hired through the *kongch'ae* at Poongsan has yet reached the top executive level because the history of the *kongch'ae* at Poongsan is relatively short; it was begun only in 1976.

Although the *kongch'ae* has become institutionalized in large Korean business and industrial firms, this practice has had a relatively short history. For instance, Lucky-Goldstar hired three persons by the *kongch'ae* for the first time in 1956. According to Jung's (1987:127) survey of 108 Korean enterprises, before 1960 only 13.4 percent of all employees were hired by the *kongch'ae*. These numbers steadily increased for a time. From 1971 to 1975 the use of the *kongch'ae* reached a peak of 28.9 percent, but between 1976 and 1980 the usage rate decreased to 21.6 percent. Since 1980 usage has dropped sharply to 7.2 percent. Although 21.1 percent of all managing executives of large Korean *chaebŏl* groups were hired through the *kongch'ae*, only 7 percent of Poongsan executives were hired through the *kongch'ae*, and they occupy the lower echelon among the top executives (see Jung 1987:127).

In 1988 Poongsan suspended the *kongch'ae* temporarily. The turnover rate of the *kongch'ae* employees at Poongsan seemed very high. For instance, out of six who were hired through the *kongch'ae* in 1976, only one remains; out of nineteen employed through the *kongch'ae* in 1977, only six are still at Poongsan.

Poongsan's connection-hiring and standard hiring.

It is difficult for anyone to figure out the number of employees at Poongsan who are related to the chairman and founder: that depends on the definition of relatives. Among the executives, there are two of the chairman's immediate family: one son and one brother. There were two brothers-in-law (both retired while I was in the field) and the husband of one of the chairman's cousins (he also retired while I was in the field). If one defines members of the Ryu lineage and clan as relatives, there are several of these, including a senior vice president, one plant manager, and several managing directors.

The kin network develops when one executive member who is related to the chairman then hires his own kin members, either consanguineous or affined relatives or both. The person who is hired through this kin network is not directly related to the chairman. This is the reason that the chairman himself does not recognize how many of his employees have been hired because of their family relationships, and who is related to whom.

In many ways, Poongsan is not a typical Korean enterprise. Though the ownership and management are separated in most of the Japanese *zaibatsu*, Korean *chaebŏl* group owners are also the managers, mainly because of the short history of entrepreneurship in Korea

(Hattori 1986:198–201). The utilization of kin members in business has been widely practiced, as evidenced in the several large Korean *chaebŏl* groups delineated by Hattori (1986:181–98). The presence in management of a large number of relatives of the founders of Korean *chaebŏl* groups is inevitable and will remain so until ownership and management are separated as in the Japanese *zaibatsu*.

The remaining employees whose educational attainment is less than a four-year university degree, including university dropouts and the graduates of two-year junior colleges, are recruited and employed individually in each plant at any time during the year, as the need for labor arises. The procedures used varies. Unlike the *kongch'ae* candidates, these job candidates have been out of school for some time and have worked elsewhere. The hiring through connections by way of the kin network and the recommendations of friends and acquaintances also occurs at this level.

In Poongsan's recruitment and employment of university graduates through the *kongch'ae*, the company recently has made a deliberate effort to attract well-qualified candidates. Poongsan not only sends out brochures advertising the company to the schools, but also invites students to make a three-day tour of the four plants and the main office in Seoul at the company's expense. (From 25 to 27 July 1988, for instance, Poongsan invited twenty-five senior university students from the ten most reputable universities.) Their major fields are not limited to science and technology but also include some liberal arts. For the participants, Poongsan provides a booklet describing the company's history, structure and organization, business philosophy, and policies, as well as the contents of its production, its operation, its research and development plan, its fringe benefit programs, and its welfare programs for the employees.

Although some large Korean enterprises administer both written and oral examinations through interviews in the *kongch'ae*, Poongsan does not administer a written part but instead emphasizes the interview. The company asks the selected few universities to recommend the qualified candidates. If one does not attend a selected school, one does not have a chance to be recommended for the candidate pool. The results of the competition in the Poongsan *kongch'ae* are severe. In 1986, 288 were recommended, but only 72 were hired; 123 were hired out of 1,052 in 1987; and 118 were hired out of 899 in 1988.

Poongsan goes through a rather elaborate and thorough oral examination and interview process that is conducted by the personnel office director, vice presidents, and president. Their evaluation is directed mainly at finding out whether the candidates in the recommended pool are suitable to meet the motto of Poongsan—*ch'angŭi, silch'ŏn,* and *hwakin* (creative; action, performance, and execution; verification and confirmation). Ideally, the company looks for a creative person, a person who is group-oriented rather than individualistic, and a person who is future-oriented. Even though the company does not like to admit it, the company likes to avoid anyone who is pro-union or a union-sympathizer.

In the past a candidate's written examination score and school grades were primary and the interview was secondary. In fact, in 1989 most Korean firms that used both the written test and an oral interview revealed that they emphasized the interview over any written examination or school grades (*Hankook Ilbo,* 11 Oct. 1989: 11). The main reason for such a switch was the intention to avoid hiring potential labor agitators. Poongsan is no exception.

Since adopting the *kongch'ae* system in 1976, Poongsan has hired 785 employees through this system (table 2.3). The number of *kongch'ae* employees each year has fluctuated with the state of the Korean economy and the prosperity of the company. In 1979 the number declined because of the slow growth of the Korean economy resulting from the second "oil shock" imposed by the Organization of Petroleum Exporting Countries (OPEC). Also, because of the company's financial difficulties in 1981 and 1982, a limited number of *kongch'ae* employees were hired. In fact, Poongsan laid off 162 rank-and-file workers in 1981 at the Bupyung plant, and in 1982, 405 rank-and-file workers were terminated at the Bupyung plant. In 1989 because of labor unrest and slow production resulting from a prolonged strike at the Angang plant, Poongsan suspended the *kongch'ae.*

The blue-collar candidates who did not graduate from four-year universities are hired as openings occur. In earlier years when a large number of workers were needed, the firm sometimes posted openings on company bulletin boards. However, according to the personnel section manager at the plant who has worked for Poongsan for more than ten years, the candidates who are recommended through connections always outnumber the openings; the plant thus does not feel the need to recruit workers.

Table 2.3 Number of Poongsan Employees Hired
Through *Kongch'ae*, 1976–1988

Year	Number
1976	6
1977	92
1978	84
1979	21
1980	101
1981	9
1982	29
1983	35
1984	43
1985	52
1986	72
1987	123
1988	118
Total	785

SOURCE: The author's field data.

During my fieldwork thirty applications were filed in the personnel office of the Bupyung plant, but no placements occurred because
of over-staffing. Anyone who wishes to work at the plant must submit a résumé to the plant's personnel office. This standard résumé
includes the applicant's name, date of birth, national identification
card number (any Korean who is sixteen must have the identification
card and number, which is equivalent to the Social Security number
for U.S. citizens), current address, relation to the head of the household, educational record, and previous job experience, if any.

If there are openings and a candidate seems to meet the qualifications on the basis of his or her résumé, the candidate is notified to
appear at the personnel office of the plant. The candidate then has to
fill out a form for further consideration and submit to an interview.
The form requires not only information already contained in the
résumé but also the prospective employee's place of origin, or *ponjŏk*

(some Koreans believe that this is the source of regional or provincial favoritism or discrimination), and birthplace, mode of dwelling, family assets, family income, personal hobbies, religious affiliation, and specific skills, if any. The form also provides a space for writing in the name of anyone who recommends the candidate. Nowadays, because the company is so concerned about potential labor agitators, and because some university graduates active in the labor movement have disguised their educational backgrounds and have sought blue-collar jobs to organize labor movements after being employed, the identity of any person who recommends a candidate would carry more weight than any other criteria. Another space is left for writing in whether the candidate has any relatives at Poongsan. If the candidate is recommended by a company executive who happens to be the candidate's relative, the candidate's chances for employment will be enhanced. This would be a classic case of connection-hiring. All of this information has to be written by the candidate himself or herself in the presence of the personnel officer. Since blue-collar work requires physical endurance, detailed information about the candidate's health, especially blood pressure, eyesight, and possible color blindness is also required.

After the interview form is completed and if everything looks fine, then the personnel officer (the *taeri* or assistant section head at the plant) interviews the candidate. If his recommendation is positive, then the candidate has a second interview with the prospective *kwajang* (section head). Personnel officers and section heads told me that during the interview they concern themselves mostly with whether there is any discrepancy in the candidate's records, whether the candidate has hidden his or her university education. If everything is satisfactory and there is an opening, then the candidate is recommended first to the *pujang* (division head), then to the *yisabo* (assistant managing director), then to the *yisa* (managing director), and finally to the plant manager. If there is an opening, and if the personnel officer and the section head recommend the candidate, approval from the above section head is mostly a formality. If there is more than one candidate for the same position, of course the most qualified candidate is chosen. In such cases, the selection is classified as a *kongch'ae* or standard hiring, not a connection-hiring.

In the case of a connection-hiring, the hired employee always feels that he or she owes a personal debt to the person who made the referral. The relationship between these two, the candidate and the person who arranged the employment, resembles the Japanese patterns of *senpai* and *kohai* (Cole 1971:189–224). The employee hired through the connection visits the person who arranged the job during the holidays, particularly during the New Year's holidays, and presents some gifts. On New Year's Day in 1989, I met an angry uncle whose nephew works at the Bupyung plant and was employed through the connection. The nephew visited the plant senior who had played the role of broker for his employment but did not visit his uncle, who lives nearby. The uncle told me, "You know, I can't believe young people nowadays. He has the time and courtesy to visit someone who arranged his job but neglects to stop by and see his own uncle." The ties between the job-seeker and the broker who arranged his employment seem to be stronger than kin ties. The relationship is almost the same as *oyabun-kobun* or the patron-client relationship in Japan (Cole 1971:196–99). And in fact, when tension was growing on the eve of a strike, I noticed that management did not try to talk directly to the most vocal union activist but looked for the patron who had arranged the employment of the worker in an attempt to neutralize the worker's participation.

My survey indicated that 73.1 percent of all Bupyung plant employees had been hired through the recommendation of friends, relatives, and acquaintances (table 2.4). Connection-hiring in the Bupyung plant is higher than in Japanese industry in the 1950s and 1960s and local U.S. industry in the 1950s (see Cole 1971:195; Reynolds 1951:129). However, it is less than that of the Hyundai automobile industry (Bae 1987:44). Further analysis indicates that among the employees who have worked less than one year at the plant, no one was hired by way of connection-hiring. The company is apparently moving more toward the use of open competitive examinations. Of the workers who were from rural farming villages, 44 percent had been employed through connection-hiring. Among those hired through a personal connection, production department workers outnumbered the others; they represented 61.6 percent of all workers so hired. Whereas 70 percent of four-year university graduates had been hired through the *kongch'ae,* only 2 percent had been hired through connection-hiring. In contrast, 77.2 percent of those who had not completed a four-year university degree had been employed through connection-hiring. The less education a person has, the more likely

Table 2.4 Manner of Employment at the Bupyung Plant

	Sex		Row Total N (%)
Manner of Employment	Male N (%)	Female N (%)	
Open Competitive Examination	19 (18.3)	1 (1.0)	20 (19.2)
Through Friend	6 (5.8)	0 (0.0)	6 (5.8)
Through Relative	17 (16.3)	0 (0.0)	17 (16.3)
Through Acquaintance	50 (48.1)	3 (2.9)	53 (51.0)
By Chance	7 (6.7)	0 (0.0)	7 (6.7)
Other	1 (1.0)	0 (0.0)	1 (1.0)
Total	100 (96.2)	4 (3.8)	104 (100.0)

SOURCE: The author's field data.

he or she has in becoming employed through a connection.

It is difficult to trace the entire network of connection-hirings among Bupyung plant employees. There were a few known networks. Among the brokers, two managing directors had assisted the most in hiring workers; one managing director had assisted in hiring fourteen and the other had assisted in hiring sixteen workers. Interestingly enough, both managing directors are related to the chairman: one belongs to the same lineage as the chairman; the other is an affine of the chairman (kin by marriage). It appears that both of them could be more influential than the plant manager in hiring new employees; the plant manager had assisted in hiring only two workers.

Connection-hiring can grow geometrically (Figure 2.1). When one is employed through connection-hiring and later arranges in turn for the hiring of kin, friends, and acquaintances, this process can become extensive.

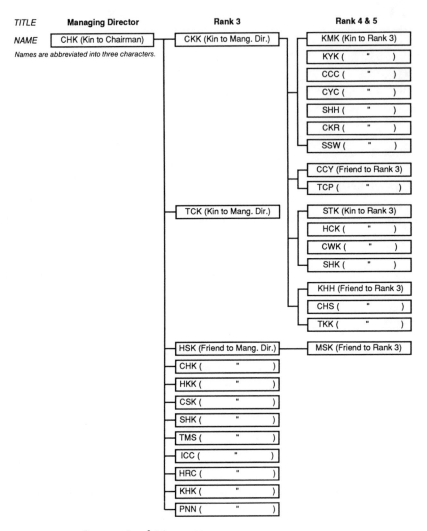

FIGURE 2.1   Connection-hiring patterns.

Current trends.

Before 1976, Poongsan's employment had been based on various forms of connection-hiring. With the adoption of the *kongch'ae*, Poongsan gradually reduced its reliance on the traditional methods of employment and moved toward the more open, competitive modern

method. In fact, in 1978 Poongsan used the *kongch'ae* even for high
school graduates and began announcing openings in Korean daily
newspapers. In 1983 and 1984 Poongsan made inquiries to the labor
department to recruit qualified workers in an effort to adopt more
standard employment methods. These trends are reflected in table
2.5.

Nevertheless, since the four-day strike from 13 to 16 August 1987
at the Bupyung plant and the seventy-two days of strikes from 1
January to 13 March 1988 at the Angang plant, and in apparent response to the continuous labor unrest, Poongsan has shifted its employment policy back toward traditional connection-hiring. For
example, the hiring of the four-year university graduates was suspended for the fiscal year 1989. The personnel officer of the plant told
me, "At the present, we do not have any openings. Even if we were
to have some openings, we have to have someone who can assure us

Table 2.5 Manner of Employment of Bupyung Plant Employees by
Length of Service

Manner of Employment	Length of Service					
	Less than 1 Year N (%)	1–4 Year N (%)	5–10 Year N (%)	11–15 Year N (%)	16–20 Year N (%)	Charter Member N (%)
Competitive exam.	2 (1.9)	3 (2.9)	6 (5.9)	8 (7.7)	1 (1.0)	0 (0.0)
By a friend	0 (0.0)	1 (1.0)	3 (2.9)	1 (1.0)	1 (1.0)	0 (0.0)
By a relative	0 (0.0)	3 (2.9)	8 (7.7)	5 (4.8)	1 (1.0)	0 (0.0)
By an acquaintance	0 (0.0)	19 (18.3)	13 (12.5)	18 (17.3)	2 (1.9)	1 (1.0)
By chance	1 (1.0)	0 (0.0)	1 (1.0)	4 (3.8)	1 (1.0)	0 (0.0)
Other	0 (0.0)	0 (0.0)	0 (0.0)	1 (1.0)	0 (0.0)	0 (0.0)
Total	3 (2.9)	26 (25.0)	31 (29.8)	37 (35.6)	6 (5.8)	1 (1.0)

of the candidate's credentials." In short, the labor movement's push for liberalization in the form of guarantees for the rights to organize unions, to negotiate by collective bargaining, and to strike tends to push the company into setting back the recruitment and employment policy from reliance on the open, competitive examinations based on merit to the traditional connection-hiring.

Labor Turnover Rates

Despite the fact that labor shortages are occurring in certain manufacturing sectors, especially in small and medium-sized plants, Poongsan's labor turnover rates for the past six years seem very low. An optimistic executive told me that the rate is the result of workers' job satisfaction.

However, my survey of workers' attitudes toward their jobs indicates otherwise. My own observations indicate that the low turnover is largely the consequence of the fact that the large manufacturing firms offer a stable, secure job and better benefits than do the small and medium-sized firms. The workers' preference for the larger manufacturing firms is the same as that in Japan: Cole (1971:37–40) describes the "dual economic structure" among the Japanese blue-collar workers. As in Japan, the large-scale firms in Korea pay relatively higher wages, offer good working conditions, and are unionized and highly capitalized, whereas workers in small and medium-sized firms have less job security because the company often faces the possibility of bankruptcy.

The retention rates among the four-year university graduates who were employed by the *kongch'ae* are interesting (table 2.6). Whereas retention rates among those who were employed in the 1970s and early 1980s are low, the rates among those who were employed more recently are much higher. Two possible factors have to be considered. First, when Korean industry was expanding during the 1970s, many new industrial firms scouted for qualified workers among the employees of firms like Poongsan. Some of the firm's *kongch'ae* employees had been attracted to other firms by better offers. Second, because Poongsan is a defense contractor, employment there exempts workers from active military duty if they work for five consecutive years at Poongsan. As a consequence, most of the newly employed

Table 2.6 Employment and Retention of University Graduates
Hired Through the *Kongch'ae*, 1976–1986

Year	No. of Employees Hired per Year	No. of Employees Currently Working	Retention Rate (%)
1976	6	1	16.7
1977	92	16	17.4
1978	84	28	33.3
1979	21	5	23.8
1980	101	26	25.7
1981	9	5	55.6
1982	29	18	62.1
1983	35	25	71.4
1984	43	39	90.7
1985	52	43	82.7
1986	72	58	80.6

stay on the job to meet the five-year requirement. There is a tendency, however, for them to move to other firms as they complete their five years' tenure. The director of personnel admits that such a trend occurs. At any event, the retention rate of Poongsan employees is very high.

In summary, although Poongsan employees have exhibited remarkable success, demographic characteristics indicate that they are not unusual as compared with other Korean manufacturing workers.

In the early 1960s, before Korean industrialization took root, Poongsan, like many other Korean enterprises, had an abundant labor supply. Recently, however, since the number of job openings exceeds the number of job applicants, the Korean manufacturing industry has experienced a shortage of labor. The situation is progressively deteriorating because the younger Koreans, taking economic growth and employment opportunities for granted, like to avoid jobs in one of the "three Ds"; "difficult," "dirty," and "dangerous" jobs.

So far, taking advantage of being a large enterprise that offers better fringe-benefit programs and job security, Poongsan has acquired its needed labor through the methods of connection-hiring and standard hiring (*kongch'ae*). Viewing connection-hiring as traditional, noncompetitive, and less rational, Poongsan has attempted to change its recruiting and hiring practice from connection-hiring to standard hiring. However, recent labor strife and slow growth have forced the company into setting back the recruitment and employment policy.

3

Reward, Compensation, and Promotion

The reward system is the major pillar of sound industrial relations. The rules regarding monetary compensation and promotion are the keystones of the reward system. A close look at the system at Poongsan will offer insight into the firm's reward and promotion systems. They are by and large similar to those of the well-publicized Japanese systems, yet they are different in some significant aspects, particularly the length-of-service wage and promotion (*nenkō joretsu chingin*) system.

Recent Korean Wage Hikes

In gathering information on the reward and compensation structure of Poongsan, I found an astonishing trend toward rapid wage hikes among Korean manufacturing workers. It was a common belief that as a late industrializer Korea took advantage of its "cheap" labor in its industrialization process. Despite this image of the past, during my fieldwork from 1987 to 1990 I witnessed the most spectacular wage increase among Korean manufacturing workers in general (Amsden 1989:197–99, 1990; Steers, Shin, and Ungson 1989:126)

Table 3.1 Wage Increase of Poongsan Employees, 1987–1991
(in *wŏn*/month)

Category	Year				
	1987	1988	1989	1990	1991
Wage of white-collar worker	342,603	373,153	476,770	516,670	571,197
Wage of blue-collar worker	259,366	292,016	391,011	426,548	472,041
Increase rate (%)	24.9	12.2	33.3	9.1	10.5
Dollar/*wŏn* exchange rate	1/871	1/730	1/670	1/708	1/725

SOURCE: The author's field data.

and Poongsan in particular. As shown in table 3.1, from 1987, when my fieldwork started, to 1991, when this book was completed, wage rates of Poongsan rose 90 percent (the rate of increase for the average Korean manufacturing worker from 1987 to 1990 was 76.5 percent).

It is indeed an astonishing increase. Perhaps Korea set another world record with this wage increase. Amsden (1990:81) recognizes that "the seventies were a period of rising real wages in all of these countries [Brazil, Argentina, Mexico, Turkey, India, and Taiwan], but in Korea wages rose spectacularly: the index of real wages increased from a base of 100 in 1970 to 238 in 1979." She further states (1989: 197), "While it took English workers seventy years to raise their real earnings by roughly 150%, Korean manufacturing workers achieved a comparable gain in about 20 years (from 1955 to 1976). In just one decade, 1969–1979, real wages in Korea rose by more than 250%."

Regarding such a phenomenal wage increase, the responses from Poongsan workers and management were different. One worker told me, "Such an increase is inevitable and natural, because our wage started from an exceptionally low base." The management responded, "Our profits no longer can catch up to the rate of wage hikes. I can understand why some Korean companies began almost at once to look for cheaper sites offshore, most notably China, Indonesia, Malaysia, and Sri Lanka." Interestingly, Poongsan started its subsidiary in the United States (Cedar Rapids, Iowa), where the cost of labor is relatively high.

Before discussing the specific wage structure and promotion system of Poongsan, I have to remind the reader that the nominal wage figures of the Bupyung plant employees of Poongsan shown in various tables are on the basis of the 1988 wage schedule. Their wages later rose 52.9 percent from 1988 to 1991; hence, the amounts shown in each table may have little meaning other than the proportional distribution by white/blue-collar, standard/supplementary wage, sex, educational level, and rank. Also, the average wage of the Poongsan employees as a whole shown in table 3.1 differs slightly from those figures in the rest of the tables in this chapter, for they are the average wage of the Bupyung plant employees only.

Standard and Supplementary Wages

The determining factors of Poongsan wages.

Generally, there are two well-established payment systems: payment in accordance with employees' social status and obligation, a system widely adopted by Japanese firms; and payment based on employees' job skills and market demands, the system employed by most Western industrial firms. Poongsan's wage system falls between the two. At best, Poongsan's wage rate structure, as measured by the formal criteria of the Western economist and sociologist, is industrially underdeveloped, but it is further evolved than that of Japan, as described by Cole (1971:72–100). At Poongsan, previous work experience determines an employee's starting salary, but unlike Japanese industries, Poongsan does not use age and the family situation as determining factors. The wage system of Poongsan, as is the case for most Korean enterprises, is not a *nenkō joretsu chingin*, the wage system of large Japanese firms. In the Japanese *nenkō* system, age and the length of service play a role in determining wages (Cole 1971:75). Nonetheless, the Poongsan wage structure does include extensive welfare benefits that resemble the programs offered by large Japanese firms: free transportation, free meals during working hours, medical services, bonuses, on-the-job training, and scholarships for the children of employees.

Table 3.2 Wage Structure of the Bupyung Plant Employees, 1988
(in *wŏn*/month)[a]

Wage Structure[b]	A White-Collar N (%)	B Blue-Collar N (%)	B as a percentage of A[c]
STANDARD WAGE			
Basic wage (*Ponbong*)	360,717 (42.7)	234,478 (34.7)	65.0
Position allowance (*Chikch'aek sudang*)	86,532 (10.2)	87,160 (12.9)	100.7
Service allowance (*Kŭnsok sudang*)	17,996 (2.1)	20,618 (3.1)	114.6
Bonus (*Sangyŏ kŭm*)	177,779 (21.0)	107,469 (15.9)	60.5
Work allowance (*Kŭnmu sudang*)	36,915 (4.4)	22,528 (3.3)	61.0
SUPPLEMENTARY WAGE			
Overtime (*Yudong sudang*)	36,272 (4.3)	92,912 (23.8)	256.2
Meal (*Siksa*)	16,638 (2.0)	16,638 (2.5)	100.0
Uniform (*P'ibok*)	1,833 (0.2)	2,000 (0.3)	109.1
Safety equipment (*Anjŏnp'yŏgubi*)	1,993 (0.2)	2,198 (0.3)	110.3
Welfare and others (*Pokjigigŭm*)	108,670 (12.9)	88,932 (13.2)	81.8
Total	845,345 (100.0)	674,933 (100.0)	79.8

SOURCE: The author's field data.

[a] The official dollar/*wŏn* exchange rate in 1988 was $1/730 *wŏn*.

[b] Not included are the allowances for special licensed skills, ranging from 30,000 to 10,000 *wŏn* per month; responsibility of being in charge of a machine, 25,000–20,000 *wŏn* per month at Bupyung; shift change allowance, ranging from 1,330 to 1,000 *wŏn* per month; safety allowance, ranging from 1,300 to 400 *wŏn* per month; free company housing for some workers; and scholarships for employees' children (up to two) until the completion of high school.

[c] B/A × 100.

Poongsan's wage structure consists of the standard wage plus supplementary wages, including overtime, meal allowances, and other welfare allowances. These are summarized in table 3.2, using the average wage for all Bupyung plant employees. The factors that determine the levels of Poongsan employees' wages are job classification (white- and blue-collar) plus the employee's skill, previous job experience, sex, and educational level.

Wage differences by job classification.

An examination of table 3.2 reveals that the wage structure of Poongsan is similar to the Japanese wage structure described by Cole (1971:76) in his study of Takei Diecast Company in 1965. One obvious difference is that while the Japanese blue-collar workers were paid a family allowance (2 percent of their total monthly income) and a housing allowance (3 percent of their total wage), Poongsan employees do not receive those allowances. Poongsan, however, provides free company housing for a limited number of employees. Those who could not take advantage of free company housing would not be paid a housing allowance. The Japanese worker's wage is 56 percent of the total monthly wage, but the Poongsan blue-collar worker's basic wage is only 34.7 percent of the total wage, and the white-collar employees receive a basic wage that constitutes only 42.7 percent of the whole.

Although blue-collar workers at Poongsan receive more than do white-collar employees for position allowance, overtime, uniforms, and safety equipment, there is still a wide gap between the basic wages of the white-collar and blue-collar workers. The blue-collar workers' total monthly average wage is barely 80 percent that of the white collar workers. If there were no overtime pay, the gap would be even wider.

Even when employees have the same educational qualifications, as shown in table 3.3, white-collar employees are paid better. This is perhaps a reflection of Confucian values, which place commerce and industry beneath the work of the *sa* (scholar or official), the *nong* (farmer), the *kong* (artisan), and the *sang* (merchant). Using survey data on the marital preferences of Ewha Womans University students from 1964 to 1971, Jones and Sakong (1980:252–53) concluded that "the *sa, nong, kong, sang* ranking was no longer operative in the

Table 3.3 White- and Blue-Collar Workers' Standard Wages at the Bupyung Plant by Level of Education, 1988 (in *wŏn* per month)[a]

Educational Level[b]	Sex	A White-Collar	B Blue-Collar	B as percentage of A[c]
Junior college	Male	210,700	201,900	95.8
	Female	187,700	_[d]	_[d]
High school	Male	204,700	177,000	86.5
	Female	181,700	157,000	86.4

SOURCE: The author's field data.

[a] The official dollar/*wŏn* exchange rate in 1988 was $1/730 *wŏn*.

[b] Since no four-year college or university graduates are included in production work, and no middle-school graduates are placed in the white-color work, no comparative data on them are available.

[c] B/A × 100.

[d] No starting wage for females is built into the schedule.

period of rapid growth and had probably lost its sway over several generations, beginning with the colonial period." However, the wage gap between white- and blue-collar workers, especially when educational levels are the same, is clear evidence, in my opinion, that Koreans continue to value the scholar-bureaucrat over others.

Since Poongsan is the top Korean enterprise in its field and the largest producer of its kind in Korea, its wages are higher than those of small and medium-sized firms. As is the case for large firms in Japan (Cole 1971:37–40), Poongsan is highly capitalized and specialized, and it therefore pays higher wages, has better working conditions, and has fewer industrial accidents than do smaller firms. According to Lee (1988), the wages paid by small Korean manufacturing firms employing from 10 to 29 workers in 1986 was 83 percent of those of large firms that employed more than 500 workers. Indeed, the average wage of Poongsan employees is 17 percent higher than of those working for small and medium-sized copper manufacturers. Whereas the average wage of the Bupyung plant blue-collar workers in 1988 was 434,859 *wŏn*, including base wages, bonuses, and overtime pay but excluding other welfare benefits, the wage of the average Korean manufacturing worker was 398,777 *wŏn* (National Bureau of Statistics 1989:91). (The official U.S. dollar/*wŏn* exchange rate in 1988 was 1 U.S. dollar/730 *wŏn*.)

Wage differences by gender.

The worker's level of educational attainment, work experience, gender, and assigned rank are the key determinants of his or her starting wage. These four factors are reciprocally interrelated with each other to form a standard wage schedule. There are two salary schedules: one for different job assignments and titles; the other for the level of educational attainment. Each schedule is categorized by wage rank (or *hobong*), the starting standard wage, the allowance for location (in case a worker's assignment is to a plant other than the Seoul headquarters), the allowance for welfare, and gender. The female worker who works in the same plant with the same educational level and with the same wage rank is paid less than her male counterpart. The standard wage schedule by the level of education is summarized in table 3.4, and by the job assignment and title, in table 3.5.

Poongsan specifies no wage levels for female employees with educations beyond the four-year university, technical high school, and two-year technical junior college. One reason is that the firm expects to have no such female employees. Moreover, Korea has no technical high school or two-year technical junior colleges for women.

The wage schedule by job title and assignment does not specify salaries for women at the rank of assistant section head or above, either for managers or for engineers. Apparently, Poongsan's female workers do not have much of a chance to advance above this rank. This is evidence of job discrimination against women.

Not only are women excluded from the highest levels of employment at Poongsan, but they are offered lower wages than their male counterparts, even when rank, titles, and qualifications are the same (see table 3.6). Among blue-collar workers who are non–technical high school graduates, women are paid about 81 percent of the male wage, and about 83 percent of the male wage of those who graduated from middle school. Among white-collar workers, the wages of female workers are a little over 80 percent of the wages of males in each educational level, but the wage gap by sex among the blue-collar workers is narrower than that among white-collar workers. For instance, the wage of female workers at the rank 1 (1-*kŭp*) level is almost 99.3 percent of the male wage. This pattern may be based on the assumption that in simple manual work, women are considered to be as good as men.

At Poongsan, the yearly raise, like that in the Japanese system, is not determined by performance and job competence but is instead based on the yearly "base up" (Cole 1971:77). The Poongsan labor union negotiates for the lump sum of the total wage cost of the com-

Table 3.4 Standard Starting Wage by the Level of Education, 1988 (in *wŏn* per month)[a]

Level of Education	Sex	Salary[b] Rank	Starting Wage	Allowance	Total Wage
WHITE COLLAR					
Graduate school	Male	4-21	315,200	50,000	365,200
	Male	4-17[c]	307,200	50,000	357,200
College/university	Male	4-17	307,200	50,000	357,200
	Male	4-17[c]	299,200	50,000	349,200
	Female	4-7	234,000	50,000	284,000
Junior college	Male	5-6	210,700	50,000	260,000
	Female	5-6	187,700	32,000	219,000
High school	Male	5-1	204,700	50,000	254,700
	Female	5-1	181,700	32,000	213,700
BLUE COLLAR					
Junior college (tech.)	Male	3-20	201,900	50,000	251,900
	Male	3-16[c]	195,900	50,000	245,900
Tech. high school	Male	4-17	185,400	40,000	225,400
	Male	4-17[c]	180,600	40,000	220,600
Non-tech. high school	Male	4-10	177,000	40,000	217,000
	Female	4-5	157,000	20,000	177,200
Middle school	Male	4-3	168,600	40,000	208,600
	Female	4-1	152,400	20,000	172,400

SOURCE: The author's field data.
[a] The official dollar/*wŏn* exchange rate in 1988 was $1/730 *wŏn*.
[b] Salary rank is a classification of starting wage of each rank. The first number denotes the employee's job rank (*kŭp*), and the second number indicates the subcategory within the given rank (*hobong*).
[c] Those who have not completed military service and those exempted from active duty.

Table 3.5 Standard Starting Wage by Job Title, 1988 (in *wŏn* per month)[a]

Title	Sex	Wage Rank	Starting Wage	Allowance	Total Salary
WHITE COLLAR					
Asst. manag. director	Male	–	1,004,000	70,000	1,074,000
Division head	Male	1-A-1	658,000	220,000	878,000
Asst. div. head	Male	1-B-1	574,000	180,000	754,000
Section head	Male	2-A-1	474,000	150,000	624,000
Asst. section head	Male	2B-1	424,000	110,000	534,000
Rank 3	Male	3-1	347,000	50,000	397,200
	Female	3-1	268,000	50,000	318,000
Rank 4	Male	4-1	275,200	50,000	325,200
	Female	4-1	222,000	50,000	272,000
Rank 5	Male	5-1	204,700	50,000	254,700
	Female	5-1	181,700	32,000	213,700
BLUE COLLAR					
Special rank	Male	T'ŭk-1	299,200	50,000	349,200
Rank 1	Male	1-1	257,200	50,000	307,200
	Female	1-1	255,200	50,000	305,200
Rank 2	Male	2-1	211,500	50,000	261,500
	Female	2-1	209,700	33,000	241,700
Rank 3	Male	3-1	173,400	50,000	223,400
	Female	3-1	171,600	32,000	203,600
Rank 4	Male	4-1	166,200	40,000	206,200
	Female	4-1	152,400	20,000	172,400
GENERAL LABOR					
Labor	Male	L-1	168,900	20,000	188,900
	Female	L-1	149,100	20,000	169,100

SOURCE: The author's field data.
[a] The official dollar/*wŏn* exchange rate in 1988 was $1/730 *wŏn*.

Table 3.6 Monthly Wages of Male and Female Workers by Level of
Education, 1988 (in *wŏn*)[a]

| Educational Level | Job[a] Class. | Wage Rank | Starting Wage | | B as percentage of A[c] |
			Male (A)	Female (B)	
College/university	W	4-17	307,200	234,000	76.2
	W	4-17[d]	299,200	234,000	78.2
Junior college	W	5-6	210,700	187,700	89.1
High school	W	5-1	204,700	181,700	88.8
High school	B	4-10	177,000	157,000	88.7
Middle school	B	4-3	168,600	152,400	90.4

SOURCE: The author's field data.
[a] The official dollar/*wŏn* exchange rate in 1988 was $1/730 *wŏn*.
[b] W indicates white collar; B indicates blue collar.
[c] B/A × 100.
[d] Those who have not completed military service and those exempted from active
duty.

pany, which is then divided among the total number of regular workers either in the form of a fixed amount or a prorated increase in
accordance with their base wage. In 1989, for instance, the lump
sum was divided evenly to everyone regardless of base salary; thus,
although the average raise was 33.3 percent, a higher raise was given
to the employees with lower pay. In 1990 the raise was 9.1 percent
across the board to every employee.

Poongsan's wage rate structure tilts more toward the Western pattern than toward the Japanese. The worker's age, marital status, family obligations, and seniority are less emphasized in Poongsan's wage
rate structure than they are in the Japanese *nenkō* system. Poongsan's wage structure is also similar to that of a Korean automobile
manufacturing plant (Bae 1987:51–69; Bae and Form 1986:120–31).

In their evaluations of the Korean wage rate structure as it is manifested in the Poongsan system, some social scientists have concluded that the impact of Confucian norms is minimal (Bae 1987:
54–56, 69), but my observations indicate otherwise. The remnants
of Confucianism are evident in the discrimination against females,
in the preference given to white-collar employees over blue-collar

workers, in the emphasis on educational attainment over skill level, and in the paternalistic welfare and benefit programs. Perhaps from the Japanese point of view the Korean wage rate structure resembles the Western, but from the Western point of view the Korean system appears to favor the Japanese. Thus, the Poongsan wage rate structure can best be described as occupying a middle point on the continuum between Japan's *nenkō* system and the Western market system.

Promotion

Even without being promoted, every Poongsan employee receives the yearly "base-up" increment. Nevertheless, promotion to the next rank has many meanings to the individual who receives it. It means an increase in wages, the ability to exercise authority over subordinates, and the opportunity to receive high status recognition within the company and in society. Promotion is considered to be the same as *ipsin ch'ulsae* (getting ahead) among Koreans and *risshin shusse* (making something of yourself) among the Japanese; the Chinese characters for the two are identical. How an employee moves up, which employee moves up faster, and what organizational factors influence such promotions are alike in Japan and Korea. At the same time, there are some differences. As is reflected in the *nenkō joretsu chingin*, the Japanese promotion system emphasizes age and length of service, but the Korean system as exemplified by Poongsan emphasizes length of service and merit of service. Both systems acknowledge the importance of the length of service, but the Korean system emphasizes merit more than does the Japanese system, while the Japanese system emphasizes age. Age-grading is not formalized in the Korean promotion system; it is not represented in the Poongsan system.

Criteria and procedures for promotion.

The criteria determining the regular promotion of Poongsan employees are length of service; achievement, including awards; training; foreign language competence for university graduates; and merit of performance. There are specifications for each of these criteria, and each is quantified. However, temporary employees, including consultants and advisers, general laborers, and executives at and above the rank of managing director (yisa) are excluded from this career ladder.

The first and most important determinant is the length of service. Sixty points out of one hundred possible points are based on the length of service. For the white-collar employees, to be promoted to rank 5 (5-kŭp) one must have spent four years in the previous rank; rank 4 (4-kŭp), two years; rank 3 (3-kŭp), three years. For blue-collar workers, to be promoted to rank 3 and rank 4, one has to work two years in the same rank; to rank 2 (2-kŭp), rank 1 (1-kŭp), and special rank (t'ŭk-kŭp), one has to stay in the lower rank for three years. No one may skip a rank. In special cases, when an employee is extraordinary in some other respect, the company does waive the length-of-service requirement, although such cases are rare.

When the employee meets the requirement for years of service specified at each rank, the candidate can earn sixty points. As time passes, one additional year earns the employee two extra points; for a two-year delay, four points; and five additional points for three years. Interestingly, when a candidate's promotion consideration is deferred for four years, the candidate can earn only three additional points. When the employee is not promoted to the next rank after five years of eligibility, no additional points are awarded. After a six-year delay, the employee is penalized three points per year. In other words, the candidate for promotion can earn the highest number of points in the third year after meeting the length of service requirement. The number of earned points for those who have worked six years beyond the minimum are equal to the points earned by those who have worked one year less than the minimum. The longer one stays in the same rank, the less likely one is to get promoted. Failure to move ahead is a sign that the employee is viewed by his or her immediate supervisors as inept.

The penalty points hinder the chances for promotion of many Poongsan employees. A fifty-two-year-old material section worker with a high school education who has been at Bupyung plant since Poongsan was established claimed that over the past twenty years he has never been promoted. He said, "In earlier years, there was no clear-cut job distinction between white- and blue-collar workers. I guess I started as a blue-collar worker. Now, I am a sort of white-collar worker. I have never been promoted, because I was not considered to be a 'docile worker' in the eyes of middle management." Currently, he is at rank 3. The personnel office considers this rank to be the highest rank that most ordinary high school graduates can attain. The personnel office also told me that his rank was adjusted when Poongsan adopted the current ranking system. Nearly 40 percent of Bupyung plant employees have never been promoted since Poongsan adopted the current ranking system. Indeed, although the length of service is the single most important criterion for advancement, it does not warrant an automatic promotion without meritorious service.

The next most important consideration for promotion is any achievement (especially any award), training, and possession of foreign-language competence for university graduates. Such a skill or achievement counts twenty points (20 percent) toward promotion consideration. To test foreign-language competence, Poongsan uses the Test of English for International Communication (TOEIC). (This test was developed by the Educational Testing Service in Princeton, N.J., for use in non–English-speaking countries for testing knowledge of English. Almost 300 business and industrial firms in Korea use the TOEIC to measure their university graduates' knowledge of English. It tests listening ability, not speaking ability.) However, one may lose points for disciplinary action or suspension from work. These points are either added to or deducted from the allocated twenty-point pool.

The third determinant for promotion is merit performance, which counts as another twenty points (20 percent). Merit performance, unlike the previous two categories, is hard to quantify. Evaluation is subjective, and the issues involved are complicated. The evaluation form requires the evaluation of two immediate supervisors, with a third higher-ranking officer confirming the results of the two evaluations. The form requires the evaluators to write an average score of their results.

The evaluation of blue-collar workers is initially made by the foreman, assistant section head (taeri), or section head (kwajang) and is finally checked by the division head (pujang) or assistant division head (ch'ajang). For white-collar workers and engineers whose rank is 3 or below, the initial evaluation is made by the assistant section head, followed by the assistant division head; it then goes to the division head. For the rank of assistant section head or above, the initial evaluation is made by two evaluators who rank above the candidate, and it is forwarded to the executives.

The evaluation focuses on a mixture of individual ability and personal character and attitudes. These traits reflect the company motto. This category has three components: (1) contribution to the company; (2) ability and performance; and (3) personal character and attitudes. Ability includes knowledge about the job, the ability to plan creatively, the ability to understand and make judgments, and the potential to grow and develop. As for personal character and attitudes, evaluators take into account seriousness, responsibility, effort devoted to self-development and improvement, and human relations. The assessment of personal character and attitudes covers a broad area and includes abstract concepts. Judging such traits is a very subjective process.

Because my fieldwork took place in the midst of labor unrest, I received the impression that although the management and superiors expected hard work and loyalty, they preferred moderate behavior and dependability over active, positive, and assertive leadership. It was my impression that they would prefer someone who was courteous and obedient over someone who was aggressive and independent. In fact, the old promotion guidelines I obtained in the plant personnel office included the traits of hard work and positive attitude, but these were deleted in the revised version in 1988. In their place were seriousness, cooperativeness, and harmonious behavior. A candidate for promotion who is industrious, vital, and able, yet aggressive and straightforward, will not be as favored for promotion as is someone who is docile and obedient. An old employee who worked in the plant for nearly twenty years but who has never been promoted lamented, "If I had been polite, regardless of my other qualifications, I could have been promoted."

Apparently, the employee's level of educational attainment is not highly important. The promotion system at Poongsan does not discriminate against the workers on the basis of their formal education, but it does rely on their abilities. Nonetheless, non-university graduates have little chance of being promoted over university graduates, especially among white-collar employees. Among the top 100 managers, only 1 graduated from middle school and only 10 graduated from high school, but 89 graduated from a four-year university. The 11 non-university graduates have either exceptional individual talent or a specific connection with the founder of the firm. In fact, the executive who graduated only from middle school started as a chauffeur for the chairman and later was promoted to an executive position. Furthermore, the non-university graduates are relatively old (fifty-six and older), and are part of a generation that experienced considerable educational disruption during the two wars, World War II and the Korean War, which makes their educational background rather unrepresentative. In the future, given the abundance of university graduates, it is inconceivable that many high school graduates will be promoted to the top management.

As in Japan, those who graduate from top universities have a better chance to be promoted. The top universities are those that are the most difficult universities to enter because of the stiff competition. Seoul National, Yonsei, and Korea University are considered to be the most prestigious. In fact, at the annual stockholders' meeting on 27 February 1989, a fifty-year-old Seoul National University graduate was named as Poongsan's new president. He passed over other senior vice presidents. Parenthetically, his predecessor was also a graduate of Seoul National. Among eleven newly promoted top managers in 1989, six were Seoul National University graduates.

Another possible factor in gaining promotion is influence through connections. It is very difficult to confirm or deny the role of influence, particularly among blue-collar workers in the lower echelon. When connections play a role in the promotions of top management, people talk about them. In fact, in 1988, when a number of appointments of top managers were being made, a forty-six-year-old president of a subsidiary company of Poongsan, who is the chairman's younger brother, was promoted to vice chairman. At the same time, a fifty-one-year-old managing director became one of five vice presidents, and a forty-year-old division head was elevated to assistant managing director: both are Ryu clan members. Since their credentials were good enough, it would be difficult for anyone to say that the two clan members' promotion depended at all on kinship connection or nepotism. And no one seems to have been surprised by the appointment of the vice chairman, because the pattern of nepotism in Korea is rather well established, and no one believed Poongsan would be an exception (*Hankook Ilbo*, 12 Oct. 1988:8; Park 1978).

According to a survey of 108 large Korean enterprises, 8.8 percent of the people in top management are close relatives of the owners and founders of the enterprises (*Hankook Ilbo*, 27 Apr. 1987:23). Hattori (1986), a Japanese anthropologist, has pointed out in his comparative study of large enterprises in Korea and Japan that although the separation of ownership from management in Japan is well established, the process is still in its embryonic stages in Korea. The participation of close family members in large Korean business enterprises is common. He indicates that close kin members range from 4.7 percent of the top management at Samsung to 9.7 percent at Lucky-Goldstar and 7.6 percent at Doosan. At Poongsan, 3 percent of the top management are close family members of the founder, which is less than half of the Korean average; others in management are from the same clan as the founder and chairman. Although their relationship with the chairman may be remote, they nonetheless share with him a common ancestor.

I did not observe any occasion when an executive who either recommended or arranged the employment of rank-and-file workers could exercise any influence on their promotions. One executive who arranged for the employment of fourteen rank-and-file workers was very supportive of the promotion of one close kin member from rank 3 to assistant section head, but the kin member's promotion has been delayed two years. His promotion, in fact, occurred after the departure of the executive from Poongsan. It appears that it may not be easy for an executive to influence the promotion of any particular individual. Everyone likes to avoid using such influence.

By and large, promotion is considered to be a very important means of upgrading employees' morale and motivation, but the impact on blue-collar workers is less profound than on white-collar employees and managers. One blue-collar worker who has been promoted to foreman told me,

> In honesty, it means very little. After thirteen years of service, I became a foreman because they believed that I have enough experience in the job and have some leadership ability. As foreman, I have the responsibility of coordinating twenty-five workers. It is not easy. Nowadays, it is very difficult to coordinate young workers, yet there is very little reward. I only get paid some allowances for my responsibility of being in charge of the machines, about 25,000 *wŏn* for a month. I don't believe being a foreman has much prestige. I often feel like I am a double-boiler: heat comes from the bottom without knowing what is cooking upstairs. I don't really care much about my promotion to foreman.

The foreman echoes the views of most blue-collar workers who do not have university degrees. They know their chances to reach the top positions are remote.

The procedure for a promotion is initiated by the personnel office of each plant. The regular promotion takes place annually in March. Before 1 March, the personnel office prepares a list of candidates who meet the requirements for length of service and compiles their credentials, including those for achievements and merit service, which is reviewed four times a year for blue-collar workers and once for white-collar employees. At the plant level, when the employee achieves more than 70 percent of the possible points, the candidate's records are presented to the plant's personnel affairs committee. The committee consists of seven members, including the vice plant manager (who serves as chair), five division heads, the personnel officer, and the president of the Bupyung chapter of the Poongsan labor union. The decision for promotion is based on the majority of votes; two-thirds of the members must be present. The credentials of the recommended candidates whose ranks are rank 5 or below are forwarded to the division head; with the division head's approval the plant manager will make the final decision. The committee is an advisory, not a decision-making, body. For the promotion to rank 4 and above, the recommendations of the plant committee endorsed by the plant manager are forwarded to the personnel office at the main office. Similar procedures must to be repeated in the main office. The higher one goes up, the more complicated the procedures for promotion become.

New challenge for promotion.

Currently, Poongsan faces a new challenge in regard to promotion. When the firm was expanding rapidly in the 1970s and the early 1980s, there were plenty of openings for the promotion of employees. However, more recently, since there has been virtually no growth, the number of openings is limited, as is the case for most Japanese large enterprises. Many qualified candidates are awaiting their turn for promotion. There are thirty-one foreman's positions at the Bupyung plant, for instance, yet more than twice that number are qualified to be elevated to foreman. Recent extension of the retirement age from fifty to fifty-five in most Korean companies makes the situation even harder than it used to be.

For white-collar employees, especially those in the upper ranks, the room for promotion is tight. In one section in the main office of Poongsan, there are three section heads, although the section needs only one. The two junior section heads are doing the jobs of assistant section heads. The accumulating numbers of candidates for promotion can potentially cause low morale and frustration. Some Korean *chaebŏl* groups such as Hanjin, Lucky-Goldstar, and Samsung have already extended the minimum length of service (*Dong-A Ilbo*, 29 Apr. 1989:7).

In the 1970s when Korean business firms were expanding, and scouting was conducted vigorously to fill the ever-increasing number of positions, capable university graduates could be promoted to division heads within ten years or so. Recent surveys show that in the late 1980s it takes almost twice the time it did in the 1970s, although the figure varies slightly from company to company. Nevertheless, the age of Korean employees in comparable firms at equivalent ranks averages six years younger than that of Japanese workers (*Dong-A Ilbo*, 29 Apr. 1989:7).

To ease the problem, some have discussed creating new ranks between the existing ranks. In fact, the rank of assistant managing director was the product of just such a necessity in the past. One reflection of such difficulties was Poongsan's announcement that the 1989 promotion list would be delayed for three months. I was informed that the ratio between the recommended employees and those who actually received the promotion was about nine to one. Competition becomes severe.

By and large, the Korean promotion system as it is represented at Poongsan tends more toward promotion by ability than does the Japanese system, but not as much as the Western system, because it takes into account the length of service more than do Western companies. The Korean system's midpoint position on the continuum between the Western and Japanese systems is the result of its socioeconomic and cultural heritage and the specific labor-market situation in Korea.

4

Career Planning

During my fieldwork, I assumed that employment would be of utmost concern to Poongsan employees. For many industrial workers in the United States, especially the millions who lost their jobs and those whose jobs lay insecure during the most recent recession, job security can seem far more important than other major industrial relations rules such as rewards and promotion. It was, however, surprising to learn that very few Poongsan employees expressed concern about their job security. This does not indicate that Poongsan has never laid off any of its employees; on the contrary, Poongsan once laid off a significant number of employees during the worldwide recession in 1982 following the "oil shock" imposed by OPEC in 1979.

It appears that Poongsan employees' feelings concerning their job security stem from the Korean ethos that managers terminating employees against their will is shameful and dishonorable. Poongsan employees, therefore, trust that their company will make every effort to avoid terminating its employees. Such a trust in management may be grounded in the family analogy, which stems from Confucianism, that likens management and labor relations to that of the patriarchal head of the household and his family members. Even in the case of financial exigency, the regular work force can be retained by terminating temporary workers, general laborers, and women first. Because of this practice, even in the absence of an institutionalized lifetime employment as is widely publicized in some large Japanese firms, Poongsan employees feel that their job security is well protected.

In this case, lifetime employment (at least partial lifetime employment) means that the worker enters a large firm upon graduation, receives in-company education and training, and remains in the same company until the retirement age set by the company (Cole 1971:113). At Poongsan, the retirement age is fifty-five, with the exception of executives. Such an employment system governs the entire passage and career-plan of an employee in a company until his or her retirement.

Although the employment security system is a major concern of this chapter, my description begins with the Poongsan training program, followed by security and retirement, in accordance with the definition of lifetime employment. In addition, the unique nature of Poongsan training, particularly at a Confucian academy (sŏwŏn) near the chairman's hometown, requires a detailed description.

Training

In Poongsan, regular training for its employees was not institutionalized until the early 1980s. An engineer who joined Poongsan in the early 1970s told me,

> When I first came to the Bupyung plant and looked around the shop floor, I got an impression that it was not a modern industrial plant by any standard. If I may use an analogy, the operation then was as if an old auto mechanic wanted to assemble a new car by collecting old parts in order to drive on a modern highway. Some parts were new, but some other parts were unavailable. When we obtained some parts, the hard-sought parts did not fit in together with other parts. Poongsan's startup and its facility were not comparable to those of POSCO. POSCO had new machines and technical advisers from Japan, but Poongsan bought mostly used machines from overseas without much technical assistance from the sellers. We reassembled them and often rebuilt them. Virtually everyone was new to the rebuilt machines. However, like someone who drove a secondhand car eventually became a semi-mechanic, we all became experts. Not many

were then able to teach others. We were about the same. . . . I honestly believe that not many people in the world other than Koreans might be able to do such a startup. You might say that training was then on-the-job, mostly by repeated trial and error. Indeed, Poongsan came a long way.

Before the early 1980s, training was mainly on-the-job training given by the skilled senior workers to the entering workers as needed. Even now, most entering blue-collar workers receive such training.

For entering blue-collar workers, training concerning safety is considered to be of the utmost importance and is mandatory. The personnel officer in the plant instructs the entering employees on safety rules, and the appropriate section head again trains them on safety rules. Safety has become a prime concern of the company.

Until 1982, Poongsan's industrial accident rate was higher than the average for Korean manufacturing workers. Beginning in 1983, Poongsan's rates became much lower than the average. From 1979 to 1988, Poongsan's four plants had 1,292 industrial accidents, including 19 deaths. In the Bupyung plant alone, four deaths occurred between 1978 and 1988; none were reported, however, from 1984 to 1988. In Bupyung, the overall accident rate was reduced from 1.62 percent in 1984 to 0.97 percent in 1988. During this period there were seven minor injuries, yet these cost a total of 547 days of one worker's work, for a total cost of 77,279,000 *wŏn*. Given the high costs of such industrial accidents, safety training has priority over all other training.

Poongsan training is divided into three categories. The first category is on-the-job-training in the plant when a new employee is hired or a new machine is introduced. Such training can be done whenever it is needed and as often as it is necessary within the plant. In a sense, this type of training is taking place all the time. The method of training varies from demonstration to practice. As this training is not institutionalized, no further examination is necessary.

The second category of training, self-development, is that which white-collar employees receive to improve their communication skills and competence in foreign languages. This training is not mandatory, but voluntary. For those who wish to develop foreign-language competence, Poongsan provides videotaped instruction in English conversation and the Japanese language. Because these skills are reflected in their TOEIC scores, which affect their chances for promotion, those employees who graduated from universities and those who are headed for promotion are likely to undertake this training voluntarily.

The third category of training, off-the-job training, offers different programs to the different ranks. It includes management improvement programs, management training programs, management-by-objective training, and a management basic training program for assistant section heads or higher ranks. Also, there is a four-day course for quality-control training designed for rank 3 and rank 2 engineers, and a four-day course in workmanship training for foremen, designed for blue-collar workers. Training for the entering employees, particularly for *kongch'ae* employees, Pyŏngsan Sŏwŏn training, and training for entering female employees all belong to this category as well.

Training for the entering *kongch'ae* employees.

For the entering *kongch'ae* employees who graduated from universities and were hired through open competitive entrance examinations, Poongsan offers fifteen days of intensive training beginning in the middle of January each year. Since Poongsan does not have its own training center or facilities, this program uses the training facilities of the Korean Development Institute (KDI) for the first five days.

The *kongch'ae* employees assemble at the main office in Seoul early in the morning on a designated day in January and turn in all the papers and documents that are necessary for their employment. Then they move to the KDI training center. The trainees receive a 400-page training manual, which includes the company motto, the company song, a welcoming statement from the company president, goals for training, and a detailed training schedule. The director of planning and research lectures on the history of Poongsan, its current state, and its future plans. Then the president makes a brief congratulatory statement.

Actual instruction begins with a long speech from the personnel director. He discusses how one can make a smooth transition from being a student to an employee of a firm, how the superiors in the company differ from professors in the universities, fathers in the families, seniors in the schools. This is followed by specific instructions on how to be an ideal employee in performing one's job assignment and how to report to the superiors. He concludes with a six-point pedagogical paradigm on the successful employee, which is identified with a successful life. As the session ends, the trainees learn the company song together.

As the training manual states, the goals of the students in this program are to familiarize themselves with the business activities of Poongsan, to acquire the right attitude toward their job, to enhance their ability to perform their jobs effectively, and to form basic values as new employees. Daily training starts at 6:00 A.M. with a morning exercise and 30 minutes' practice of the company song, followed by breakfast. After a one-hour lecture by one of Poongsan's executives, the trainees learn about Poongsan management, production, marketing, and sales, as they also learn about the appropriate manners and etiquette required of new employees. Essentially, the curriculum seeks to promote teamwork and safety training.

The final ten days of training takes place at the four plants, with the trainees traveling from plant to plant. Instead of attending lectures in a classroom, the trainees observe and participate in actual plant operation. During the KDI training, guest lecturers are utilized for their expertise, but in the training at the plants, all Poongsan employees serve as mentors and trainers. After the ten days of plant training end at the Angang plant, all the trainees receive certificates for the successful completion of the program, a step that signifies that they have become officially recognized Poongsan employees with rank 4 (4-kŭp). Some are engineers who majored in technical subjects, and others are assigned to managerial positions as white-collar employees.

During their training, trainees are paid 85 percent of the regular wage of rank 4. Since the training is completed in the middle of February and their commencement is scheduled around the end of February, they return to the company and resume their assigned duty upon their graduation, usually on 2 March. In 1988, 116 university graduates completed this training as new employees.

Compared with the training for entering employees in Japanese firms, which normally lasts three months for males and two weeks for females, Poongsan's training is shorter than that for Japanese males but longer than that for Japanese females (Rohlen 1974:192–211). (In 1988, the program trained all males.) Such a short period of training is dictated by the budgetary allocation. The director of Poongsan training told me that whereas most of the Japanese firms allocate nearly 1 percent of their total sales for training, Poongsan spends about 0.03 percent. Because of the confined time framework, Poongsan's training for entering employees does not include some of the Japanese programs, such as the development of spiritual strength and the psychology of accomplishment, Zen Buddhist meditation, visits to military bases, doing *rotō* (the Japanese trainees were instructed to go down into town and find work from the residents, cf. Rohlen 1973:1550; 1974:203), a twenty-five-mile endurance walk, and spending a weekend in the country (see Rohlen 1973; 1974:192–211). However, similar spiritual training is available at Poongsan in the *sŏwŏn* training.

Training for the entering female employees.

The annual training for Poongsan's entering female employees, most of whom are clerical workers and secretaries, also takes place at the training facilities of KDI. This training takes place in the middle of June for two days. The goals and purposes differ from those of male *kongch'ae*; the emphasis is on ways to achieve mutual understanding and teamwork, cultivating a positive attitude toward the job, improving general knowledge about the job, manners and etiquette, and self-development.

As they check into the training center, trainees receive the training manual, which includes the company motto, the company song, and the purpose of training, just as does the *kongch'ae* manual, although this manual is much thinner. Although the trainees are briefed about the state of the company, lectures are mostly about the value of teamwork and about the right and appropriate attitudes toward the job. Since Poongsan sees the role of female employees as supportive of the male employees, not as managerial, the focus of the training is on the manners and etiquette required of the female employees.

Training in etiquette includes teaching the women the right way to bow. The training manual is specific, illustrating the correct posture: the employee is instructed to close her two feet tightly together, to bend her upper body down at a 45-degree angle, and to lower her eyes to the ground, focusing about one to two meters ahead of her standing position. She is instructed not to stare up at the person she is greeting. Etiquette training also includes the proper usage of honorific words toward superiors, colleagues, and visitors, the proper way to answer telephones and take messages, and the use of appropriate language. Specific instructions are given on the way the female employee should open office doors to conduct a visitor to her superiors, to the car, and to the elevator. I was interested to note that when a female employee rides in a chauffeur-driven car with her superiors, she is expected to sit either in the front seat next to the chauffeur or, if the car is crowded and she has to sit in the back seat with two superiors, to sit in the middle, which is less comfortable than seats beside the door.

The female employees at Poongsan have obviously been thoroughly instructed in etiquette. During my fieldwork, whenever I walked into the offices of the executives, including the chairman, president, and vice presidents, all the receptionists would stand up to greet me, bow to me as the training manual shows in the picture, and ask me the purpose of my visit as cordially as they could. If the person I was visiting was not available right away, the women always led me to a waiting room and served either coffee, tea, or soda automatically without asking me. Although their manner of offering these refreshments is not included in the instructions in the training manual, someone must have instructed them carefully, because their manners were uniform.

During 1988, eighty-four female employees completed this two-day training. Again, whereas a Japanese bank requires two weeks of training for its female workers (Rohlen 1974:193), Poongsan's training is just two days long. Because of the time limit and also because the participants are, by and large, clerical workers and secretaries, Poongsan training for its female employees is confined mostly to instructing them in etiquette. Hardly any production workers are included in the program.

Sŏwŏn training.

As mentioned briefly in chapter 1, Poongsan offers an annual *sŏwŏn* training for eighty employees, forty at a time twice a year for those who occupy managerial positions and for engineers whose ranks are rank 3 (3-*kŭp*). In many ways, this training resembles the Japanese spiritual education described by Rohlen (1973:1542–62; 1974:192–211). Different from the other training programs, which usually take place in a modern training center such as the KDI facilities, this train-

FIGURE 4.1   An overview of the Pyŏngsan Sŏwŏn.

ing takes place in early July at a *sŏwŏn*, a Confucian academy for *yangban* scholarship in the tradition of the Yi dynasty. The Pyŏngsan Sŏwŏn, which belongs to the prominent *yangban* clans of Kyŏngsang province, is located in the vicinity of the chairman's hometown, Hahoe.

The *sŏwŏn* was originally established to serve as a combination of private academies and shrines dedicated to past Confucian worthies. Although the function of the *sŏwŏn* as an academy to train young men in Neo-Confucian ideology, manners, and morals was virtually eliminated because of modern school systems, it still retains some of its functions as a sacred shrine. In fact, during the filming at the Poongsan *sŏwŏn* training by the Pacific Century filming crew in the summer of 1990, the producer asked the director of Poongsan training to have the traditional mask dancing performed in the main court of the *sŏwŏn*, so that the filming crew could harness their lighting equipment to the power line in the main building. The director sought permission to do so from the *sŏwŏn* officials, but the request was denied, for the mask dancing originally had been performed in Hahoe by commoners hidden by the masks to satirize the *yangban* class, and so the mask dancing could not be allowed in the main courtyard of the *yangban* shrine.

At any event, for Poongsan's *sŏwŏn* training, forty trainees at a time are selected from four plants and the Seoul main office; they meet at the railroad station nearest the *sŏwŏn* after traveling about five hours from Seoul by train. Under the guidance of the director for training, they make the nearly one-hour bus ride to reach the village where the *sŏwŏn* is located and where the first program starts. All the trainees and instructors visit the birthplace of the late prime minister Sŏae (the chairman's twelfth-generation ancestor), which is the current residence of the *chongson* (main heir of the clan) of the village.

As the trainees assemble on the floor of the house, the *chongson's* mother gives a "pep-talk" on Confucian teachings, the strength of the traditional family, and the possible application of these principles to the management of large industrial firms. Her talks are largely grandmotherly advice and wisdom. After refreshments are served to the visiting trainees by the *chongson*, the trainees, under the direction of the *chongson*, pay a visit to Yŏngmokak, a museum in which relics of the late prime minister are displayed. Then they make a grand tour of the entire village. I followed them as if I were one of the trainees.

Some participants told me that this occasion was their first visit to such a traditional *yangban* village, although they have seen the villages on television or in movies. A young participant was very critical, and even resentful, of the former *yangban* class as he was touring the village. In front of a huge *yangban* house, he even mimicked a cowardly *yangban's* gesture as often portrayed in a comedy. He satirized the *yangban* without any mask.

Trainees are impressed by the special location and beauty of the *sŏwŏn*. The *sŏwŏn* faces southeast toward the Nakdong River. It is reached by a winding road to the chairman's village, with the river on the left. Entering the front gate, a visitor has to climb up the stone steps below the Mandaeru pavilion, the largest *sŏwŏn* pavilion. Emerging from under the pavilion, one must climb up a few more stone steps to reach the lecture hall, where lectures for the trainees take place. In front of the lecture hall is the dormitory, which parallels the library, where the trainees are assigned. Behind the lecture hall, one comes to the shrine. There is a storage room to the west of the shrine and a memorial service preparations office and the duty officers' quarters to the east. The two-story pavilion has seven bays across the front and two in the sides, and it commands a view of the whole surrounding area. There is an artificial oblong pond near the wall to the west of the pavilion.

Upon arrival, the trainees change their outfits to company-made athletic uniforms, which are designed to be comfortable for their activities. Then the orientation, loaded with the prohibitive norms such as "no card games, no alcoholic beverages," begins immediately. The curriculum includes lecture series, team sports, workshops, problem solving, speeches, and an endurance test as the final event. There is also a lecture on traditional Korean culture by a folklorist who specializes in Korean folklore. The traditional mask dancing is performed at night in an open square in front of the main building of the *sŏwŏn* (not inside the *sŏwŏn* building) by the students of Andong University, who wear the masks of scholars, monks, maidens, old women, butchers, commoners, and servants.

The entire four-day program, beginning at 6:00 A.M. and ending at 11:30 P.M. every day, is centered on teamwork. The great emphasis is on group activities to enhance the development of teamwork over individuality. According to Rohlen's report, Japanese spiritual education includes Zen meditation; visits to military bases; *rotō*; spending the weekend in the country to demonstrate the trainees' aggressiveness, boldness, and courage; and an endurance walk for twenty-five miles. Poongsan's *sŏwŏn* training does not include meditation, but the atmosphere surrounding the Confucian *sŏwŏn* resembles that of a Zen temple. Visiting military bases would be a useless exercise for the Poongsan employees, who, unlike the Japanese, face mandatory military service. Most Poongsan employees (except the exempted workers at Angang munitions plant) have finished their military service. In fact, my survey of the Bupyung employees indicates that 86 percent of the employees are veterans. Also, the *rotō* is not included in the Poongsan curriculum, apparently because there is not enough time to allow one day's working experience for a strange employer. Otherwise, the Korean and Japanese programs are very similar.

Japanese trainees are required to walk for twenty-five miles to test their endurance, whereas Poongsan's *sŏwŏn* training program adopts *kŭgi'hulyŏn*, a team effort to achieve certain goals under the most difficult circumstances. The *kŭgi'hulyŏn* takes place at night in the rugged mountains. As a combination of Japanese endurance work and teamwork, the *kŭgi'hulyŏn* not only requires trainees to solve a given task collectively in teams of four members, but it also requires a walk in the rugged mountains for ten miles using a map and a compass to reach an appointed destination. The team tasks vary from year to year and from team to team. Some examples of these problems include showing drawings of a sailboat, wristwatch, telephone, and the like and asking the participants to figure out what is missing. Others include showing pairs of numbers and asking the team to figure out how many of those pairs can make 1001. Some teams are asked to write a five-line structured poem using the title of Poongsan. All the problem-solving games are difficult and time-consuming.

Although every trainee seems to be attracted by the aesthetic beauty surrounding the *sŏwŏn*, the limited lodging and bathroom facilities bother the trainees the most. Ten trainees are assigned to a small room; it is literally crowded. In the morning, forty trainees have to compete with each other for two bathrooms. At night, they have to fight against mosquitoes. Mosquitoes are the "enemy number one" in the night sessions, even though the trainees draw nets to keep them away (Figure 4.2). Although a good many of the trainees are from rural villages, they seem to have already forgotten their village lives of the past. When I mentioned the difficulties of trainees in their *sŏwŏn* training because of its poor facilities, the chairman of Poongsan responded to me that "that is the precise reason why we are having our training over there. If we look for a good facility and comfort, we would have it in a modern hotel with air-conditioned system. They have to think about how we lived in the past, even in such a short period of time. We have to know our roots, where we are from." Perhaps, for the trainees, coping with the given situations may be the biggest *kŭgi'hulyŏn*, or learning endurance. Although Poongsan's *sŏwŏn* program is relatively short, it seems to serve the same purpose that Japanese spiritual education serves.

To relieve the trainees' anxiety at the end of the program, Poongsan *sŏwŏn* training uses drinking as a release. Drinking any alcoholic beverage during the training is strictly prohibited, but on the final night, all the trainees are encouraged to drink as much as they can the at company's expense. All the trainees are expected to drink to their maximum capacity and to express their views and feelings freely and loudly, without fear of any repercussion from management. The Pyŏngsan Sŏwŏn training so closely resembles Japanese spiritual training that I wondered whether it had been modeled after the Japanese program. However, the founders of the Pyŏngsan Sŏwŏn (not the chairman, but a few executives) assured me that its design originated with them. Perhaps their denial of Japanese influence may be necessary to preserve the nationalistic aura. Nevertheless, because the chairman lived and conducted business in Japan for a decade, it is difficult to rule out the possibility of Japanese influence on Poongsan's training.

At any event, when I first heard about the sŏwŏn training, I thought it was a technique of manipulation to indoctrinate Poongsan's middle managers with the Confucian virtues. My assumption was on the basis of three indicators. First, regardless of whether his managerial philosophy was based on the Confucian virtues, the chairman of Poongsan is, in my judgment, a strong Confucian advocator, so that he had a great temptation to exert the Confucian-oriented

FIGURE 4.2 Mandaeru pavilion, where lectures for the Poongsan trainees take place.

FIGURE 4.3   The Poongsan chairman, wearing a traditional Conufucian robe for his ancestral rites, standing in front of his ancestor's shrine with the anthropologist.

family analogy to his firm: bound to a common fate, workers and managers should work harmoniously to achieve their goals and enjoy their common prosperity. Second, the training takes place in a Confucian academy. Third, it takes place in the vicinity of the chairman's hometown, Hahoe, a stronghold of the Confucian culture in Korea.

As I observed the training program twice in 1987 and 1988 and participated as a special guest speaker in the 1991 training sessions, I was not certain about my presupposition. In the training curricula, there was no single agenda or item about Confucianism. The contents and curricula of the training program were developed by an independent training firm and handled by the personnel office of the firm in the form of subcontracting. The chairman is for the most part unaware of the details of the training. The folklorist who delivers lectures on traditional Korean culture does not include any segment on Confucianism (as far as I know, he is not known to be a Confucian advocate). Rather, his emphasis was on the pre-Confucian era of Korean culture. The most surprising thing is the performance of the mask dancing as a part of integrated curricula, even though it was performed outside the premises of the *sŏwŏn*. The mask dancing in essence satirizes the negative elements of Confucianism and the *yangban* who politicized it in ruling the Yi dynasty.

Perhaps the hidden meaning of the training can be best explained in terms of searching for national identity. The chairman of Poongsan is a cultural nationalist first and a Confucianist second. Poongsan's training at the *sŏwŏn* may be the product of a reaction against both the loosening of traditional Korean culture in contemporary Korean society and the Western influence that is blamed for this trend. In fact, Eckert and his associates have observed this trend (Eckert et al. 1990:414):

> The cultural challenge has been to retain and develop a unique Korean identity while absorbing a constant and intense barrage of foreign cultural influence. . . . Recently the pendulum has moved toward the latter, and traditional culture (both high and low), disdained as late as the 1960s by many South Koreans as unprogressive or simply embarrassing in a Western-oriented world, has been enjoying a renaissance of interest and respect. Folk culture in particular has become a new source of pride and inspiration, especially to nationalist (*minjok*) or populist (*minjung*) artists who have consciously identified the core of the nation with the history of the common people (or masses).

Poongsan's training at the *sŏwŏn* thus may be an unintended consequence of the chairman's belief and values. Tu's (1984:67) explanation may be applicable; he has written that an individual "may unconsciously translate values in his religious belief system into factors that motivate his economic behaviour." Additionally, the Poongsan trainees have an opportunity to learn something about their chairman's roots and the reputation of his clan.

The director of the Poongsan training program, who happens to be a member of the same Ryu clan as the chairman, sums up the theme of the *sŏwŏn* training:

> Well, if Poongsan had its own training facility somewhere in the countryside like some of the other *chaebŏl* groups, we might not

have this training at this *sŏwŏn*. Then we could avoid any possible criticism regarding a possible Confucian indoctrination. The *sŏwŏn* was available, its aesthetic beauty is exceptional, and it is away from the plants, so we took advantage of it. Honestly, not many Korean *chaebŏl* groups have access to such a facility. In fact, some years ago, a canoe team of an Ivy League school from the United States came here and spent that summer in canoeing because of its scenic beauty. What we are hoping to accomplish during this training is to provide an opportunity to rediscover our traditional culture, and to examine two contrasting cultures, *yangban* and commoners. By living a few days in a *yangban's* academy and acting [as one watched the mask dancing; in that dancing the audiences also act and participate] as commoners in the mask dancing, they [the trainees] may be able to understand both sides well.

Most trainees seem to be exhausted when the training sessions come to an end. Yet, no one appears to be resentful about the training, including the one who was mimicking the *yangban's* gesture, except for the inconveniences in lodging and toilet facilities. The topic given to me as a special guest lecturer was "Traditional Korean Culture in the World Context." The trainees raised more questions than I asked them. It looked as if they were the anthropologists.

Whatever the intended purpose of this training at a Confucian academy might be, it certainly has an unintended consequence, as Tu (1984:67) has indicated. It has an impact on the Poongsan workers' view of Confucianism. In my survey of the Bupyung plant employees, I learned that a great majority of those who have had the training believe that the company should be run on the basis of Confucian values rather than on Western democratic values (the ratio is 5 to 1). Nonparticipants preferred Confucian values only 3 to 1.

Expansion of the concept of the *sŏwŏn* training.

In 1988, a total of 2,264 (1,246 blue-collar workers and 1,018 white-collar employees) Poongsan employees participated in some sort of training offered by the company. My survey of the Bupyung plant employees indicated that 37.5 percent received training in 1988, while 62.5 percent had not received any formal training other than on-the-job training within the plant. However, beginning in 1989, a three-day training course focusing on harmony, cooperation, and mutual understanding between employees and the management was required of all Poongsan employees in the four plants, including the plant manager. The requirement is likely a response to the labor unrest and strikes facing the company since 1987. Instead of using KDI facilities, each plant uses the convention facilities of a nearby hotel. All the Bupyung plant employees completed this training at Hotel Yangchi in seven sessions attended by about 100 workers at each session. The training manual resembles that used for *sŏwŏn* training, except that it is not as comprehensive.

In terms of the goals of the training, the thinking of management and trainees differ. Whereas management emphasizes the goals of harmony, cooperation, teamwork, and understanding, the employees, particularly blue-collar workers, focus on the acquisition of new skills and techniques related to their jobs. Regardless of the wishful thinking of the blue-collar workers about acquiring valuable mechanical and technological skills, the automated machines and the computer-oriented operations of the Poongsan plants make blue-collar workers simple laborers. The few engineers who know how the automated machines work are the only exceptions. Certain skills and craftsmanship that one might learn from the senior workers and foremen in the plant are often rendered obsolete overnight, as new automated machines are installed. Therefore, it may be appropriate that management gives priority to training that fosters workers' docility, cooperation, and meekness.

Security and Lateral Movement

Poongsan does not have the institutionalized *nenkō* type of promotional system that is used by some large Japanese firms, although there is increasing pressure to change the traditional system "to cope with the new technology which makes it hard for them [older foremen] to be effective leaders" (Cole 1971:106). In a similar vein, as far as job security is concerned, Poongsan does not make any commitment to guarantee permanent or lifetime employment, as some large Japanese firms do. As Cole (1971:113) defines it, lifetime employment in a firm means that "the worker enters a large firm after school graduation, receives in-company education and training, and remains in the same company until the retirement age of fifty-five." The apparent absence of a lifetime employment system in Korea, and at Poongsan in particular, stems from the different historical and socioeconomic conditions of the two countries.

Historically, the Japanese practice of lifetime employment was institutionalized at least partly as a response by management to the high labor turnover during World War I and as a union and worker response to job scarcity in the post–World War II period. In his interpretation of the institutionalization of permanent employment, Abegglen (1958) sees it as having grown out of traditional social relations, while others such as Taira (1962) see the system as having developed because of economic reasons after World War I. Even in the 1960s, Cole (1971:125) has reported, "the growing labor shortage, caused by the expanding economy and demographic changes resulting from a declining birth rate, pressures the permanent employment practice and encourages workers to look for alternative job offers. The structure of the labor market increasingly comes to resemble that of other advanced industrial societies." According to the recent observations of a Korean reporter in Japan, a study of Japanese university students indicates that almost half of the sampled students do not want to stay in one company for life. Indeed, in 1988, more than 2 million Japanese changed their jobs. Almost 26 percent of Japanese business firms believe that the lifetime employment system will fade away, mainly because of rapid technological development, the elimination of the dual economic structure between the large and small firms, and the narrow and delayed promotion path of large firms. Some Japanese prefer to face the challenge and opportunity of small and medium-sized firms.

In contrast, rapid Korean economic growth and industrialization has created ample room for employment opportunity. At the same time, the suppression of the agricultural sector in favor of the export-oriented manufacturing industry has caused massive migration from rural to urban industrial areas since the mid 1960s. This migration has created a huge and cheap work force for labor-intensive manufacturing industries (S. Cho 1989:10). Particularly with the dual economic structure, the large manufacturing industry has never experienced a labor shortage. For the large enterprises, as far as the labor force is concerned, it is a buyer's market. The large industrial firms do not feel they have to guarantee lifetime employment to attract the needed work force.

Furthermore, there is a strong tendency in Korea to stigmatize those who change jobs often. One's value, status, and dependability tend to be measured by the duration of one's stay in a group. The more one moves around or changes one's job, the less dependable one is thought to be. Korean managers label the manufacturing workers, especially those in textile industry, who move from company to company as *ch'amsaejok*, "a flock of sparrows" flying over the fields in search of better crops. Employers try to avoid hiring those frequent movers. In my survey of Bupyung plant employees I learned that the employees themselves believe that those who change jobs often have something wrong with them (56.7 percent), are unreliable (12.5 percent), or have no loyalty to the company (17.3 percent). Only 5.8 percent of the sampled workers believe that workers who change jobs often are capable and able workers.

The large firms do not have to resort to lifetime employment. And at Poongsan, even those who would like to change their jobs to other firms that require similar skills are faced with few alternatives, since Poongsan is the largest manufacturer of copper and copper-related products in Korea. Usually, the small and medium-sized firms offer less desirable working conditions, lower pay, and an uncertain future because of poor finances. These factors reinforce the low rate of labor turnover. In my survey, I learned that those who are satisfied with their jobs are not in the majority (10.6 percent). The results of the survey seem to indicate that even though employees may not be quite satisfied with their current jobs, they are there to stay because alternative jobs are limited.

Although Poongsan does not have institutionalized lifetime employment, the firm assures the workers of its moral obligation to retain good workers. Most employees expect to be employed as long as the company does not face a financial crisis. In fact, 181 (25 percent) of 724 employees at the Bupyung plant have worked there more than eleven years, and 64 (8.84 percent) have worked there more than sixteen years. Since Poongsan has been in existence for only twenty years, and started with 83 workers at the Bupyung plant in 1970, the figures indicate that Poongsan in effect has a partial lifetime employment system. In fact, article 28 of the personnel rules specifies that an employee cannot be arbitrarily dismissed from the company unless the employee receives a criminal sentence in court or violates certain rules listed in articles 29 and 30. The moral obligation of the company delineated in article 28 is not any less stringent than the tenure system of American universities.

Under a system of partial lifetime employment, managers do not usually terminate any employees, even if they are not happy with them. Other mechanisms are utilized to solve problems. In fact, a member of the plant's personnel affairs committee told me that during the six years he served on the committee, they had never acted to terminate any single worker for the worker's own mistakes. Rather, the company terminated workers only when it was faced with financial exigency. However, Poongsan does not rule out the dismissal of its employees. There are several conditions for possible dismissal, as specified in article 30 of the rules and guidelines for personnel affairs:

1. When an employee wishes to resign;
2. When an employee's work ability or efficiency is inferior to the general level;
3. When an employee's dismissal is determined by disciplinary action;
4. When it is known that an employee was hired under falsified credentials;
5. When an employee's performance is hampered owing to physical or mental disorder, physical weakness, or chronic disease;
6. When there are superfluous personnel because of readjustment and curtailment of business, or to rationalize operations, or for other unavoidable reasons;
7. When an employee has not been given any duty assignment within three months from his or her discharge from the previous assignment (in this case, the matter must be reviewed by the personnel affairs committee);
8. When an employee instigates illegal strike, sabotage, or other collective means to disrupt the normal work;
9. When there are other reasons corresponding to one of the above items.

These nine conditions are very similar to those of a Japanese company. However, the most striking difference between the dismissal conditions in Poongsan and the Japanese company Cole (1971:117) described is the fourth Poongsan rule: when an employee has been hired under falsified credentials. This rule is a response to the possible employment of potential union advocators and instigators who, though they are graduates of universities, seek employment as rank-and-file blue-collar workers under falsified credentials. This possibility has become a major concern of company personnel officers in their recruiting of prospective employees.

As for the sixth rule, Poongsan dismisses employees only when it does not have any other choice. As has happened elsewhere in Korean industry, Poongsan has had to face the termination of some workers. In 1982, because of the economic slowdown at home and abroad after the "oil-shock" imposed by OPEC in 1979, which resulted in especially drastic reductions of orders from the defense department, Poongsan terminated large numbers of its employees. The Angang plant reduced its work force from 4,489 employees to 3,280, dismissing 1,209 employees, and the Bupyung plant terminated 405 workers, reducing its work force from 1,058 to 653. These were the largest number of dismissals Poongsan has ever faced.

Even then, Poongsan terminated temporary workers and general laborers first. Then termination was aimed at female employees who worked in producing coin blanks. Poongsan switched coin blank production to another plant, excepting only the production of precious metal commemorative medals and coin blanks for the 1986 Asian Games and the 1988 Olympic Games in Seoul.

The reduction of the work force resulting from financial hardship is a situation that can face any industry anywhere. It must have been a particularly painful experience for the owner of the firm with any form of permanent employment system. As a Japanese management official explained to Cole (1971:118), "My idea of a good manager is one who does not fire workers" even when the company faces economic difficulty. In the difficult years from 1979 to 1982, according to the memory of Poongsan employees, both executives and rank-and-file workers worked together to overcome the difficulty. In an effort to avoid a massive termination, all Poongsan employees voluntarily returned their bonuses and other allowances to the company. Despite their effort, the money was not enough to avoid the termination of such a large number of employees.

Poongsan's chairman recalled his feeling of those days for a reporter (*Chaegae Journal*, 1 June 1986:44): "When the interest rate was going up, the monetary exchange rate of the Korean *wŏn* was going up against the U.S. dollar in the international monetary market to discourage exports, and oil prices were outrageously high, I was very close to being bankrupt. Because of the financial crisis, when I had to face terminating hundreds of my own employees, I even thought about committing suicide."

His statement was not an exaggeration, but seemed to express his genuine feelings. For Korean managers, terminating their employees against their will is considered to be shameful and dishonorable. This feeling may stem from the analogy that likens industry to the family, with the owner and manager of the industry as the patriarchal head of the household and the employees as family members. The head of the household is responsible for supporting his family members. If the head of household is unable to support his own family members, he is considered to be irresponsible, and thus shameful and dishonorable. This closely resembles the Korean father's affection described by Janelli and Janelli (1982:35).

If an employee is less productive and is undesirable in the eyes of the management, immediate dismissal of the employee is not considered; first, an effort is made to transfer the employee to an unimportant position. Cole (1971:119) described such positions as undesirable and harmless positions where the transferred workers do not interfere with production. In his study of a Japanese bank, Rohlen (1974:149) has witnessed such a policy when the bank sent an employee to an isolated and unimportant place, which was "a kind of exile worse than a simple reduction of command."

Everyone at the Bupyung plant knows which positions are considered to be unimportant and undesirable. Moreover, transfer to other plants involves many personal sacrifices on the part of the transferring employee. Some may turn in their resignation promptly to protest such transfers. In that case, the company has accomplished its purpose without terminating the employee. Others who do not have alternatives just accept the transfer as a sign of management's dissatisfaction. When undesirable transfer is used as a mechanism for dismissal, it allows both the management and the employees to save face.

During my fieldwork I witnessed several such cases, including two top executives in the main office and several rank-and-file workers at the Bupyung plant. An assistant managing director (*yisabo*) and director of a unit in the main office, who had been one of my informants, anticipated a promotion after the annual stockholders' meeting. Instead, the same rank holder in a subsidiary company was promoted to managing director (yisa), assigned the person to the same unit, and became his immediate boss. The director who was excluded from the promotion displayed his dissatisfaction. Then his attendance at work became irregular, and he was absent from work for a month. After four unhappy months, he finally turned in his resignation. Currently, he is running his own small business. In another instance, a plant manager who is a distant relative of the chairman was transferred to a harmless position in the main office after one outburst of most furious labor unrest; later, he also resigned from his post.

At the Bupyung plant a rank-and-file worker who had been handling the labor relations affairs at the management office became sympathetic to the union organizers. He had been trained in labor relations and had obtained a certificate as an expert in labor relations affairs, and he became quite knowledgeable about labor relations. At the same time, he became a strong advocate of the labor movement. Despite warnings from the assistant managing director not to do so, he was giving technical advice to the union, even though he could not be a member of the union, according to company bylaws. Suddenly, one day, he was transferred to a new department. This transfer did not stop him from advising the union. Finally, in early June 1989, less than one month after his previous transfer, he was transferred again to the security department, which is not considered to be a desirable position and required him to make no personal contact with union members. Finally, the union took this transfer seriously, and with the support of the union he took his grievance to the plant manager. The union newsletter published the case in detail. Finally, the plant manager bowed to union pressure and promised to restore the employee to another department.

During this commotion, the management began to ask the employee's relatives who are also employed at Poongsan, particularly the one who recommended and arranged his employment, to calm him down. Ironically, however, the managing director who was initially responsible for his employment had been forced to resign earlier because of the union's demands during the 1987 strike. I asked the employee who was going through the agonizing moments, "Why do you have to go through such a commotion?" I trusted that he would answer me honestly because he happened to be one of my remote kin.

He commented,

> I know that if I keep my mouth shut, the manager will transfer me back to the original position since there is union pressure. But I know too well that labor relations in the plant need to be improved. Instead of management's trying to work together with the union, since we do not have any previous experience in labor movements, the middle managers in the plant see the union as an enemy rather than a partner. But the union movement is not right either, because they do not know what they are doing mainly because of the lack of knowledge and experience. The management should allow me to be involved in their union affairs. I can be really helpful to the company as much as I can be to the union, because I know something about them, and union members trust me.

If his transfer was based on what he was doing, as he claims, his punishment was not based on any wrongdoing but rather was based on his disobedience of his superiors. The company's action may stem from the traditional Korean values manifested in Korean childrearing practice. As Brandt (1971:173) recognized nearly two decades ago in an ethnographic study of the rural Korean village, when rural Korean children are "beaten or slapped, it is usually for disobedience rather than wrongdoing." Indeed, "children are encouraged to be dependent, obedient, and cooperative." In Korea, maintaining an independent idea seems to be less appreciated than is remaining dependable, conformative, and cooperative.

The transfer or lateral movement of an employee to an unimportant position is sometimes related to the status of the employee's patron who was instrumental in the initial employment. When the managing director resigned in 1987, several of his clients who were employed by his connections were transferred to relatively unimportant positions. They ended up working in simple jobs where they could not demonstrate their abilities. In cases like this, it is very difficult for the fieldworker to discern whether the new assignments are based on merit. One thing that is for certain is that any change occurring in a high echelon usually brings about shifts of low-echelon, rank-and-file workers.

When undesirable transfers take place in top management, such high-ranking employees tend to resign: either they go to other firms or they start their own business. When such transfers or different assignments take place at the lower levels, employees usually accept them. This submissiveness is particularly true among blue-collar workers. For them, quitting and leaving the company means that either they would not have any job at all or they would be going to less desirable firms, usually with poor working conditions, less pay, and poor fringe benefits.

Managers' reluctance to dismiss their own employees is also reflected in their restraint in hiring new employees. Poongsan had experienced hardship from 1979 to 1982, and its financial state in 1988 was not strong. Because the appreciation of the Korean *wŏn* against the U.S. dollar in the international monetary market discouraged export, because the workers' wages increased, and because prolonged labor unrest reduced production, the company decided to halt its hiring of *kongch'ae* employees for two years, 1989 and 1990. In fact, in 1989 the total wages of Poongsan employees (111.5 billion *wŏn*) were nearly double the wages of 1988 (59.9 billion *wŏn*) as shown in table 3.1. Wages in 1989 constituted 24 percent of the total output, but had been only 14 percent in 1988. If production decreases further and wages continue to increase at the current rate, there is no guarantee that Poongsan can maintain its current work force. To prevent the dismissal of some employees, Poongsan decided not to hire any new employees, hoping that its restraint and the number of retirees would be sufficient to meet its needs.

Retirement

As prospective retirees reach their fifty-fifth birthday, they quietly prepare for retirement. There is neither an individual retirement ceremony nor a golden watch. At most, fellow workers throw a party or two.

Except for executives whose ranks are managing director and above, the mandatory retirement age at Poongsan is 55. The retirement age used to be 53, but it was extended to 55 starting 1 September 1987. Even with the extension, there has been growing pressure from the workers to extend the retirement age further, mainly because average life expectancy is growing. In fact, the average life expectancy of Koreans in 1960 was 52.7 years for males and 57.7 for females; in 1970, it was 62.5 for males and 69.1 for females. The World Bank (1989:165) reports that in 1987, the average Korean life expectancy for both males and females is 69. In 1989, it became 66.9 for males and 70.8 for females (Hankook Ilbo, 24 Feb. 1990:7). And it was estimated that by 2000 it will be 69.3 for males and 76.2 for females (T'ak 1984:37–38).

The present-day average Korean blue-collar worker who reaches retirement age is likely to have children who have not quite completed their education, especially when they pursue education after high school. Furthermore, most retirees have to spend money for the weddings of their children, and many are still supporting their surviving parents. In many ways, the retirees need more income than they have ever needed in their lives, yet they have to face the cutoff of their regular source of income.

Almost all Korean firms have a retirement pension system. Most private firms employ lump-sum pension systems, but the pension for civil servants in the government pays almost 70 percent of their basic salary for life (Choi 1984). Because of this stable and lifelong pension, even though it is insufficient for their livelihood, prospective employees tend to choose jobs on the basis of stability (43.1 percent) over prestige (4.3 percent), size of income (25.0 percent), meaningfulness (12.8 percent), and promotion opportunities (14.5 percent) (National Bureau of Statistics 1988b:101).

Schemes and formulas to calculate retirement pensions in private industry vary. The Poongsan retirement pension pays a lump sum upon retirement, an amount based on the amount of monthly wages the employee has been paid and the length of service of the employee. The higher the wage, the larger the pension, and the longer the service, the larger the pension. The formula for the retirement pension calculation is this: to a standard one month's wage (an average monthly salary of the last three months), add one-twelfth of the last year's monthly allowances, bonuses, and other wages, and then multiply this amount by the number of years of service. This lump-sum pension is slightly more than one full monthly wage for each year's service. If an employee worked for twelve years at Poongsan, his or her lump-sum retirement pension would be slightly more than one full year's wage. Retirees can hardly meet their needs for the rest of their lives on such an amount.

It is difficult to trace what retirees do after leaving Poongsan.

Since almost all Korean manufacturing has a retirement age of fifty-five, it is difficult for any rank-and-file retiree to seek regular employment in other plants. Among the recent retirees, some report they are working as temporary workers in small manufacturing plants; others work as night watchmen; and one company driver now drives a taxicab. One retired managing director runs a small shop on his own with the help of his sons and does some subcontracting work with one of the affiliated companies. However, since Poongsan does not have many affiliated companies and the nature of Poongsan's products does not depend on much subcontracting, retirees do not have many opportunities like this.

Recently, several small firms launched a bold and innovative step to hire "not-so-old" retirees to make use of their labor, maturity, and experience. Seoul High Speed Bus Lines plans to fill half of its seventy positions for ticket-counter clerks with retirees whose ages range from sixty to sixty-five. The Hotel Ambassador hired thirty-five retirees who are fifty-five and older; the Yulsan Farm, which raises chestnut trees, fills 80 percent of its work force with retirees; and the Consumer Protection Agency hired ten retirees and assigned them to work as counselors. All of the employers have expressed their satisfaction with the retired workers and plan to expand this practice if positions are available (Dong-A Ilbo, 20 July 1988:9). Those who were hired are of course the lucky ones, a tiny minority among the nearly 10 percent (4,024,182) of the current Korean population (40,419,652) whose ages are fifty-five and older (National Bureau of Statistics 1988a:44–45). The proportion of Koreans who are older will be greater in the future.

There being no records tracking Poongsan retirees, in my survey I asked a question concerning employees' plans upon retirement. The majority of the sampled employees (45.2 percent) do not have any definite plans. About 9.6 percent of the respondents hope that they might be able to do some business in connection with Poongsan. Others urge that the current retirement age should be extended, and some plan to go back to their hometowns, since a majority of them were from rural villages. However, no one suggested that the current retirement pension plan be upgraded.

According to a nationwide survey by the National Bureau of Statistics, based on a sample of 17,500 households, 64.9 percent, a much larger percentage than at the Bupyung plant, do not have any plans at all after their retirement; 11.5 percent of the respondents count on their retirement pension; 9.4 percent on savings; 14.3 percent plan to depend on some combination of insurance, fraternity (*kyae*, referring to a revolving credit society), real estate, and stocks and bonds (National Bureau of Statistics 1988b:277). Among the 64.9 percent who have no provision for retirement, most will have to count on filial support from their children, particularly by the firstborn son. Of the Bupyung plant employees surveyed, only 10 (9.6 percent) said that they cannot save at all. The majority (50 percent) save between 80,000 *wŏn* and 100,000 *wŏn* per month, which is about 14 percent of their monthly wage. According to a recent survey done by Chubu Kyosil (Circle of Housewives) on manufacturing workers in the Sŏnsan and Kumi industrial zones, 38 percent of the sampled 773 workers save nearly one-third of their monthly wages (*Dong-A Ilbo*, 28 June 1988:7).

Traditionally, Koreans are unaccustomed to receiving aid or support from anyone, including the government, other than members of the immediate family and close relatives (Kim 1988b). This filial support is rooted in the traditional Korean family system with its emphasis on filial piety. The tradition of filial support is strongly prevalent among the Confucian-oriented East Asian families, and remnants of the tradition have also been demonstrated among Asian Americans (Homma-True 1976; Koh 1983; Ryan 1965).

My fifty-three-year-old informant who worked in the Bupyung plant for nineteen years and is ready to retire in two years told me,

> I was born in Beijing, China, where my father was a wanderer fleeing from the Japanese. When the war was over [World War II], we returned to my father's hometown, a small farming village in Kyŏngsang province. I was nine years old then. When I graduated from high school, my father passed away, leaving my mother and four children, including myself. From then on, I, as the first son, was managing my family. As soon as I completed my military service, I had a job in a slate factory in Taegu, a provincial capital. My two sisters married later, but I had to take care of my mother and a younger brother.
>
> My younger brother was so brilliant, and always made the top grades in his class. I finally decided to help his schooling by sending him to the best high school in the country, so that he could be somebody. I wished my brother would have the best college education, which I never had. I guess it was my *han*. With the arrangement of the chairman's relatives, I got a job at the newly created Bupyung plant of Poongsan. We were so poor that we could hardly eat three

meals a day. My mother and my wife got odd jobs to ease our family finances. I did not even ride the bus, to save the bus fare. Luckily, my brother entered the best high school in Korea, which was the hardest high school to enter, and went on to the best university in Korea. From then on, he helped me by tutoring high school students until he finished at the university. Thanks to his excellent grades and hard work, he received a scholarship from a prestigious university in the U.S. He finally received his Ph.D. from that university, specializing in semiconductors. He was employed by the largest firm in Korea and elevated to the rank of executive.

My daughter graduated from a top university in Korea and is ready to get married. My first son is a senior at one of the most prestigious universities in Seoul, majoring in computer science; his job is already secured in a company where his uncle is an executive; and my second son is a high school senior who is preparing for college next year. My younger brother and children are appreciative of my support for their educational opportunity.

It was not easy for me to support the education of my brother and three children, and to support my mother. Honestly, I was not able to save a penny, and I did not have any time to think about my retirement. I do not know what I will do after my retirement. I have to support my last child until he completes his college. If my company had not extended the retirement age from fifty-three to fifty-five, I would be retiring this year. See, I have a son in high school!

He hopes that his brother and his sons will help him when he retires, but he is uncertain about his future. He continued,

I know that they would like to help me. But with their limited income, I do not know how they can. I know by my experience that it is very difficult. I have had to sacrifice almost everything for myself. I ought to do something so that I don't have to be a burden. If I can, I would rather like to work, but I don't think I can find any suitable job. The only asset I have is this house, and my lump-sum retirement pension for over twenty years' service by the time I retire. Perhaps it will be around ten million *wŏn* [roughly 13,600 U.S. dollars at the 1988 currency exchange rate].

His house was small and humble, located not far from Yongsan subway station. It is difficult to believe that, living in such a humble house and having a monthly wage of only 560,000 *wŏn* [roughly 767 U.S. dollars per month], he could help send two children to college and one to high school and send a brother to earn a Ph.D. from one of the most expensive American private universities. Perhaps such a burning desire for higher education has made the Korean economy what it is today.

My informant's statement reveals some changes in the inherent Korean values on filial support. Even though he deserves to be supported by his children and younger brother after his retirement, he is reluctant to be a burden to them. Indeed, according to a Korean Gallup Poll survey of 1981, 34 percent of the 1,642 sampled Koreans who were sixty and older wanted to have jobs (men, 43 percent; women, 28 percent) either to support themselves or to reduce the burden on their children (Son 1984:384). Not only my informant but also many Koreans who belong to the informant's generation are indeed those who have spent the most years supporting their parents, but perhaps they will receive the least support from their children because of the changing family system, urbanization, and industrialization. Nevertheless, instead of expecting support from their children to match the support they gave to their parents, aged Koreans desire to be independent.

A new challenge in Korea is the growing demand that aged retirees be supported by society through social welfare and other public pensions. The demand is steadily increasing, from 3.6 percent in 1979 to 5.0 percent in 1988 out of 17,500 sampled Korean households (National Bureau of Statistics 1988b:276), although a majority of the respondents still think that the children of the retirees should be initially responsible. Also, in a 1979 survey 30.6 percent believed that it was the responsibility of the first sons; in 1988 the portion who so believed decreased to 25.2 percent. However, the belief that filial support has to come from both sons and daughters increased from 6.4 percent in 1979 to 35.8 percent in 1988. Nonetheless, the notion of self-support by the aged parents decreased between 1979 and 1988. It is probably realistic to assume that without a major change in the social welfare system, aged parents in Korea will not be able to support themselves.

As people's beliefs that daughters are equally responsible for aged parents increased, the retirement age of female employees has also come under challenge. Regardless of the equal rights for retirement age for females in the Korean Constitution (Article 11) and the Equal Employment Opportunity Act (EEOA) promulgated in April 1988, most of the females stay in the labor force only until their marriage, as is the case in Japan (Cole 1971:147–48; Rohlen 1974:78–79). Since the average marriage age of Korean females is 24.8 years old, the average retirement age for females is around the same age (National Bureau of Statistics 1988b:270). In Poongsan as a whole, out of 1,175 female employees, nearly 80 percent are younger than 26 years old. This statistic confirms the customary retirement age for Korean females.

Not only does the Korean law not allow discrimination against female workers, but also, in principle, there are no Poongsan personnel rules regarding retirement age that discriminate against females. Nor was there any direct pressure exerted upon the female employees to take early retirement. In fact, eighteen Poongsan female employees are fifty-six or older. Except for one at the main office, seventeen of them are at the Dongrae plant.

The early retirement of female employees is related to the Korean sociocultural milieu as well as to the support system for the female workers. According to a recent survey by the Center for the Development of Korean Women of 1,107 Korean workers, "The number of female workers who do not desire to keep on working until their age limit (62.1%) exceeds that of those who desire to do so (37.9%), and the reason brought forward by most of the former (52.9%) is that it is hard to do it in parallel with the home life. . . . 50.6% of them replied that they would work up to the age limit, if proper nursing facilities are provided in their workplaces" (Shin et al. 1988:215–16). Furthermore, working housewives are still stigmatized unless they are holding professional jobs.

The loss of so many females in the work force to marriage carries a great cost, considering the fact that there is already a labor shortage in the manufacturing sector, particularly in small and medium-sized firms. Indeed, 40 percent of the total Korean work force is female, and more than 42 percent of the manufacturing work force is female (National Bureau of Statistics 1989:84–85).

Nonetheless, there is a new movement to encourage females to continue employment after their marriages, although it is low-keyed and not very vocal. According to the same survey cited above by the women's organization, "more than two thirds (75.5%) of those who are under the survey, replied that the retirement for marriage is unreasonable and it should be corrected" (Shin et al. 1988:216). In the future, it is anticipated that more female workers will be willing to work after marriage. Increasingly, stronger labor unions will be important advocates for this movement.

At the same time, there is increasing demand to extend the retirement age for all workers beyond the current level of fifty-five years old. In 1989 the Korean government began to study the possibility of extending the current retirement age for low-echelon civil servants, especially rank 6 (6-*kŭp*) or below, from fifty-eight to sixty-one in certain areas where more labor is demanded (*Chosun Ilbo,* 19 May 1989:14). Most Korean commercial banks already have extended the retirement age of chief of a branch (*chijŏmjang*) from fifty-five to fifty-eight. The extension of the retirement age in most Korean manufacturing industries may be unavoidable in the future. Nonetheless, the simple extension of the retirement age alone is not sufficient to meet the ever-increasing needs of aged Koreans.

In a rapidly industrializing society like Korea, "formal social security has to complement the declining function of informal social security based mainly on filial support. Otherwise, the gap created by these two—the decline of filial support and the lack of formal social security—will further aggravate the existing social problem. The extension of life expectancy by the development of knowledge in curative and preventive medicine in particular will even escalate the situation towards disaster" (Kim 1988b:133).

5

Social Interaction Among Employees

During the filming at Poongsan by the Pacific Century filming crew in 1990, the producer asked a section head of Poongsan to capture a scene concerning the section head's visit to his subordinate to give some instruction. My wife and I were assisting the filming crew as the interpreters. The section head told me in Korean, "We don't do that. I call him up to relay an instruction or direction rather than going to him." The American film producer was unaware of the authoritarian Korean norms. This episode epitomizes the social interaction patterns between superiors and subordinates in the rules for Korean business and industrial relations. They are indeed formal, bureaucratic, and authoritarian.

This chapter describes social interactions among Poongsan employees in their work setting, as well as their social interactions through various informal organizations. Social interaction refers to the behavior of the employees that is influenced by the prevailing norms associated with the status they hold and the roles they play.

Social Interactions in the Work Setting

Except for the executive suites where the offices of the chairman, vice chairman, president, and vice presidents are located, Poongsan has three types of work settings: the offices in the main office in Seoul, the managerial offices in the plants, and the large open complexes of the shops where the production takes place. The activities of employees in these settings vary, particularly between the white-collar employees in the office and blue-collar workers in the plant. Here, I attempt to portray the activities and atmosphere of an average office in the main office and the general affairs office and production floor of the Bupyung plant, since Poongsan is an industry consisting primarily of plants and our concern on rank-and-file workers is particularly central. Also, I briefly describe the office of the local chapter of the Poongsan labor union at the Bupyung plant.

Relations at the main office.

A typical day in an office at the main office in Seoul starts at 9:00 A.M. Except for the private offices of the top executives, the large open offices are occupied by twenty employees each, all of whom belong to a single section. Two rows of desks and chairs are arranged to face each other. Some bigger offices contain some forty employees. The lowest-ranking employee sits next to the entrance door, next to the female clerks, secretaries, and typists. The female employees' seats are next to a semicloset with a kitchen facility, from which they serve tea, coffee, and soft drinks to superiors and visitors. One deputy sits at the left side of the back facing the side view of his subordinates, so that he can see their activities and can keep in close contact with the people he supervises. The desk of the head of the section is not in a separate room but at the back and center of the office, right next to a tea table, several comfortable chairs, and a couch, where the head calls up his subordinates for small group meetings or where he receives visitors. A telephone is located on an end table, and cigarettes and an ashtray are provided for visitors. The head can oversee all his subordinates.

A chauffeur-driven car brings the head a few minutes before 9:00 A.M., and his deputy drives his own car. Chauffeur-driven cars are available only for those whose ranks are managing director and above. The rest use all modes of transportation, including subway, bus, and taxi. Because the Seoul headquarters office is located near a subway station, a good many use the subway. Until nine, there is an air of genial informality as people exchange greetings and make small talk while they are going about their own preparations. They talk about the morning's traffic, the weather, and politics, while the head and the deputy are talking about the day's agenda and priorities. There is no formal ceremony or ritual, nor is there any speech or formal instruction by the head. Everyone seems to know what to do, and much of the work appears to be routine. The deputy is seemingly busy reviewing and approving the memoranda and reports prepared by his subordinates. The deputy approves those documents by signing with his personal signature or by stamping with his red personal seal. The section head has to attend numerous conferences with his superiors and fellow managing directors, as well as call upon other sections.

There is no official coffee break. It is not needed for those in managerial positions, because coffee or tea is served by the secretaries. It is also perhaps taboo for the low-ranking office workers to drink coffee or tea from the office kitchen, because I have not observed anyone doing that unless he entertains a visitor. Although there is no institutionalized break time, everyone seems to have a break before lunch.

Lunch hour is from 12:30 to 1:30 P.M. Since there is no company restaurant or cafeteria in the headquarters office building, everyone has to find a place to eat nearby. There are hundreds of restaurants, ranging from inexpensive and filthy ones to expensive and luxurious ones. The price ranges from 1,000 wŏn (roughly 1.40 U.S. dollars) to 10,000 wŏn (roughly 14.00 U.S. dollars) per person. Since everyone can find an appropriate place suitable to one's own budget, no one brings a sack of lunch. For the employees, going out during the lunch hour seems to be more important than eating itself. Unless there is a special occasion, it is very rare for an entire section to go for lunch. In fact, it is difficult to find a place for more than twenty people at one time because almost all of the dining facilities are crowded. Usually, two to four make up a group for lunch, which is a manageable number. Lunch groups usually consist of those with similar ranks in the section. Sometimes employees call friends from other sections and assemble in the entrance of the elevator. Unless there is a special occasion, the executives, head, or deputy of the section seldom go out together with subordinates for lunch. Whenever one goes out with his superior or senior member for lunch, the superior or the senior usually pays for the subordinate or junior. Among colleagues and friends, "Dutch treat" is common nowadays. A young member told me, "It is more comfortable to go out with my own peers, so that we can have some relaxed atmosphere for flirtation. Most of all, we can find a place, so that we can afford and can do Dutch treat."

After lunch, most of the lunch mates go on to a tearoom for an extension of the lunch hour. Some have their shoes shined while they are drinking tea or coffee and smoking cigarettes. Some who own stock go down to a stock brokerage firm located a block away from the headquarters building to check stock prices.

Before 1:30 P.M. they all return in much the same way they came in the morning. The seat of the head of the section is often empty because either he is having an extended hour of lunch or he may be attending another conference. Sometimes the section head calls a meeting, which often lasts two hours or so. Indeed, working hours are long, the average being nine hours a day during the week and another six hours on Saturday. However, these white-collar employees do not receive overtime pay. One employee told me, "Recently, especially after the labor unrest had begun, our working hours have been shortened, in comparison with those of the pre-labor movement days. In those days, we couldn't tell when we would be closing." As far as working hours are concerned, white-collar employees in the main office have been able to take advantage of the blue-collar workers' demands for shorter working hours.

After work, employees in the same section seldom go to a bar or dinner together. Instead, they go with friends from school or other connections. Except for special occasions such as a New Year's party, Poongsan superiors seldom treat their subordinates after work to an informal gathering for just drinking or dining. The Korean custom on this differs from the Japanese practice, as described by Rohlen (1974: 97–100); Japanese white-collar workers frequently meet and party after work, in gatherings that include superiors and subordinates. The social atmosphere among Poongsan employees and their relationships are seemingly similar to those of Western firms: there is a homeward rush right after work. Perhaps this pattern may be related to the dual nature of the Korean ethos of individualisr as C. Chang (1989:196–97) has pointed out: "They a. pendent and competitive in pursuing personal succes education and promotion, but they are expected to be dedicated members of many social groups and organizations at the same time."

The relationship between the supervisor and the subordinates in the work setting appears to be formal, distant, and authoritarian.

Very similar patterns were observed by Silin (1976:73) in the large Taiwanese business enterprises. The subordinate maintains a strict attitude of subordination to the higher-ranking employees, using honorific words and humble gestures. Among their own peers their behavior is more relaxed and varied. Because interaction patterns among Poongsan white-collar employees tend to be highly bureaucratic, they lack a personal touch. Maybe this stems from the fact that the majority have been in the military, which has such an authoritarian culture.

In fact, when an executive goes to a subordinate, the subordinate stands up much as an enlisted soldier faces a general in the army. When an executive walks into the shop of the plant, the rank-and-file workers stand at attention as if to a general. When I visited a steel plant, the plant workers saluted the plant manager.

Relations at the Bupyung plant.

The work setting of the general affairs department at the Bupyung plant shares one half of a large open office space with the engineering department, which includes high-ranking engineers and the quality control section. The arrangement of the desks and chairs is the same as at the main office. The seat of the section head faces the side view of the section workers and is located in the center of the two rows of desks at the back, so that he can keep in close contact with the people he supervises. The assistant managing director is located not in a separate room but at the back and center of the general affairs department, keeping some distance from his subordinates. Right next to his desk, there is a reception and small conference area with a few chairs, a couch, and a tea table. It is almost the same arrangement as at the main office.

Work in the general affairs office starts at 9:00 A.M. The head of the general affairs office, as an assistant managing director, rides in a chauffeur-driven company car. The rest may elect various modes of transportation. A good many choose to walk, especially those who live in the company apartment, about fifteen minutes away on foot. Others who live in Inch'ŏn or Seoul take company buses free of charge if they live near the route of the company bus. Although they are white-collar employees according to their job classifications, they wear the same gray uniforms the production line workers wear.

At 9:00 A.M. there is no signal to start work. Everyone takes his or her seat and starts working. By 9:30 the assistant division head and higher-ranking employees go to the plant manager's conference table for a daily conference of an hour or so. The rest of the workers do the unfinished work of the previous day and await the day's agenda, usually set during the daily conference. During the conference of top managers, the rest of the workers make small talk on a wide range of topics while they go about their own preparations.

After the conference is over, the assistant managing director calls up his deputies and instructs them as to the day's business, showing them the priorities, which are usually set by the main office. There is no direct interaction between the assistant managing director and the rank-and-file employees. Direction and supervision go through the middle managers. The distance between the assistant managing director and his subordinates appears to be great, the relationships are formal, and any signs of personal affection are hardly observable.

During the lunch hour, from 12:30 to 1:30 P.M., almost everyone eats in the plant cafeteria because it is convenient and free of charge, and the food is better than that of restaurants near the plant. One large dining table can accommodate six people, and tables are set together in pairs. One front table is always open for the top managers, the plant manager and two managing directors, and the division heads. No rank-and-file workers, especially blue-collar workers, dare to take the unmarked yet customarily designated seat for the top manager in the plant. To the American-educated observer who is accustomed to the concept of equality, such a separate seating arrangement appears strange. Even at the head table, hardly any subordinate talks to the plant manager unless he asks questions of them. They eat and leave after they finish. As they finish eating, they take the empty trays to be washed, but the service-line ladies take the tray of the plant manager as an expression of respect.

During lunch, all female employees sit together in a corner section of the cafeteria. Since the Bupyung plant has a small number of female employees, the segregation does not seem obvious. But in the Dongrae plant cafeteria, the seating arrangement by gender is prominent, since the Dongrae plant has 490 female employees. Not only do employees sit with workmates of similar rank and type of work, they sit with colleagues of the same gender.

I thought that the lunch hour would be an ideal time for the top management in the plant to interact with the rank-and-file workers by sitting with them. When I asked a managing director about it, he answered, "If we were to do that, we would be overwhelmed by their personal requests and favors from the workers." I put the same question to a blue-collar worker. He commented, "How could I dare to bring my tray, sit next to the plant manager, and carry on a conversation? Perhaps my stomach could not digest the food. I don't want to have such stress during the lunch hour." He added, "Nowadays, it is a great improvement. We used to have a separate dining hall." In fact, during my visit to Angang plant, I dined with the plant executives in a separate dining room.

The cafeteria meal does not take a full hour. Some people take less than fifteen minutes to eat. A crowded cafeteria may not be a place to rest during the remaining time. Some workers play volleyball or soccer at the plant yard, while others sit on benches and smoke cigarettes. During the lunch hour, hard-core labor union members get together, sing songs, and march toward the administration building to demonstrate union power. Others just enjoy idle talk. Cross-rank contact or conversations were not observed. Most workers get together with peers of similar ranks and age. As the top managers come back to their office, the secretaries serve tea or coffee. They relax until the afternoon work starts.

The afternoon work also begins without any signal or mark. Everyone comes in and continues the day's routine. The assistant managing director is busy with calls to his deputies, instructing, and signing papers. There is no specified break time. As quitting time nears, some go to the dressing room and change their uniforms to plain clothes. A few minutes after closing time, they start leaving one after another, without saying any particular words. Unlike the main office white-collar employees, the white-collar employees in the plant leave even if their superiors are still in the office. A managing director told me, "In the past, every subordinate waited until the superiors left, but nowadays, thanks to the union, no one waits beyond the time, unless there is a particular instruction. Rather, we wait until they leave." As the plant manager and managing directors leave, secretaries await them at the front porch and bow to them as the cars leave.

Departing workers may go together if they are going the same direction. Others wait for their friends. The pattern is almost the same as for any industrial worker in America. They appear to be individualistic and are seemingly eager for the homeward rush. I asked one worker, "Don't you have an after-work drink with your coworkers?" He said, "Sometimes we do, either when we are frustrated or have something to celebrate. But, you know, with our income, it is difficult to do it so often." One supervisor told me,

> I heard that Japanese workers get together very often, and the superiors and the people whom they supervise go to a bar and drink together. But with my income, I just cannot afford to do it. See, in the wedding season [spring and fall], I have to spend so much money for wedding gifts for workers and their immediate family members. [Usually, Koreans put a 10,000 wŏn bill in an envelope and present the envelope to the receptionist at the place where the wedding takes place, an alien custom to Westerners who are familiar with church weddings and bridal showers.] I wish the company would give us such an allowance.

Except for special occasions such as company picnics and sports events, informal gatherings and drinking parties are rare. In sum, the interactions among the white-collar employees in the managerial office at the plant are formal, distant, and authoritarian.

The relations of blue-collar workers.

The work setting for the blue-collar workers in the production line differs from that for white-collar employees. Their work schedules also differ. Until 1985, the Bupyung plant had a two-shift system. In 1987 it changed to three shifts. The first shift is from 7:00 A.M. to 3:00 P.M., the second shift replaces the first shift from 3:00 P.M. to 11:00 P.M., and 11:00 P.M. to 7:00 A.M. is covered by the third shift. Workers cannot work overtime except on weekends. Overtime comes on the weekend if necessary, a decision made by the section head. Because of the extra income, workers usually accept the overtime offer. At the same time, the plant makes every effort to offer overtime work to secure some extra pay for workers.

Regular working hours for the blue-collar workers were forty-eight hours per week until 1989. In March 1989 their regular working hours changed to forty-six hours, eight hours per day, including mealtime, from Monday through Friday, and six hours on Saturday. However, most blue-collar workers have overtime on weekends. With these overtime hours, Poongsan working hours are similar to the fifty-four-hour average for Korean manufacturing workers as a whole for the ten years from 1978 to 1987 (National Bureau of Statistics 1988b:116).

Bupyung production workers are divided into thirty-one groups (*pan*); each group has a foreman (*panjang*) and an average of twenty-five workers. But some groups have thirty-one workers, and other have less than twenty workers, depending upon the department. Some workers in certain sections do not compose any group, because the number of workers is too small. A foreman is appointed by the plant on the recommendation of assistant division head on the basis of his work experience, leadership quality, job knowledge, and dependability. None of the thirty-one foremen has less than ten years of work experience. Workers' interactions in the work setting are centered on the group.

As an example, the rolling section, which is the largest section in the Bupyung plant, is supervised by one assistant division head, assisted by one assistant section head and three engineers (*kisa*). There are six groups, each group consisting of twenty-five workers and one foreman. Two groups make up a team (*cho*), and each team rotates the three shifts once a week. The shift is not fixed permanently. The assistant division head and assistant section head do not follow the shift, but come in at 9:00 A.M. and leave at 6:00 P.M., as do the other managers. However, three engineers follow the rotation of the shift. For the shift, an engineer actually supervises the work of the team while the assistant division head and assistant section head are off duty.

Each worker comes in about ten minutes before each shift starts. Many use the company buses. As they arrive, they have to pass through the security check. As soon as they change into their uniforms, in accordance with the direction of a foreman they prepare for the day's work. Each worker goes to his machine. There are eighteen machines for the rolling section; two or three workers are assigned to each machine. The nature of the work is repetitive and well automated, with the assistance of computers. The work itself does not appear to be as physical as I had assumed. Large fans and open floor space provide enough air circulation, and the temperature inside even in the summertime is tolerable. Overall working conditions inside the plant are more comfortable than in paper mills in

America where I did my fieldwork in the late 1960s. However, the noise level of squeaking metal sounds and machines inside the plant is so high that ordinary conversation is difficult. Furthermore, like all assembly-line work, the operational system does not allow any worker to be idle or away from the job unnoticed.

As long as the machines are functioning normally, workers do not need to call up their superiors. A fifty-two-year-old foreman who had worked nineteen years in the plant and had been foreman for ten years told me that his role is mainly for coordination and harmony rather than supervising. "Although I have been here long, as far as knowledge on the machine is concerned, the workers who are assigned to a particular machine know it better than I do. I cannot be an expert on all those new machines." A small unit within the group based on the machine is almost autonomous in their own operation. Also, most of the activities are centered on the machine. The foreman said, "Because of the three-shift system, when they work on second and third shift they do not have time to mingle with fellow workers after work. Sometimes, when they work on the first shift, they get together and drink *soju* [clear distilled Korean liquor, probably the nearest Western equivalent of vodka or possibly rum]. But, even in this case, workers who work with the same machine usually get together once or twice a week at the most."

To promote the unity and cohesion of the group and section as a whole, knowing that the workers' interaction boundary is confined to a particular machine, the section used to have sporting events once or twice a year for all the section employees, as well as a New Year's gathering. However, since the rolling section has 155 workers, the group is too large to manage. Thus, currently such gatherings take place by a team, which is made up of two groups. This arrangement can be coordinated by the shift and is also small enough to be orderly and manageable.

Out of the occasional gathering of all the employees of a group and team, the interactions among blue-collar workers on a typical day are very formal, routine, and bureaucratic. A worker commented to me, "What else can we do in the plant after the work? I cannot just fiddle around." In fact, there are no company recreational facilities at the Bupyung plant, and workers spend little leisure time together. The same is true of the white-collar employees in the main office.

The Bupyung chapter of the union.

The work setting of workers in the office of the local chapter of the
Poongsan labor union is like that of the workers in the management
offices; they also start work at 9:00 A.M. and close by 6:00 P.M. The
union office was first placed in a small barracks and later was moved
to a small single-story brick building. The local chapter president,
vice president, general secretary, and female clerk are the only full-
time union workers. They have been relieved from their production-
line duties. The general secretary is busy calling and answering the
telephone calls from other local chapter offices. He prepares posters,
which are usually placed on the wall of the cafeteria where all employees go once or twice a day. The vice president entertains visitors,
like myself, and takes the complaints of workers against management. The president of the local chapter does not take part in the
daily routine, for he has to coordinate activities with the management office and attends meetings in the headquarters office in Seoul
and with presidents of other local chapters regarding new wage negotiations. At the time I was in the field, for six months in 1989, the
union and management were negotiating new wages.

The vice president of the local chapter told me, "This is the most
difficult time for anyone to be a labor leader. We, as union officials,
are caught in between labor and management. Knowing something
about the difficulty the company has faced, we like to be sympathetic, but members charge us with being pro-company. When we are
sympathetic to the problems of labor, management thinks of us as
'radical.' There is no way of winning." Indeed, many members of the
union express their skepticism about the role of the current union
leadership. This will be discussed further in the following chapter.

Informal Organizations

Because informal social interactions among employees are limited
during working hours, largely because of the difficulties stemming
from the shift changes, the rigid hierarchical ranking order, and the
lack of recreational facilities, most informal activities take place
through various informal organizations. Among Bupyung employees, there are thirteen organizations, clubs, and teams with 546

Table 5.1 Informal Organizations of the Bupyung Plant Employees

Organization	Members	Frequency of Regular Meeting	Membership
Hiking club	64	1/month	Open to everyone
Fishing club	18	1/month	Open to everyone
Tennis team	43	3/month	Open to everyone
Soccer team	39	1/month	Open to everyone
Baseball team	25	4/month	Open to everyone
Kangwŏn-hoe	27	4/year	Kangwŏn only[a]
Kyŏngsang-hoe	130	2/year	Kyŏngsang only[a]
Honam-hoe	58	4/year	Honam only[a]
Ch'ung-u-hoe	24	6/year	Ch'ungch'ŏng only[a]
Ch'ungnam-hoe	57	6/year	Ch'ungnam only[a]
Engineers club	37	1/year	Engineers only
Material section club	12	1/month	Material section employees only
Nŏngk'ul-hoe	12	1/month	Females only
Total	546		

SOURCE: The author's field data.
[a] Includes only those who were born in that province.

members. Some employees belong to more than one organization, but nearly 75 percent of the Bupyung employees belong to at least one of the organizations. There is a hiking club, a fishing club, a soccer team, a baseball team, a tennis team, five regional friendship organizations, a female club, an organization for engineers, and a friendship organization for material section employees. The names of the organizations, their membership, and the frequency of regular meetings are shown in table 5.1.

Employees are also interested in organizing a plant band, a vocal group, a photo club, and religious groups. Some executives consider the existence of many informal organizations and the emergence of new organizations as a positive sign of fellowship among the employees. But others see it as a "sign of weakness in human relations, because among true friends 'organized friendship' would not be necessary," as Cole (1971:139) heard from a Japanese worker who was commenting on the informal organizations in a Japanese firm.

The managers of large Korean *chaebŏl* groups perceive the activities of informal organizations as positive and functional, as they foster friendship among their employees, reduce the conflicts and tension existing across ranks, and enhance mutual understanding and harmony among the employees. As the labor unrest has become an acute problem faced by Korean industries in 1987 and 1988, many *chaebŏl* groups have used these organizations as a channel of communications and a mechanism for establishing unity and harmony among their employees, encouraging the active participation of executives in these group activities. In 1988 Samsung Mulsan, one of the largest subsidiary companies of the Samsung *chaebŏl*, which has not yet recognized a labor union, allocated some 105 million *wŏn* (roughly 143,836 U.S. dollars in 1988) to support 48 informal groups for 2,500 employees. This represents a 70 percent increase over its budget for such groups in 1987. Samsung Electronic, another subsidiary, increased its budget from 70 million *wŏn* for 1987 to 190 million *wŏn* in 1988 to support 107 informal organizations for company employees (*Dong-A Ilbo*, 8 July 1988:13). Ssangyong, Lucky-Goldstar, Hyundai, and many other *chaebŏl* groups follow similar policies.

The members of informal organizations at Poongsan's Bupyung plant complain about the lack of such support. Nonetheless, for sporting teams the company provides uniforms, equipment, and fees to join leagues. One baseball player told me, "Company support for the baseball team has improved. In the past, we had to pay for our own uniforms. Now, not only does the company pay for the uniforms and equipment, the company pays for our meals and drinks after the game." A member of the hiking team still complains about the lack of company support. Said he, "In a gathering of hiking teams of large Korean firms, the Poongsan team was the only team not accompanied by a top executive."

Since my fieldwork was carried out during the baseball season, I had a chance to observe the games between the Bupyung team and the main office in Seoul. The games took place on a Sunday morning in a high school field in Bupyung near the plant. The main office team is led by the division head. The main office team rides in a large van that also carries their equipment, and some players drive their own cars. As team members assemble, they greet each other and spend some time in informal conversation. The pattern of interaction among the players differs from patterns in the office setting. In the work setting the relationships between people of different ranks are formal and remote, but on the baseball field everyone occupies an equal position regardless of his rank in the firm. Even the division head has to chase the ball when it comes to him, and the rest of the players jeer when the division head makes errors. Baseball skill dominates in the field. None of the players seems to be aware of the ranking in the firm.

After the game is over, players drink cold drinks, exchange news about the main office and the plant, and renew their fellowship. Since they have been playing some years together, they seem to be well acquainted. Then the two teams go together for a long lunch and cold beer. The atmosphere is friendly, informal, and congenial. Included among the players were several union instigators during the 1987 strike at the Bupyung plant and a division head who is in charge of the public relations department in the main office. Yet they were friendly. No mention was made of the strike. No one seemed to be interested in talking about matters relating to the company and the union. One Bupyung player who works in the managerial section told me, "This kind of association through sport is really good for making friends. When I go to the headquarters office in Seoul, I feel like I have some friends over there. Sometimes, we have lunch together when I visit. They are very helpful." Such an association seems to be helpful in maintaining a good working relationship between the headquarters office and the plant. Also, it seems to serve as a bridge between the high-ranking employees and rank-and-file workers. Within the office, such interaction does not occur among the various ranks, but such fellowship allows the higher ranks to learn about those below them.

Some informal organizations, such as the five regional organizations based on the origins of the workers by provinces and the engineers' club, serve as interest groups. For instance, on 30 March 1989, thirty-four engineers of the thirty-seven who belong to that club released a joint statement declaring their wish to join the union, although the company's rules prohibited them from joining. The union promptly accepted them. They are all university graduates, while a great majority of the existing members are not. It remains to be seen what their role in the labor union will be, how they will mingle with the blue-collar workers, and how the management of the company is going to deal with them. However, a reporter from a Korean daily newspaper union that combines blue-collar workers and white-collar reporters told me that blue-collar workers dominate the union and are its major beneficiaries because of their sheer numbers. Also, he said that the blue-collar workers in his union tend to be more vocal.

The friendship groups are organized according to the regional ties linking those who are from the same provinces. Since those who belong to the same organization share regional subcultures, including the use of regional dialects, group cohesion among the members is as strong as one sees in kin group solidarity and school ties. Among the five regional organizations, Kyŏngsang-hoe is the most influential, because it has the largest number of members, and also several distant relatives of the company chairman are included. Any rank-and-file worker who is interested in running for a leadership position in the union likes to win the support of this organization. There is latent competition among the five organizations. One Kyŏngsang-hoe member told me, knowing that I speak with a thick Kyŏngsang accent, "I don't believe anyone dares to seek the union presidency without getting our endorsement, because our organization is the largest and most influential." Even the managerial office is aware of the potential importance of this organization as an interest group.

For those who are not actively involved in any of those organizations, relations within the company and with fellow workers remain latent once they leave the plant. However, for the sixty Bupyung employees and their family members who live in the company apartments, ties with the company extend beyond their working hours. Although an elected president (the spouse of an employee) coordinates relationships and promotes fellowship among the residents, the interactions among the residents are clearly divided along blue-collar and white-collar lines. White-collar employees tend to associate with other white-collar workers, and blue-collar workers prefer to mingle with other blue-collar workers, due largely to the different shifts they work. Friendship among the wives of the employees follow the same pattern. Similar patterns have been witnessed in Japan by Nakane. She (1970:30) indicates that "when wives meet, they, too, will behave towards each other in accordance with the ranks of their husbands."

Until recently, a certain building was designated for the blue-collar workers, and their numbers were limited. However, recently an effort was made to mix the groups. Currently, almost even numbers of blue- and white-collar workers reside in company housing. The company makes an effort to give priority to the blue-collar workers whenever a vacancy occurs. Yet vacancies occur rarely, and the waiting list is long, for it is a major fringe benefit in the form of virtually free housing (the occupants pay only utilities and maintenance fees). A plan to construct additional units is underway in response to the increasing demand by the union.

Since housing prices in Korea are extremely high and the waiting list for the company housing is very long, competition for such housing is intense. Some occupants stay on beyond the maximum time allowed for one to occupy company housing, even though they know that the housing was originally built for workers to use temporarily until they find their own places. It was not easy for me to discover why some stay on even when they should have their own housing.

Living in the company housing is a privilege, because it is limited to only sixty workers and none of the rest are paid a housing allowance, as in some Japanese firms. As a consequence, there is a significant income difference between those in company housing and nonresidents. Moreover, the company residents can have a small garden plot nearby, which allows them to enjoy gardening as a hobby and also to help keep household costs for vegetables down. Most important, since the housing is located within easy walking distance of the plant, the residents do not have to struggle to beat the rush-hour traffic and save money on transportation. As long as the use of company housing remains such a privilege, the competition over and demand for company housing will grow more severe. As long as the housing shortage in Seoul and Inch'ŏn remains as it is now, and the price of housing and rental fees remain unaffordable for the average industrial worker, even the construction of additional units of company housing may not be sufficient to ease employees' anxiety over company housing. To ease the housing situation, for instance, the Hyundai automobile plant "built and sold 1,108 condominiums to the employees at cost, about ten percent off the market price," in addition to providing family housing for 254 families and dormitories for about 2,100 bachelor employees. Nonetheless, Hyundai company housing can accommodate only 45 percent of the employees, far short of the demand (Bae 1987:73).

Workers' Interaction After Work and on Weekends

According to my survey of the Bupyung plant employees, after a day's work the plant employees (55.8 percent) tend to associate most often with their fellow plant employees. The second most frequent association is with their former school friends (16.3 percent); the third is with their hobby club members (15.4 percent). They infrequently associate with their hometown friends (5.8 percent), but they associate with their relatives the least (2.9 percent).

According to the same survey, although blue-collar workers are more likely to associate most often with fellow workers (62.7 percent), white-collar employees' associations are more evenly distributed among fellow workers (33.3 percent), former schoolmates (33.3 percent), those who belong to the same hobby clubs (20.0 percent), and others (13.4 percent). Comradeship among blue-collar workers seems to be much stronger than among white-collar employees. This pattern seems to follow the educational level, if we assume that the white-collar employees are better educated than the blue-collar workers. University graduates among the employees like to associate with their former schoolmates (50.0 percent), but only 7 percent of the workers who had high school educations or below associate with their former schoolmates. For male workers, the phrase "former schoolmates" means the ones who went to the university together. The survey results are well confirmed by my direct observations.

The association patterns among the employees after work when these are broken down according to gender and length of service are unambiguous. The number of women in the sample is small because the number of female workers is small, but the pattern is nevertheless a clear one: no female employees associate with their coworkers after work. The majority (75 percent) associate with their former schoolmates. Perhaps for the female workers high school friends are the equivalent to the university classmates of their male counterparts. The female employees' ties with the company appear to end when the workday ends. It may be that the customary early retirement of women at marriage and their limited career opportunities hinder the development of comradeship as well as group identification among them.

In terms of length of service, the workers who have worked a lengthy period of time in the plant tend to associate frequently with their coworkers. Among those who associate with fellow workers after work, 75.8 percent have worked at the plant for more than five years. No one among those who have worked less than one year at the plant associates with coworkers. Friendships, apparently, have not had the time to develop.

A majority of married workers tend to associate with their fellow workers (63 percent), but the majority of the single men like to associate with their former schoolmates (55 percent). Employees from rural villages tend to associate more with their fellow workers (62.0 percent) than do those urban dwellers who are from Seoul and provincial capitals (36.0 percent). People with urban origins instead tend to associate with fellow hobby club members (28.0 percent) and their former schoolmates (20.0 percent). Comradeship among plant employees is thus stronger when the workers have rural backgrounds.

As already commented on with the meaning of religious affiliation on the entrepreneurs' origin in the Korean cultural context (Jones and Sakong 1980:222), religious preference plays an extremely minor role in interactions among workers after work. Workers who belong to the same religious group do not necessarily interact with each other more often than with those who belong to other religious affiliations.

Employees' interaction patterns on weekends differ from those of weekdays. No one category dominates, although the survey reveals that workers do tend to spend time with family members and relatives more on weekends than on weekdays. The distinctively different patterns of weekday and weekend socializing are shown in table 5.2. During the weekdays they spend more time with their fellow workers, but on weekends they tend to spend time with family or with fellow hobbyists. As evidence of this trend, on weekends the streets of Seoul and Inch'ŏn are less crowded, and most bars and drinking places have fewer customers.

Table 5.2 Comparison of Weekday and Weekend Associations of the Bupyung Plant Employees

	Weekday		Weekend	
	Freq.	%	Freq.	%
Colleague in the company	58	55.8	20	19.2
Former schoolmate	17	16.3	20	19.2
Hobby club member	16	15.4	24	23.1
Hometown friend	6	5.8	10	9.6
Family member/relative	3	2.9	26	25.0
Other	4	3.8	4	3.8
Total	104	100.0	104	100.0

SOURCE: The author's field data.

Workers' Attitudes Toward the Company and Management

Ever since labor unrest became an acute problem in the summer of 1987, the company has made every effort to enhance harmony among Poongsan employees. Posters promoting harmony and unity are everywhere. One executive commented, "If we were to adopt a company motto nowadays, without any doubt it would be 'unity and harmony.'" Indeed, unity and harmony are the main themes of the employees' training. Despite the company's effort, there remain structural characteristics that hinder unity and harmony and that can lead to some divisiveness. The divisions follow the lines separating the different ranks and age groups and the blue-collar workers and white-collar employees.

As mentioned earlier, social relations in the Poongsan work setting are formal. Indeed, cross-rank associations other than directly job-related supervision occur seldom and are discouraged. One blue-collar worker commented, "It is worse than in the military." In fact, as high-ranking executives enter the plant, rank-and-file workers salute, just as in the military. The worker went on to say, "I don't believe the top men know what we think. They just listen to the middle managers. But they don't know much about us either." In fact, 63 percent of workers sampled in my survey believe that there is no meaningful communication between the management and the workers. "If the company has financial difficulty, why haven't they communicated with us about it, using a newsletter? I first learned through the news media that the Angang plant strikes cost some 300 million *wŏn* a day," commented one worker. More than 40 percent of the sampled employees believe that an increasing dialogue between the management and workers is the most urgent need, whereas 31.7 percent of the sampled employees consider that the company ought to respect the workers as "decent human beings," not as "the instruments of production," and 26.0 percent of the respondents consider wage increases as the most urgent need. Workers consider dialogue and communication between the workers and management to be more important than increases in their own wages.

One division is readily apparent, that between blue- and white-collar employees. This split is rooted in the structure of Korean society. Traditionally, from the time of the Yi dynasty in Korea, Confucianism has placed scholars or officials on a higher level than farmers, artisans, and merchants. Although such perceptions have changed as Korea has moved rapidly toward industrialization, a social stigma is still attached to blue-collar work, which is still perceived as hard, unclean, and lacking prestige. In reaction to such a negative image, blue-collar workers are almost hostile toward white-collar employees.

In return, some white-collar employees believe that the average wage of the blue-collar worker is higher than that of the white-collar employee because of overtime pay. A comparison of the wages of the two groups among the Bupyung employees reveals that the average white-collar employee's overtime pay (36,272 *wŏn*) is indeed much less than that of the average blue-collar worker (92,912 *wŏn*); the blue-collar worker's monthly overtime earnings average nearly 2.6 times those of the white-collar employee. The bonuses and allowances for the length of service for blue-collar workers are slightly higher than those for white-collar employees, but the remaining categories of pay for white-collar employees are higher. Despite the longer hours of hard work for blue-collar workers, their earnings average 220,412 *wŏn* less than those of the white-collar employees. The white-collar employees' typical belief about the wages of blue-collar workers is unfounded. Furthermore, blue-collar workers endure disadvantageous working conditions. Not only does the work of white-collar employees not demand physically hard labor, but blue-collar workers have to accept assignment to constantly changing midnight shifts, which disrupt normal family life. Although some white-collar employees have to agree to midnight duty, they must do so much less frequently than do blue-collar workers.

As for promotion, white-collar employees can expect to progress toward the top management positions. In contrast, promotion for blue-collar workers ends after they have reached the foreman level, which does not have great meaning financially or in terms of status. Most engineers who graduated from technical universities feel the same as do blue-collar workers. One engineer who had reached the managing director's position said, "Although this is a manufacturing industry that requires the work of engineers, I do not believe I can expect any further promotion. Look who are the top managers! They are all nonengineers." Among the eight in top management, excluding the chairman but including the vice chairman, two presidents, and five vice presidents, only two vice presidents are engineers. And the two vice presidents are plant managers who are located far from the headquarters office.

Age marks another division among employees. By and large, younger workers tend to believe that older workers are too docile, meek, and even servile toward the management. Although it is difficult and even arbitrary to distinguish between the old and young, if we consider thirty years old and under as young, 76.7 percent of younger workers consider older workers to be too conformable, too naive, not demanding enough of their rights; they see older workers as being concerned about their own interests only and rarely concerned about the welfare of the junior workers. Only 6.7 percent of the younger workers consider the older workers to be an asset for the company, and only 10 percent of the younger workers view the older workers as capable of leading the junior workers. The younger workers' distrust of the older workers is more prominent among blue-collar workers, who also tend to criticize the older workers as being too conformable (66.9 percent of blue-collar workers are critical of the older workers).

The older workers are less critical of their younger counterparts, however. Among the sampled respondents, 44.1 percent of the older workers consider the younger employees to be too radical, too egoistic, and too Westernized, because they do not respect the older

workers and often ignore seniority. Yet a majority of the older workers (52.9 percent) trust that younger workers are self-controlled,
wise, and able to demand their own rights much better than older
workers can.

The older workers who believe that the younger workers do not
respect the older workers enough and thus disregard seniority based
on age are in supervisory positions, including the foremen for blue-
collar workers. One aged managerial person at the plant told me, "In
the past I used to address most younger workers whose ages are almost same as my sons without using honorific words. Often, I would
call their names without suffixing with *ssi* [Mister]. They took such
a practice as an indication of informality, familiarity, and closeness
[much as Americans view the usage of first names]. But nowadays, if
I do it to them, they do not appreciate it. They interpret such practice
as an indication of disrespect." One foreman said, "I would rather
deal with older workers than deal with younger workers. They are
not like us any more. They don't give a 'damn' about the older workers. Nor do they care about the foreman." There is certainly a generational conflict between young and old among the Bupyung plant
workers. Generational conflict is not unique to Poongsan workers
but is common among all Korean industrial workers (see Cole 1971:
267–68; Erikson 1968; Lenski 1966:426–28; Rohlen 1974:199).

There is a general myth that since Korean culture emphasizes hierarchical order according to age, younger Korean industrial workers
respect older workers and tend to be obedient (Shin 1986:46–48).
However, according to my observations, instead of respecting the
older workers, they are critical of older workers for their docile attitude toward the management. At the same time, the militant attitude of the younger workers toward the company has become a major
topic of conversation among some older workers and management.
Management continually worries about potential trouble in dealing
with younger workers.

No matter what effort management and older workers may make
to reach younger workers, the younger workers can hardly understand the years of hardship during the Korean War and the poverty-
stricken postwar years that lasted into the 1970s. They take Korea's
economic growth for granted. Younger workers were taught democratic values and egalitarian concepts in schools, through textbooks
at least, and they witnessed economic injustice during the spurt of

economic growth and rapid industrialization in Korea. Most younger workers were born in cities as sons and daughters of industrial workers, not on rural farms. Hence, they are marked by their urban sophistication, cynicism, and militancy. A similar pattern has been observed by Rohlen (1974:199) in Japan during the 1970s.

Currently, however, 76 percent of Poongsan employees are from rural farming villages; the farm-oriented workers are more likely to be docile and responsible, as agricultural societies are apt to stress obedience and responsibility in their socialization (Barry, Child, and Bacon 1959). Because of this, Japanese industrial firms at home and abroad have sought workers whose backgrounds are rural, hoping that they would bring their rural work ethic to the factories (Ouchi 1981:11; Willigen and Soffle 1986). Nonetheless, future industrial workers in Korea, including those at Poongsan, are more often likely to have urban origins; most are the offspring of industrial workers who were uprooted from the farming villages. Given this, as has been shown in Japanese industry by Cole (1971:71), "the future is likely to show a reduction in worker subservience based on uncritical acceptance of company goals." Furthermore, as some have recognized, when farm-oriented workers are uprooted and join the industrial work force, they develop a radical proletarian militancy (Bae 1987:102–103; Hamilton 1967; Leggrett 1963). This tendency has been evident in the labor strikes, where the division nearly took the form of a class conflict between the management and the workers.

6

Labor Relations

My fieldwork from the summer of 1987 to the summer of 1989 and additional field trips in the summers of 1990 and 1991 provided me the opportunity to witness the most furious labor unrest in Korean history. For the Korean labor movement, major changes took place during my fieldwork. When I began my study, there was no organized labor union at Poongsan. But the Poongsan labor union was born while I was still in the field. In the midst of my second year of fieldwork, I observed the worst labor unrest in the history of Poongsan.

Without predicting such an eruption of labor disputes in Korea, some scholars have generalized, portraying workers in the newly industrializing Asian countries, including Korean workers, as cheap, docile, loyal, and productive laborers because of their cultural heritage of Confucian doctrine (Benjamin 1982; Chen 1981:269; Hofheinz and Calder 1982:112; Winckler 1984). Nevertheless, as evidenced in the rate of wage hikes of Poongsan employees described in chapter 3, the cost of labor in Korea is no longer cheap, and docility is no longer a trait of Korean workers, as will be described in the following passages.

On the contrary, by observing Korea's recent labor unrest in the late 1980s, some scholars characterize Korean labor-management relations as a confrontational mode of interaction rather than the cooperative mode that is manifest in Japan (Chung and Lie 1989:217). Deyo (1989:4, 139) has pointed out that the Korean workers' labor movement is exceptional among other East Asian countries that share the Confucian heritage. However, the most recent report on Korean labor-management relations indicates that the confrontational mode is changing toward the cooperative mode. Specifically, according to the statistics of the Korean Labor Department, all the figures regarding labor disputes by August 1991 have been reduced by 29.1 percent of the levels in 1990, showing a cooperative mode between labor and management relations (*Hankook Ilbo*, 30 Aug. 1991:14).

Regarding such turbulent labor unrest after 1987, *Chosun Ilbo*'s special report of 20 May 1989 (p. 3) cited Hŏ Sang-yong, president of the Korean Central Association of Small and Medium Size Enterprises, as providing a possible explanation, that is, "a sudden manifestation of Korean workers to fulfill their accumulated *han* for years." In fact, for generations the Korean workers' labor union movements had been hampered, oppressed, and often misled. One top Poongsan executive used a metaphor of a "track race" to describe Korea's recent labor disputes. Said he, "We were so anxious to run fast to beat others that we forgot our belts were loosened up. Consequently, we showed up our naked bodies. For the sake of the growth of the corporation so fast in such a short period of time, we have not paid close attention to our workers and their feelings. If we had walked slowly, we could have avoided such an adverse effect."

To understand the newly born Poongsan labor union after the June 29 Proclamation of 1987 and its activities, a brief history of Korean union movement may be useful.

The Korean Labor Movement

The Korean labor movement began near the end of the nineteenth century among dock workers; the unions have enjoyed a persistent and faithful membership ever since (Chŏn 1989:307–8; K. Kim 1988: 246–63). The labor unions have waxed and waned since then in response to the political milieu in Korea. Over the past one hundred years Korea has lived under many distinctively different forms of government and political atmospheres. Although each regime adopted its own policies toward labor unions, all have consistently exerted a high degree of government control over union activity in the belief that the role of labor unions is conflictive, unproductive, and disruptive of economic growth.

Consequently, much of the effort of the organized labor movement in Korea has been directed against the regimes; not much effort has been devoted to workers' rights. During the Japanese colonial period, when colonial capitalism increased the industrialization of Korea, the labor movement was considered to be synonymous with the anti-Japanese independence movement (Chŏn 1989:307). Especially since 1928, the labor movement has been conducted by progressive native intellectuals and radical industrial workers whose actions took the form of revolutionary class conflict. After the Sino-Japanese War (1937) and intensified Japanese colonial policy, the Korean labor movement went underground (see Choi 1983:72; Chŏn 1989:309; Cumings 1981:27; Grajdanzev 1978).

After World War II, a militant, left-wing union leadership emerged under the Chosŏn Nodongjohap Chŏnguk P'yŏngŭihoe (Chŏn'p'yŏng). Chŏn'p'yŏng was a part of the Communist party apparatus, and it fostered class conflict. In so doing, Chŏn'p'yŏng lost sight of workers' rights and welfare. Recognizing the potential threat of the increasingly violent left-wing labor movement of the Cold War era, the USAMGIK was instrumental in organizing the Federation of Korean Trade Unions, called Taehan Tongrip Ch'oksŏng Nodong Yŏnmaeng (Noch'ong) in opposition to the Chŏn'p'yŏng. Not only was Noch'ong an auxiliary organization for a conservative right-wing political organization, but it also set up a tense confrontation between the two labor organizations (Chŏn 1989:309; K. Kim 1988:247; Choi 1983: 46). Neither organization represented the workers; both were parts of political interest groups. In 1947 the USAMGIK declared the Communist party and Chŏn'p'yŏng illegal and eliminated them.

In 1948, when the republic under the Syngman Rhee regime was born, the new Korean Constitution guaranteed three basic rights of labor: the freedom of association, the right of collective bargaining, and the right of collective action. Yet labor-related laws were not enacted until 1953, due largely to the Korean War. Even after labor laws were promulgated, they existed only de jure, never de facto. The Korean labor unions were handmaidens of the government, not

organizations for the betterment of the working and living conditions of workers (Hahm, Yang, and Kim 1964). Noch'ong was the
only recognized, legitimate labor organization. Thus, unions became
political instruments, not meaningful organizations for rank-and-
file workers (Choi 1983:46).

The beginning of the 1960s was a time of great turmoil. The students overthrew the Syngman Rhee government in April 1960. The
short-lived Chang Myŏn regime ended by the military coup led by
Park Chung Hee in May 1961. The oppressed labor union movements
again erupted as the students demonstrated for democracy and
greater political control. In 1960, for instance, there were 227 strikes
with 64,335 workers participating, whereas in 1959 there had been
only 95 strikes involving 49,813 workers (Chŏn 1989:341). Moreover,
increasing numbers of white-collar workers' unions were organized,
including those for teachers, journalists, and bank employees. The
workers' demands were not limited to wage increases and improved
working conditions but also expanded to union democratization by
banishment of the government-patronized union leaders (ŏyong).
These ŏyong union leaders controlled company-dominated unions
or unions by appointment that were supported by company or state
authorities (Choi 1983:177).

A dissident minority group under the name of the National Council of Trade Unions, called Nohyŏp, challenged the legitimacy of
Noch'ong and launched a radical movement. It coordinated its activities with those of the well-organized and politically oriented Teachers' League (Kyowŏn Nojo) during a brief period of weak and unstable
government under the Democratic party led by Chang Myŏn. However, the union movements centered on rank-and-file workers were
halted by the military coup of May 1961. Soon after seizing power,
the military junta suspended the labor unions and banished the
Nohyŏp, which included radical union leaders. At the same time the
military junta froze wages and prohibited strikes. In August 1961 the
military government restructured the labor organizations, literally
appointing the key union leaders with the assistance of the Korean
Central Intelligence Agency and police (Amsden 1989:324; Chŏn
1989:49).

The military government set its single-minded goal of "export-
oriented industrialization and growth" through a series of five-year
economic development plans, beginning in 1962; it viewed the labor

unions as unproductive and largely disruptive of economic growth. The government made every effort to debilitate unions through legislation in 1962, 1970, 1971, and 1972, and launched a propaganda campaign calling on the workers to sacrifice. Government also increased its control over the unions, favoring management in industry by offering tax shelters and financial support. Unions were controlled by the governmental elites who wanted to be active partners in the implementation of economic planning. Korean labor relations became a matter of government versus the unions, not labor versus management. Management officials were excluded from all dealings in labor relations. The government introduced labor-management councils as substitutes for labor unions in the late 1960s; these councils were later granted legal status under the Labor-Management Council Law (Nosahyŏpŭihoe-bŏp) in 1980.

However, even during Park's military regime from 1961 to 1979, Korean workers did not simply remain docile, and there was labor strife. As the number of industrial workers grew rapidly, they learned the need for trade unions just as they learned the skills of industrial employment. Large-scale industrial disputes loomed, threatening employers. Labor disputes occurred at a number of industries: foreign-owned electronics firms in 1968; industry-wide strikes by textile workers hit the sixteen cotton textile firms and metal workers struck at a government-run company in 1969; chemical workers held a hunger strike in 1970 and 1971; the Hanjin labor strike occurred at the Korean Airline (KAL) building in 1974; and the Hyundai construction workers struck in 1978, to name just a few (Chŏn 1989: 344–51).

A garment shop worker who committed suicide by burning himself on 13 November 1970 staged the most poignant protest against low wages and inhumane working conditions. The average working day was fifteen hours long and the wage was equivalent to the price of a cup of coffee at a tearoom in Seoul. Work space was inhumane; the distance between the floor of the second level and the ceiling measured only three feet, so the laborers were unable to stand upright throughout the whole day. Protesting such unbearable working conditions in a garment industry at the P'yŏnghwa market in Seoul, workers attempted to stage demonstrations. As their protests were being suppressed by the police and the factory owner, Chŏn T'ae-il took the ultimate step, immolating himself "by pouring gasoline over himself and setting himself on fire in front of policemen and the public, shouting 'We are not machines,' 'Keep the Labor Standard Law,' 'Do not mistreat young girls'" (Choi 1983:203). This bizarre incident led to the organization of the garment workers' union and promoted workers' solidarity and self-awareness. About seventy Tong-il (Dong-il) women textile workers stood nude, forming a human barricade in front of riot police. Spurred into action by these incidents, many sympathetic intellectuals, students, and church leaders became adamant supporters of labor unions. They established the pattern of "student-turned-factory-workers," often called *wijang ch'wiŏp* (employment under false credentials), to launch the crusade of the labor movement against the suppressive government labor policy (see Park 1989).

Besides suppressing unions by legislation, the government, using the KCIA and the police force, introduced the New Factory Movement (Kongjang Saemaŭl Undong). The New Factory Movement was derived from the New Village Movement (Saemaŭl Undong) as an ideological approach to creating a harmonious relationship between labor and management. The movement began in 1970 as a state-directed effort to improve the rural economy by fostering diligence, cooperation, self-help, and active voluntary participation and to cultivate grass-roots leadership (Burmeister 1988; Hwang 1981). The underlying logic was to harness the traditional culture and value system manifest in family and kinship relations founded on Confucian virtues. With the blessing of President Park, who in November 1973 alluded to the application of the principle to work in the nation's factories, the Kongjang Saemaŭl Undong was introduced to Korean industry. The movement essentially asked workers to be as loyal to the company as they would be to their parents. The leading idea was that all workers had to cooperate to achieve high growth and productivity. Long hours and hard work without protest were taught as noble virtues that were manifestations of one's participation in the nation and loyalty to the company, just as filial piety is the basis of one's loyalty to a king. The slogan of the movement, "Treat the employees like family; do factory work as if it were my own personal work," is still posted in the bulletin boards of almost every factory in Korea, including the Poongsan plants.

Despite the governmental effort to indoctrinate workers with values of loyalty and dependability through New Factory Movement training, most Korean industrial workers who have gone through such training seem to be unconvinced by the moral indoctrination. As Bae (1987:105–6) has indicated in his study of Hyundai automobile workers, "even though Korean workers knew and approved of the Confucian ethic, hierarchy, etiquette, and wanted their employers to behave like loving and respectable parents, . . . they were not loyal and obedient servants. They saw their employers as motivated primarily by profit."

Indeed, the relative "industrial peace" during Park's regime cannot be credited either to the New Factory Movement or to traditional Korean culture. Rather, the latency of the potential labor unrest stemmed from the authoritarian control of the government. As evidence of this, explosive labor unrest erupted during the power vacuum created by the assassination of President Park in October 1979, which continued until the seizure of power by other military officers led by General Chun. During four months in early 1980, there were 848 labor disputes, compared with only 105 disputes in the entire year of 1979 (Choi 1983:456). There was "a large scale 'wildcat' revolt by 2,500 mine workers against the union leadership and the local police paralyzed a mining town with a population of 30,000 for four days. Other large scale strikes at the same time involved a 1,000 steel workers' violent strike at the Busan [Pusan] and Incheon [Inch'ŏn] factories of the Donggug [Tong'guk] Steel Co., and a 700 metal union workers' violent demonstration against the Incheon Iron and Steel Co., a branch firm of the largest conglomerate in Korea, Hyundai Heavy Industry" (Choi 1983:458–59).

In reaction to the ever-increasing labor unrest, in August 1980 the Chun government revised labor laws to make it more difficult for workers to organize unions. Union organization was restructured into a strictly enterprise-based form. This provided the legal base for the Labor-Management Council. The union shop system was prohibited, and involvement of a third party was forbidden as well. These actions aroused the sympathetic support of intellectuals, students, and church-backed labor rights groups; the Urban Industrial Mission (UIM), sponsored by the Protestant Church, and the Young Catholic Workers' Organization (Jeunesse Ouvrière Chrétienne, or JOC), sponsored by the Roman Catholic Church. Church organizations, which originally became involved in labor issues as a way of expanding church membership, played a crucial role in educating the workers, awakening their self-consciousness as factory workers. "The role of church organizations evolved as the political situation changed over the last three decades. The more repressive the government became, the more radical the church organizations' response" (S. Kim 1989:3).

Despite the suppressive labor policy of the Chun government, the organized labor movement grew on a large scale. A nationwide taxi drivers' strike in 1984, the Daewoo automobile workers' strike of April 1985, and strikes by workers in the Kuro industrial zone in June 1985 are a few examples. Labor disputes increased: only 88 in 1982, 265 in 1985, and 276 in 1986 (Chŏn 1989:351). Most important, during the seven years of the Chun regime, thanks to the support of intellectuals, students, and the church organizations, the labor movement became more well-planned and politically oriented (Chŏn 1989:312–17). However, the Korean labor union movement faced a totally new situation when the Chun regime was brought to the brink of collapse by massive antigovernment demonstrations by students, workers, and intellectuals. When Roh Tae Woo, the candidate of the ruling party, issued the June 29 Proclamation, great labor unrest was touched off by widespread demonstrations and strikes. In 1987 the total number of labor disputes reached 3,749, the largest number in a single year in the entire history of the Korean labor movement; 3,241 cases that year occurred after Roh's announcement of reform. In counting the number of labor disputes, various sources show slightly varied figures (cf. Chŏn 1989:317–18; *Nosasinbo*, 15 Feb. 1989:9).

In response to the raging labor disputes, in October 1987 the outgoing Chun government revised the labor laws. The revised laws reduced government control and made union organizing easy. Despite such conciliatory gestures, labor unrest continued: there were 1,833 labor disputes in 1988 (*Nosasinbo*, 15 Feb. 1989:8). However, the laws prohibited civil servants and workers who work in the defense industry from participating in collective action. This prohibition is also specified in the new Constitution, which was promulgated on 29 October 1987, in article 33, number 3: "The right to collective action of workers employed by important defense industries may be either restricted or denied as prescribed by law." Since Poongsan is a defense industry, its workers' union activities, any collective action or strikes, were subject to government interference.

The Poongsan Labor Union

The history.

Poongsan was established during Park's eighteen years of authoritarian labor control, a policy designed for the sake of "export-oriented industrialization and economic growth," with emphasis on the chemical and heavy machine industries. To accomplish its goal, the Park regime "had to resolve one essential problem facing a newly industrializing nation—that is, how the state integrates a rapidly growing labor force into a newly evolving industrial system and builds an effective labor force with first generation industrial workers" (Choi 1983:275). Recognizing that liberalizing policy on labor union movements would be dysfunctional for rapid economic growth, the Park regime persuaded management and workers to adopt a Labor-Management Council for each industry to promote industrial peace and productivity. As a consequence, there was no labor union at Poongsan until Roh's June 29 Proclamation. The council was the chief mechanism for communication between labor and management. The council consisted of six representatives from both labor and management. Theoretically, workers' demands regarding wages, improvements in working conditions, and any grievances became the concern of the council. The council aimed to prevent labor disputes and to improve productivity through mutual agreement.

Prompted by the rising labor disputes and reduced control over the labor unions, organizing for a labor union by Poongsan workers preceded the amendment of labor laws by the government in October 1987. I was in the field as this movement was going on, and I witnessed the movement in the Bupyung plant and was able to associate with the key instigators of a four-day strike and demonstration at the plant 13–16 August 1987. This labor unrest eventually led to the formation of a sublocal, the Bupyung chapter of the Poongsan labor union. Poongsan's union became a member of a nationwide organization of Korean metal unions.

The Bupyung labor strike.

Despite widespread speculation that the Bupyung strike was instigated by the joint action of the young, radical student-turned-workers (*wijang ch'wiŏp*) and the church-based organizations, my close observation and association with eight key organizers revealed no such activity. Rather, the strike seemed to be a spontaneous response to the nationwide labor unrest. It seemed strictly a labor movement to organize a union in the plant and to improve workers' wages and working conditions, not a movement instigated by outside forces. The demographic characteristics of the organizers indicate that they were neither young radicals nor student-turned-workers. The average age of the organizers was slightly more than thirty-three years, and seven of them were married. All of them were responsible for supporting their families, even their parents. Five were honorably discharged from their military service, and three were exempted from military service because they were working at a defense industry. Educational levels varied: two were middle school graduates, four were high school graduates, and two were junior college graduates. Seven had rural origins, and one was from an urban area; they came from various provinces of Korea.

The strikers presented sixteen demands, which could be divided into five categories: (1) to organize a labor union, (2) to increase wages and other allowances, (3) to extend the retirement age from fifty to fifty-five years of age, (4) to build more company housing, and (5) to narrow the wage gap determined by level of education. Specifically, they demanded the resignation of the managing director who was in charge of general affairs and daily operations, including labor-management relations. The managing director happened to be a relative of the chairman by marriage. During the strike there were rallies; strikers carried banners and placards, and they set up barricades of workers at the gate of the plant. They did not allow the managing director to enter the plant. The atmosphere and tone of the workers' demonstration appeared violent, but the four-day strike did not produce any violent incident. No one was injured.

In response to the workers' demand, the managing director turned in his resignation. His prompt resignation led to a mood of conciliation. On the fourth day of the strike, labor and management reached an agreement to honor almost all of the workers' demands; workers were even to be allowed to organize a local chapter of the Poongsan union. The concession was not difficult for the Bupyung plant, as the Onsan plant had already organized one four months earlier. The Angang and Dongrae plants organized their own unions not long thereafter, despite the fact that these plants, especially the Angang plant, were producing goods exclusively for the defense industry.

The Poongsan union is organized so that it has a unit at each plant. In most large conglomerates, the central union is established at the largest plant, usually close to the enterprise headquarters, but the Poongsan central union is established at the Onsan plant, the third largest among the four plants in terms of the number of employees. It is farther from the headquarters office in Seoul than is the Bupyung plant. The Onsan plant may serve as the central union because it was established earlier than other plants. The president of the Onsan plant union also serves as president of the entire Poongsan union; there are three presidents of local chapters at Bupyung, Dongrae, and Angang.

The organizational structure of the local chapters of the Poongsan union is exemplified by the Bupyung chapter (Figure 6.1). All the local chapters are structured alike. Each local chapter has one president, two vice presidents, and one executive managing director. There are two active committees: an eight-member executive committee makes routine decisions and is advised by a six-member steering committee. A legislative committee composed of twelve representatives makes overall decisions by a majority vote of the members present. For important matters, such as the appointment of officials and changes in the by-laws, decisions are made by a two-thirds vote of the members present. The number of committee members and representatives varies from one local to another.

As for union membership, nearly 80 percent of Poongsan's eligible employees, 7,473 of a total of 9,430 employees, joined the union. At the Bupyung plant, the rate of participation is slightly higher than at the other plants (82 percent). On 2 October 1987, the Poongsan union signed a collective-bargaining agreement with management. Workers' retirement age was raised from fifty to fifty-five, and the average worker's wage in 1987 was increased 24.9 percent from that of 1986 and increased 12.2 percent in 1988 compared with that of 1987. Also, the annual 400 percent bonus increased to 500 percent in 1987 and 600 percent in 1988. These appeared to be significant improvements, and I thought workers were satisfied by the raises.

Astonishingly, in my survey of Bupyung plant workers in the summer of 1988, only 10.6 percent of the sampled employees indicated that they were satisfied with their jobs in Poongsan; 43.3 percent of

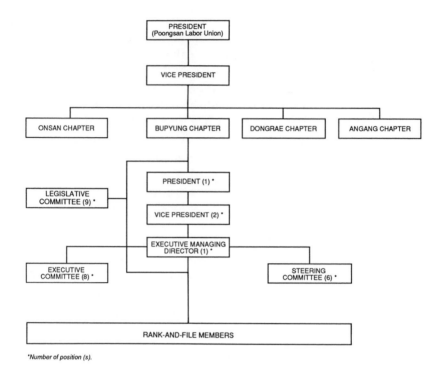

*Number of position (s).

FIGURE 6.1   The structure of the Bupyung union local chapter.

them were neither satisfied nor dissatisfied with their jobs; 40.4 percent were dissatisfied with their jobs; and 5.8 percent were so dissatisfied with that they would quit if alternatives were available.
The categories of workers who were dissatisfied were evenly distributed among all the variables: by their rural or urban origins, length
of service, kind of work, marital status, age, gender, and educational
level. (There are no significant differences at the 0.05 level in chi-
square tests among these variables.) If the results of the survey are
accurate, it is easy to forecast future turbulence in Poongsan's labor-
management relationships.

Workers are skeptical about the labor union's role, especially under the current union leadership. They suspect the leaders of being procompany. The origin of this skepticism can be traced in the history of the Korean labor movement as described earlier, in which Korean workers were not allowed to select their leaders. A new labor aristocracy was established among highly capitalized industries with rapidly rising wage rates.

Amsden (1989:195) has observed that "a new 'labor aristocracy' was established, but its skill base was nontraditional. This new labor aristocracy, moreover, was helped rather than hurt by modern machinery and, if for no other reason, played a negligible role in trade union growth in the 1950s through 1980s." The statement of the president of the Bupyung union local chapter, who was quoted in the previous chapter, is classic: "Knowing something about the difficulty the company has faced, we like to be sympathetic, but members charge us with being procompany. When we are sympathetic to the problems of labor, management thinks of us as 'radical'."

In the survey, I found that although 5.8 percent of the sampled employees think the union is running well, 1.9 percent consider it unnecessary. The great majority of the respondents (76.0 percent) maintain a "wait and see" attitude toward the union and its management for the welfare of employees. Since the union has had such a short history, workers are reserving judgment. This attitude holds across all categories, by blue- and white-collar work, length of service, marital status, age, educational level, and gender. The skepticism toward the union leadership is reflected in the collective bargaining of the Angang workers. In December 1988, all the presidents of the local chapters of Poongsan signed the collective-bargaining agreement, but the Angang workers did not ratify the agreement and asked for renegotiations, not trusting their representatives.

Given the workers' low morale and their distrust of the union leadership, it seems clear that Poongsan is vulnerable to a labor dispute at any time. Poongsan workers are especially hostile toward the laws related to their labor union activities, including the Constitution (article 33, number 3), special laws on the national defense industry (article 18), and the Labor Disputes Adjustment Act (article 12, number 2), which asserts that "the right to collective action of workers employed by important defense industries may be either restricted or denied as prescribed by laws."

The Angang plant labor strike.

Despite the skepticism of the rank-and-file workers toward the new union and its leadership, the Poongsan labor union has accomplished a formidable task: achieving wage increases through collective bargaining and raises in the workers' retirement age, as well as other advances. It seems that as the workers accomplished some of their goals, unattainable without the union, the level of their expectations also rose. Young workers at the Angang plant especially wished to test their power to challenge the existing labor laws restricting the right of collective action of those who work in defense industries. Unlike the Bupyung strike in 1987, the Angang labor strike was supported by radical student organizations at Tonguk University, Kyŏngju campus, near the Angang plant; by several church-supported organizations; and by seven other pro-union political organizations. One Poongsan executive expressed his moral outrage against the participation of third parties, particularly by the radical students. Eckert (1990:134) was told an identical grievance by a highly successful Korean exporter: "His workers had gone on strike even though he had always treated them well, providing them with relatively high wages and bonuses and a superior work environment complete with showers and other facilities. . . . The only explanation he would accept for the strike was that it had been instigated by radical students posing as workers, that is to say, that the workers had been duped into striking by sophisticated outside agitators."

The militant Angang workers were led by forty-one young workers, mainly high school graduates with rural origins, mostly single, and predominantly male. They were committed deeply to the challenge of the existing laws. The Poongsan management was a major target.

This long-lasting and violent labor strike led to the closing of the Angang plant for seventy-two days, from 2 January 1989, to 14 March 1989. It was triggered directly by the death of an Angang plant worker resulting from an industrial accident. Four workers at the plant circulated printed materials in the township of Angang at night to launch propaganda against the company, protesting its unethical way of handling the matter with the victim's family and setting the compensation for the death. The company fired the four workers on the grounds that they damaged the integrity of the company's good intentions. In response to the firings, two hundred Angang plant workers demonstrated at the township of Angang. Unionized workers at the plant demanded reinstatement of the terminated workers and sabotaged production by such tactics as refusing to take overtime work or work night shifts, leaving early from work and coming in late, and delaying lunch hours. Their campaign dragged on for seventy-nine days.

In response to the company's refusal to reinstate the four workers, the workers became increasingly militant and relations between workers and management deteriorated. On 13 November 1988, 144 Angang workers went to the Bupyung plant and occupied the plant, and the next day they went to the Seoul headquarters office and occupied the office building for eight days, pouring paint on office walls and floors and destroying some office furniture.

Pressured by the violent protest and demonstrations, the company offered a conciliatory measure by offering to reinstate the terminated workers, to pay living expenses for the striking workers during the strike, and to start negotiations through collective bargaining. The collective-bargaining agreement was signed on 22 December 1988. Although the other three plants ratified the agreement, Angang workers demanded a new round of negotiations for a different version of the bargain. The next day, 550 Angang workers left work.

On 26 December 1988, equipped with clubs and metal pipes, they marched to the Onsan plant, asking workers there for a sympathy strike. When the Onsan workers failed to respond, Angang workers began demonstrating at the Onsan plant, pouring paint and scattering human feces throughout the plant and disrupting normal work. To prevent any possible clash between workers in the Onsan plant and the "invading workers" from Angang, the company closed the Onsan plant temporarily, until 30 December 1988. Four workers were injured in the demonstrations. Two days later the Angang plant workers retreated from Onsan and returned to Angang.

All the demonstrations were still going on when I returned to Korea in the winter of 1988. The Poongsan strike was not the only one. Labor strikes were common in Korea that winter, the worst in recent Korean history. Street demonstrations were at their height, and campus unrest was also at its worst. No one could pass by any college or university without feeling the effects of tear gas. The streets of Seoul and other major cities looked like battlefields. Sometimes I had to be confined inside the bus for hours until a demonstration was over. Anti-American slogans were everywhere, and the shouts of "Yankee Go Home" pierced the ears. In fact, the street demonstrators, students and workers, were hostile toward foreigners, since some foreign firms, including Mitsui from Japan and a few banks from the western European countries and Australia, as well as foreign embassies cracked down on Korean employees because of their intention to organize unions. Some employees in those firms and agencies were terminated, and others were demoted for their active participation in the union movement. In the eyes of some Korean workers and students, foreign firms were as antilabor as the Korean government (*Dong-A Ilbo*, 22 June 1988:14). I was afraid to interview any striking worker when the militant Angang plant workers occupied the headquarters office in Seoul for eight days. I remained a bystander.

The worst was yet to come. My role as a fieldworker, a Korean-American, and a professor at an American university became increasingly difficult beginning in early January 1989. On 8 January it was widely reported in the major Korean mass media that a thirty-nine-year-old Korean-American, James Lee, hired by the Hyundai Heavy Machine Industry, an affiliated company of the Hyundai *chaebŏl* group, had led a midnight raid on the gathering of the labor leaders of that company. Anyone who was associated with America, particularly Korean-Americans, became major suspects in the eyes of the labor leaders and union members. Management, including the management at Poongsan, did not want to be associated with anyone from America. My informants and friends at Poongsan advised me not to get involved in any labor-related matters, because those who did not know me well would be suspicious of my actions. Friends worried about my safety from the angry workers. Lee's involvement in the Korean labor strike greatly hindered my fieldwork. I had to wait until the furor died down and Lee's incident was forgotten. My interviews with the striking workers took place after the strike was settled.

The workers continued to strike at the Angang plant. Their slogans and wall posters became violent: "We are not afraid of dying," "500 percent wage increase, even if the company is bankrupted," "Poke out the eyes of reactionary union members [*pandong*]," and "Stop dictatorship over the workers." They poured waste oil and paint on the heads of employees at the management office and destroyed

FIGURE 6.2   Broken office furniture and spilled paint in a managerial office
at the Angang plant.

office furniture and equipment. They even made gallows labeled
with the names of top executives in front of the storage facility
where the most powerful explosives were stored.

Striking workers threatened to blow up the plant by setting fire to
3,300 tons of explosives stored for the production of ammunition.
They scattered waste oil and gasoline mixed with sawdust around
the buildings to set them on fire. If the explosives had been set off,
the impact would have been devastating. In November 1977, in Iri,
Chŏnnam province, 25 tons of similar explosives were touched off;
59 people near the site were killed, and 1,343 people were injured.
The explosives at the Angang plant were 132 times more powerful
than those at the Iri disaster. The damage at Angang could well have
reached the township of Angang with its 34,031 inhabitants.

Alarmed by the potential danger, on 31 December 1988, the company decided to close the Angang plant. On 2 January 1989, the company notified the defense department of the imminent danger, since
the Angang plant is a major defense contractor. Company managers

FIGURE 6.3   A mass rally of the Angang plant strikers.

requested the intervention of the police. Because the laws prohibit
collective action in the defense industry, the workers' strike was considered to be unlawful; thus, on 2 January, police moved in and
seized control of the plant. Police led away thirty-seven hard-line
strikers in a predawn raid at the plant. Among them, seven labor
union leaders, including the twenty-five-year-old president of the
Angang chapter, Chŏng Chong-gil, were formally arrested. Police
also booked a twenty-four-year-old radical female worker and five
others without physically detaining them and put fifteen other workers on the wanted list for fanning unrest at a defense plant where
strikes were prohibited. Once the police had regained control at the
plant, managerial personnel could perform their duty of cleaning up
the mess, but the production unit of the plant was closed for seventy-
two days until 14 March 1989.

According to the company's estimate, the Angang plant labor unrest cost 72.1 billion *wŏn* (roughly 107 million U.S. dollars at the
1989 exchange rate) in total plant output lost, plus a 21.8 billion *wŏn*

loss of profit. This amounted to more than 300 million *wŏn* per day. But the loss was not limited to the company. More than four thousand employees at the Angang plant and their dependents lost their livelihood. Furthermore, the prolonged strike threatened the town's economy.

A new Poongsan president was appointed at the annual stockholders' meeting, and a new plant manager was named; the new team started negotiating with the acting union president of the plant as of 9 March 1989; an agreement to resume operation of the plant beginning on 14 March 1989 was reached. The agreement included these stipulations: (1) the union guaranteed the safety and normal work of the plant, and the company supported legal and normal union activities; (2) the union rejected third-party intervention; (3) the fate of key militant instigators who violated the existing laws would be left to the court's decision, but those who were suspended from the company but were not hard-core militant leaders would have their suspensions reevaluated within seven days after the operation of the plant resumed; and (4) although the government's office of labor affairs insisted on the principle of "no work, no pay" during a strike, Poongsan would pay 60 percent of the workers' basic wage, excluding allowances, and 100 percent of the bonus, for the seventy-two days of the strike.

Comparison of the two Poongsan strikes.

The strikes at Bupyung in the summer of 1987 and at Angang from the summer of 1988 to the spring of 1989 differed in both the nature of the strike and the composition of the strike leadership. The Bupyung strike was brief, nonviolent, and spontaneous; the Angang strike was prolonged, militant, and well planned. In the Bupyung strike there was no intervention by a third party; the Angang dispute was supported by radical students, church organizations, and antigovernment political organizations. The prolabor supporting organizations used the Angang strike as a means of organizing unions in defense industry firms and of testing the strength and will of the government to block collective action against management in defense industries. In the case of Bupyung, direct negotiations between labor and management were easy, as no third party was involved, but at Angang the temporary agreements often fell through because the union leaders

Table 6.1 Social Characteristics of the Key Union
Organizers of the Bupyung and Angang Strikes

Characteristics	Bupyung	Angang
Average Age	33.0	23.0
Marital Status		
Married	87.5%	14.6%
Single	12.5%	85.3%
Education		
Less than high school	25.0%	0.0%
High school graduate	50.0%	97.6%
Junior college	25.0%	0.0%
College graduate	0.0%	2.4%
Military Service		
Honorably discharged	62.5%	9.8%
Exempted	37.5%	90.2%
Religion		
Christian[a]	12.5%	26.8%
Buddhist	12.5%	12.2%
Confucianist	12.5%	2.4%
No preference	62.5%	58.5%
Origins		
Rural	87.5%	100.0%
Urban	12.5%	0.0%

SOURCE: The author's field data.
[a] Including Roman Catholic.

had to consult with third-party organizations even after having
reached preliminary agreements with management.

The most obvious difference between these two strikes lay in their
respective leadership. As shown in table 6.1, Angang organizers were
on the average ten years younger (the average age was twenty-three)
than were Bupyung organizers. Moreover, they were predominantly
single (85.3 percent), mostly high school graduates (97.6 percent),
and largely exempted from active military duty (90.2 percent). Also,
more of the leaders were Christians at the Angang plant (26.8 percent) than at Bupyung (12.5 percent).

Certainly, the ideological gap between these two groups was as
important as their age differences. Workers at the Bupyung plant

tended to work with the management in improving their working conditions and wages. Angang workers employed radical and militant means to revolutionize the plant. Some Angang workers openly expressed the belief that "even if the company were crippled and current management closed the plant, some other management or government would take over the company." They did not believe the government could afford to allow the plant to close. This pattern of thinking among the young workers may match the attitudes Rohlen (1974:199) observed among young Japanese workers:

> There is no insubordination, but in the opinion of older men, even those in their late twenties, too many of the newcomers lack a sense of responsibility and commitment to their work and their fellow workers. . . . Too many are ill mannered and unintentionally disrespectful, they have no apparent resolve, and they seem unable to sustain interest and motivation. The conclusion many draw is that they have not been brought up correctly. . . . The postwar parents and school system, in their combined enthusiasm to be as democratic as possible, have produced a generation of young people who lack many of the experiences, the values, and the discipline that previously made for thorough Japanese-style socialization.

This is certainly the case of young Korean workers in the eyes of older workers and management.

Although the labor organizations of these two plants differ remarkably, the workers share one common characteristic: the origin and occupations of their parents. Seven out of eight Bupyung union organizers (87.5 percent) were from rural villages and their parents were farmers; all Angang organizers were from rural villages and their parents were farmers.

Uprootedness and Docility

Contrary to the general belief that workers from rural villages tend to be docile because of their rural work ethic, which values long hours and hard work, as demonstrated in Japanese factories (Barry, Child, and Bacon 1959; Ouchi 1981:11; Willigen and Soffle 1986:143–44), Korean workers from farming villages tend to be more class-conscious and militant than their urban counterparts. Perhaps when farmers are uprooted and became industrial workers, they tend to

adopt a militant proletarian mentality, as was demonstrated by Leggrett (1963) in his study of 375 Detroit blue-collar workers and by
Hamilton (1967) in his work on the social bases of French working-
class politics. The term "the uprooted," which was used first by
Handlin (1952), is used to describe peasants or other inhabitants of
an agrarian area who "move to an industrial region and become part
of the working class." "The process may be labeled 'agrarian-indus-
trial mobility'" (Leggrett 1963:684).

This uprootedness can possibly explain why Korean industry enjoys less industrial peace than does Taiwanese industry. As Deyo has
pointed out, labor conflict in Korea is substantially greater than that
of Taiwan, although the two nations share the same Confucian heritage (Deyo 1989:4). On the one hand, Taiwanese industrial and commercial firms are located in rural areas; thus, fewer Taiwanese rural
farm workers are uprooted (Gallin and Gallin 1982:239). The industrial decentralization of Taiwan provided the rural Taiwanese with
off-farm work opportunities (Fei, Ranis, and Kuo 1979:250). As Deyo
(1989:41) has pointed out, "Many industrial workers in Taiwan thus
reside in small, dispersed, and mixed-class communities rather than
in homogeneous-class, urban factory neighborhoods." In Korea, on
the other hand, "industrial development is focused largely on export-
processing zones located near large cities, particularly Seoul, Inchon
[Inch'ŏn], and the southern coastal port centers" (Deyo 1989:40).
Also, a great majority of Korean industrial workers are concentrated
in a few industrial and export-processing zones (Lee 1987:165; Song
1977). Uprooted from the farm, they tend to be class-conscious and
militant (Koo 1990). Furthermore, their clustering in single-class
communities and enclaves allows intellectuals, students, and church-
based organizations to concentrate their prolabor activities on a large
and easily reached population. Unionizing, teaching, demonstrations, and antigovernment political rallies are thus much easier to
organize and implement.

The Workers' View of Management

Because the strike at the Angang plant was so furious, its memories
still linger in the minds of many. The cases of the militant instigators who were arrested by the police were not yet settled when I left

Korea. Some were expecting to be drafted into the military because, as they had not completed their five-year term in the defense industry, they had became subject to the draft as soon as they were terminated from the company.

From the young workers' point of view, the chairman was willing to donate millions of *wŏn* for President Chun's Ilhae Foundation, as the story emerged in the aforementioned congressional hearings, yet he was parsimonious in sharing the profits with his workers. The workers' view of Confucian ethics and the family model in industrial management differed from that of management. To workers, employers should act as responsible parents toward their employees; then workers would return their loyalty to the company. In the chairman's way of thinking, he did the best he could to provide jobs for them and enabled them to make a living, and such a violent protest against him was incomprehensible.

The consumption patterns of the well-to-do Seoulites are another source of workers' anger and frustration: a country of frugal workaholics is turning to consumerism. Self-indulgent recreation that used to be viewed as shameful has become common among the rich, upper-class Seoulites. Casting off their traditional values of austerity and thrift, they openly flaunt their affluence. Korean newspapers report such excesses daily and criticize them, even warning against the self-indulgent consumerism (*Hankook Ilbo*, 26 Sept. 1989:1; 27 Sept. 1989:5; 29 Sept. 1989:5; 30 Sept. 1989:20; 4 Oct. 1989:1–5). A reporter for the *Washington Post* (21 Sept. 1989:E1, E10) reported, "Exhibitions of affluence are sweeping to the surface in surprising ways. A storefront sign in one of Seoul's fashionable areas advertises liposuction, and plastic surgeons in a university neighborhood do a good business performing nose jobs on coeds. . . . While successful businessmen in Seoul are chauffeured from their comfortable homes to air-conditioned offices, farmers in the countryside live in primitive houses that lack indoor plumbing." But one does not have to go to the countryside to see such uncomfortable housing conditions. There are many such houses in the outskirts of Seoul where industrial workers and day laborers live.

Furthermore, it is a well-known fact that some of the successful Korean businessmen give more in tips to the entertaining girls at their drinking parties in one evening than twice the monthly wage of a female factory laborer. In 1988, while Korean *chaebŏl* groups spent 0.7 percent of total output for research and development, they spent 0.2 percent for entertainment and 0.9 percent for advertisement (*Hankook Ilbo*, 15 Aug. 1989:5). Some spacious and luxurious apartments in the Kangnam district, south of the Han River, cost between 500 million *wŏn* and 800 million *wŏn* (over 1 million U.S. dollars at the current exchange rate). A worker whose monthly take-home wage is around 500,000 *wŏn* (above average) would have to save his total earnings for more than eighty-three years to purchase a nice apartment in Kangnam district. Such poorly distributed wealth has triggered workers' uprisings. One Poongsan worker who played an active role during the strike told me, "Korean labor unrests have a lot to do with such an economic injustice. I know some of the issues we raised during the strike cannot be met by the company. Actually, our anger was against the prevalent economic and social injustice. Since we cannot direct our frustration toward the society, we used our company as an easy target." Indeed, Bae (1987) argues that most of the complaints of automobile workers at Hyundai were directed more against inequality in the social system than against Hyundai as an employer.

As already mentioned in chapter 1 regarding the business ethics and morality of large Korean *chaebŏl* groups, public criticism against some Korean *chaebŏl* groups for their special favors or privileges from the government, "octopus tentacles" operations (concentrated and expanding business diversification to gain more power over the Korean economy), and real estate speculation are well documented. Eckert (1990:142) has noticed,

> A particular source of public anger has been the constant speculation of the *chaebŏl* in real estate, which has directed capital from productive resources and sent the price of land in certain areas of Seoul and other cities to astronomical levels. . . . Between 1960 and 1972 "*chaebŏls*—especially the largest ones—possessed (and have continuously possessed) large amounts of real estate, of which a considerable portion was non-business related, idle properties. In many cases, the *chaebŏls'* decision to build factories was more influenced by the prospective land price hike than by efforts to organize the production.

Because of all these facts, it has been difficult for Korean entrepreneurs, even those who are exempted from such charges, to mount a successful defense against the public outcry. Although the Poongsan chairman took advantage of governmental support, especially from

President Park in the formative stage of the firm, he is not involved in diversification of his business and real estate speculation. As a large entrepreneur, he suffers from the same categorical treatment as other *chaebŏl* group owners who practice unethical real estate deals.

Recently, there has been growing public criticism against the work ethics of the contemporary Korean labor aristocracy and the astonishing rate of wage hikes. According to a recent report released on 24 September 1991, on the basis of a nationwide survey done in 1990 by the Korean Chamber of Commerce, out of 4,949 workers from 644 firms, 70.7 percent of the respondents were opposed to overtime work, even if it should reduce their income (the number of working hours per week was reduced from fifty-four hours to forty-four hours by 1 October 1990). Furthermore, in the 1979 survey, 94.3 percent of the respondents had viewed their companies as their secondary homes, while in the 1990 survey, only 59 percent considered their workplaces to be their secondary homes (*Hankook Ilbo*, 25 Sept. 1991:12). The Korean media have been critical and have even warned against the loss of the frugal work ethic by the Korean workers (*Hankook Ilbo*, 26 Sept. 1991:23).

Without doubt, the living standard of the average Korean worker has improved enormously. However, since the wealth is concentrated among only a few Koreans, the workers' feelings of relative deprivation make them feel poorer than ever before. As long as the Korean system for distribution of wealth remains as it is now, whatever effort each industry and firm may make to improve the wages and working conditions of workers, serious Korean labor unrest will remain a latent possibility. As Poongsan workers told me, Korean labor unrest is directed primarily toward the existing social structure and its unfair distribution system.

Whenever the Korean economy shows slow growth, as it did in 1989 with a 6.5 percent annual growth rate compared with a 12.2 percent growth rate in 1988 (*Hankook Ilbo*, 26 Jan. 1990:7), *chaebŏl* groups mainly blame workers' rising wages. Taking seriously the outcries of *chaebŏl* groups, the Korean government put a ceiling on wages. The Roh regime started to crack down on labor strikes, as previous regimes have also done (*Times*, 1 May 1989:18–19; *Hankook Ilbo*, 6 Dec. 1989:7; *Korea Times English Section*, 20 Dec. 1989: 10). To secure the so-called industrial peace, in December 1989 the government froze the wages of upper-echelon civil servants. Several organizations representing the interests of business and industry, several *chaebŏl* groups (including Lucky-Goldstar, Hyundai, and Hanjin), and finance and banking institutions have all expressed their intention of increasing wages for their top management, despite the opposition expressed by the unions (*Hankook Ilbo*, 12 Dec. 1989:1; 15 Dec. 1989:5; 18 Dec. 1989:18; 26 Dec. 1989:17). The government announced, "If any industry increases workers' wages within the limit of their percentage increase of their industrial production, government will be in favor of offering loan and tax incentives for the industry as well as employees" (*Hankook Ilbo*, 15 Dec. 1989:1).

At the same time, the Roh regime, recognizing that the Korean economy was at a crisis point, announced measures beginning in January 1990 to stop labor unrest. The government announced a detailed plan for industrial peace. It dispatched 337 special investigators to seventy-one industrial zones for surveillance, on the assumption that left-wing communists were instigating the labor disturbances (*Hankook Ilbo*, 20 Jan. 1990:12). The government also announced a crackdown on any possible joint movement of students and workers in labor disputes (*Hankook Ilbo*, 20 Jan. 1990:1). On 20 January, the police determined that Chŏn'nohyŏp was an unlawful labor organization that promoted class struggle and unlawful labor disputes as a left-wing organization, and they blocked its organizational meeting and issued search warrants for key organizers (*Hankook Ilbo*, 23 Jan. 1990:8).

While such labor suppression by the Roh regime was being justified as necessary to stave off an economic crisis, the government issued permits to develop golf courses for five *chaebŏl* groups, including Samsung, Lucky-Goldstar, and three others. The plan was nothing more than a form of real estate speculation. Bowing to increasing public outcry against such permits, next day the *chaebŏl* groups themselves withdrew the plan (*Hankook Ilbo*, 9 Jan. 1990:8; 11 Jan. 1990:1). In the workers' eyes, the issuing of such permits to the large *chaebŏl* groups was evidence of a probusiness policy. In fact, wealthy Koreans are not even subject to financial disclosure and can hold bank accounts under pseudonyms (Amsden 1989:327). Such a practice inevitably draws suspicion to the government's motives, because large sums of money are thus not subject to income tax. In the absence of social and economic justice, the government's hard-nosed policy toward the workers' unions may not be persuasive. Whenever the government loosens its control over the unions, militant labor movements erupt.

Until now, scholars have portrayed the workers in export-oriented industries in the newly industrializing East Asian countries as cheap, docile, loyal, and productive labor, because of their cultural heritage of Confucian doctrine (Benjamin 1982; Chen 1981:269; Hofheinz and Calder 1982:112; Winckler 1984). Until recently, Korean workers' wages were indeed low, yet they were productive. But I wonder whether docility is any longer a trait of Korean workers.

There have been periods when Korean workers have seemed docile on the surface, but this is due to the high degree of government control rather than to the Korean cultural heritage. The latent unruliness has erupted whenever the authoritarian control has lessened. Even under high government oppression, Korean workers have resorted to bizarre protests to dramatize the misery of workers. Choi (1983:471) lists various means of protest: "suicide by burning, jumping from a building, sit-in fasting demonstration, a women workers' nude demonstration, the threat of self-destruction by winding a high voltage wire around the body, demonstration by taking hostages, demonstration in the building of the opposition party's headquarters, and so on."

On the basis of her work on women workers in export industries in Korea, S. Cho (1989:10) refutes the docility of Korean women workers. She reports,

> The export-led industrialization in Korea provides conditions in which young female workers' subordination in the family and their inferior position in the labor market can serve as incentives for the development of women's class-consciousness and involvement in the labor movement. . . . Employers are unduly vulnerable to workers' sabotage and have little power to exercise effective forms of labor control. This series of conditions provides women workers in an export industry a greater measure of power than is usually accorded them.

Deyo's recent work (1989:4, 139) indicates that Korean workers' labor movements are exceptional and that labor disputes in Korea are more intense than those of three other East Asian nations that also share the Confucian heritage.

Indeed, my own observations during these years of intensive labor disputes, coupled with the historical record of Korean labor conflict, lead me to believe that Korean workers are not particularly docile. Their apparent docility has been the result of governmental control, not the cultural tradition. If Confucian doctrine were the guiding metaphor for the behavior of workers, it would have been impossible for them to express their anger by threatening their chairman during the strike. As the study of Korean labor union history reveals, the more repressive the government control becomes, the more militant is the Korean workers' response. Because Poongsan is a defense industrial firm, there always will be the potential for government intervention when labor disputes erupt. Poongsan as an employer is likely to remain subject to governmental intervention. Consequently, it may not be able to develop its own means for coping with the ever-rising workers' demands. The confrontation will always be between the workers and the government, not between labor and management.

7

The Culture of Korean Industry

The foregoing ethnographic description of Poongsan has led me to conclude that the firm's industrial culture and organization can be characterized by the coexistence of the traditional and modern. Because Confucianism has been an integrated part of Korean culture since the Yi dynasty, regardless of its origin, it is considered to be a part of traditional Korean culture.

Nevertheless, I have to admit that despite the efforts by Durkheim (1947), Maine (1965), Redfield (1947), Tönnies (1963), and Weber (1957) to dichotomize and polarize the concepts of tradition versus modernity, it has been difficult for me to define the concepts. Gusfield (1967) has discussed well the myths associated with the concept of tradition. I can understand why some writers intentionally avoid defining them, leaving them to the reader's common sense. At this common-sense level, the social structure of traditional societies exhibits characteristics of inequality based on kinship ties, hereditary privilege, and established authority. Modernization tends to destroy the characteristics of traditional or premodern societies.

Some may even think of premodern in terms of present-day industrialization and technology with its jet travel, space exploration, and nuclear power. Levy (1966:11) defines modern society as a place where the "members use inanimate sources of energy and/or use tools to multiply the effects of their efforts." Still others define modernization as synonymous with Westernization or "Europeanization" (Cole 1971:7). Eisenstadt (1966) states that modernization is historically the process of change toward those types of social, economic, and political systems that developed in Western Europe and North America from the seventeenth century to the nineteenth and have been spread to other European countries and in the nineteenth and twentieth centuries to the South American, Asian, and African continents. Jacobs (1985:6) understands that for Asians modernization is usually labeled as Westernization.

In contemporary Korea the meaning of tradition and modernity varies, depending on a person's political ideology and generation. To college students and young industrial workers, tradition is viewed as exploitive and backward; thus, it is negative. To the old, established, and conservative Koreans, it is considered protective. A similar interpretive pattern occurred in Japan in the 1960s. According to Cole (1971:7), "Most Japanese intellectuals equate tradition in social or economic behavior with feudalism; tradition, in this view, is something bad that must be rooted out to build a modern society." Young Korean intellectuals and industrial workers are equally critical of traditional values. Nevertheless, in this study, tradition is understood merely "as the legacy of preindustrial values or patterns of behavior (social structure) founded in industrial society," as Cole (1971:8) defines it in his study of Japanese blue-collar workers.

The basic tenet of the existing sociological paradigms, as well as Tai's (1989) affective model of the Orient in contrast with the rational model of the West, presents a dichotomy between tradition and modernity, as if every society can be viewed as being located in one of these two polarized categories. As Bendix (1967) has pointed out, the intellectual tradition behind these polar concepts has three common assumptions: tradition and modernity are mutually exclusive, change is intrinsic, and industrialization is a largely uniform process.

In this chapter, the traditional and modern cultural traits that influence Poongsan's organizational culture are categorized to examine the validity of the assumptions pointed out by Bendix. Of particular interest is the company's shamanistic ritual of *kosa* as an manifestation of traditional Korean culture.

Traditional Cultural Traits

The *kosa*.

The most striking traditional remnant one still sees in Korean business and industrial settings is the company *kosa*. The *kosa* is a polytheistic shamanistic ritual of offering food to the god or deities of the group—the household, for instance, or the village or other group—and praying for the well-being, prosperity, and security of the group members.

Although there is a rich ethnographic literature in English on Korean shamanism and household *kosa* (Covell 1983; Harvey 1976; 1979; 1980; Huhm 1980; Kendall 1985; 1988), the literature on the *kosa* in business and industry is scarce. The company *kosa* is analogous to the household *kosa*, based as it is in the belief that there are gods (not necessarily one god but more than one) that determine the fate of the company. If company employees win the good graces of the powerful gods or deities by offering the proper food to them, the company will prosper without disaster. Unlike the household gods, the company gods are not located in any particular place such as in the roof beam above the porch; it is simply assumed that the company gods hide inside the plant or company. The employees and owners must recognize the existence of the mighty gods who have power to influence the people of the company and the physical plant. Kendall (1985:123) has observed:

> When a company opens an office, when musicians occupy a new studio, or when a restaurant relocates, the group offers *kosa* led by the director or manager. I once saw men set up *kosa* offerings in the foyer of the Garden Tower Apartments, . . . where a cement company had just opened an office on one of the upper floors. The man in business dress who was arranging the pig's head told me that the *kosa* would benefit both his company and everyone else in the building. . . . Perhaps the most elaborate *kosa* of the decade was held in 1978 to commemorate the opening of the Sejong Cultural Center, a luxurious theater complex in downtown Seoul.

Like many other industrial firms, Poongsan also observes an annual *kosa* to pray to the plant's gods for the continuing prosperity of the company, and sometimes it offers a special *kosa* when one of the plants installs a new and expensive machine to pray for a smooth operation without industrial accident or disasters. Some workers are reluctant even to operate machines without having first offered a *kosa*, for fear of a god's punishment.

At Poongsan's Bupyung plant, the annual *kosa* takes place sometime in December, and a special *kosa* takes place whenever an appropriate occasion arises, such as the completion of a new building or the installation of new machines. The specific date of the annual *kosa* is set by the wife of the chairman of the company, who decides the date after consulting with the kind of fortune-teller who chooses lucky days for weddings and other major events. The role of the chairman's wife in selecting a specific day for the *kosa* resembles the role of the Korean housewife, who petitions the household gods on her own authority, not on her husband's.

As soon as the date for the annual *kosa* is set, the chairman's wife notifies the plant manager of the date. Next, food is prepared by the plant's general affairs office: first-grade rice, sweet rice, beans, dried pollacks, various fruits and nuts, Korean rice wine, meat, and vegetables. To distribute to each employee the food to be offered, the plant prepares disposable wooden lunch boxes and chopsticks, one for each plant employee. The office also provides candles and incense. Preparations for the annual *kosa* cost the Bupyung plant 537,328 *wŏn* (about 827 U.S. dollars) in 1987; in 1988 the amount increased to 573,122 *wŏn* (about 882 U.S. dollars), which is equivalent to one worker's monthly wage.

On the day before the *kosa* offering, the plant prepares a clean table in an empty space of the casting section of the plant; it serves a bowl of pure water, changing it three times during the day. At five o'clock in the afternoon of the *kosa* day, all the foremen, ranking officers, and managerial personnel assemble in the area where the main table is located. All the food—the steamed rice cake, steamed pig's head, rice wine, fruits, nuts, dried pollacks—are placed on the table. The plant manager officiates, lighting the candles and burning the incense. He bows twice, and the rest of the participants follow. No prayers are said aloud, and no statement is made. Perhaps each participant prays silently. There is no elaborate shamanistic ritual (*kut*). As Kendall (1985:114) has pointed out, the rites of the *kosa* are indeed deceptively simple. The entire ceremony takes no more than thirty minutes.

Throughout the company *kosa*, female roles are limited as compared with the household *kosa*. For the household *kosa*, the housewife petitions the gods. However, in the company *kosa*, the officiating is done by the plant manager and mostly his male subordinates, although females are not excluded entirely. In many ways, the company *kosa* resembles the village festival (*purak chae*). It has been frequently noted that some village festivals are done on the model of the dignified male-centered ancestor *chaesa*, while others are raucous and colorful shamanistic ceremonies. Also, the company *kosa* is similar to the ancestor-worship rites of Koreans: the women cook the food for the dead ancestors, but the men make the formal offerings (Kendall 1985:114).

Perhaps the pattern is the result of diffusion of a Confucian sacrifice, *chae*, into the shamanistic ritual of the *kosa*. It is not unusual to see an inclusiveness in Korean religious belief that combines several different religions. Such inclusiveness is also witnessed in China and Japan. Hsu (1970:242) has observed the inclusive nature of Chinese attitude toward the religion. Befu (1971:96) has described the Japanese religious concept: "The same person may worship deities of different religions without feeling of conflict. . . . A Japanese religious concept of a deity may combine elements derived from different religions." In fact, to the most ordinary Japanese person, "the distinction between Shintoism and Buddhism especially is so blurred that sometimes it exists only in the mind of the scholar analyzing folk beliefs" (Befu 1971:96). Interestingly, among the participants in the *kosa* ritual of the Bupyung plant, there were several Christians and Buddhists. I asked them about their feelings toward the *kosa*; participating apparently did not bother them.

Since Koreans consider *kosa* food a sacrament, it is distributed to all employees of the plant. As soon as the offering rites are over, the food is packed in the individual wooden lunch boxes and distributed to every employee. Each box includes 200 grams of steamed rice cake, 100 grams of steamed sliced pork meat, and one orange. Almost all of the employees take the *kosa* sacrament back to their homes and share it with their family members, believing that the food brings good luck and fortune. Others do it simply to show it to their family members.

I asked the plant manager about the seriousness of the company *kosa* and its function. He was neither intensely serious nor offhand about it. Said he, "Since it has been a regular function of the plant since 1974, and most of the workers see it positively, I do not have any objection to its being observed." Nonetheless, it must have been a serious matter to the chairman's wife. One of her relatives told me that "she [the chairman's wife] wanted to be a Christian, but she could not because of the *kosa*."

Some plant managers of other companies take the company *kosa* very seriously. One steel plant manager in Inch'ŏn, whose wife is a close friend of my wife, told us during our conversation about the company *kosa* that her husband prepares for his officiating at his plant *kosa* almost a month ahead of time. He avoids any intimate contact with her for a month. He believes that such abstinence from sex during the preparation period purifies him for such a holy event. In the morning of the annual *kosa* day, which normally takes place in a winter month, he takes a shower with cold purified water. He believes in the mighty power of the plant deities that provide prosperity and safety. The steel plant manager himself told me, "If nothing else, it [his attitude] shows my sincereness about the rituals, and workers know my dedication to the plant and the safety of the workers." The plant manager happens to be a student of science and also a graduate of the school of engineering from a most prestigious university in Korea.

Impact of Confucianism.

Much greater than the impact of the shamanistic *kosa* is the impact of Confucianism on the organizational culture of Poongsan. Organized labor unions and collective bargaining are Western in origin, and yet a close analysis of Poongsan's collective-bargaining agreement indicates that it reflects a strong traditionalism in its reliance on the Korean extended family concept, which is derived from Confucianism. Prominent are the paid annual leave days for the weddings and deaths in a worker's family. Family members that are included go well beyond the immediate family members to include extended kin. Specifically, a worker is allowed a six-day paid annual leave upon the death of his grandparents, if the worker is the oldest grandson and main heir. The number of days allowed is the same as in the death of his parents or his spouse. For female workers, leave is not specified. On the other hand, only four days' paid leave is allowed for the death rites of the employee's parent-in-law. The days allowed for the death rites of a worker's father's oldest brother's wife (aunt) are the same as in the case of his sister. This does not, however, apply to other, younger aunts.

These allowances are manifestations of the Confucian-oriented Korean family system with its rules of patrilineal descent and primogeniture. The same principles are also applied to the amounts of a special payment for weddings and funerals for the workers. Since the labor contract is produced by an agreement between the management of the company and the union of the workers, it is evident that the traditional Korean family concept is valued and observed by both management and employees.

Indeed, the impact of Confucianism is profound, and it covers a wide array of characteristics in the organizational culture of Poongsan. The formal organizational chart of Poongsan, with its division of labor based on technical qualifications, a rigid hierarchical order, codified rules and regulations, and career paths is not much different from the rational bureaucratic model of the West. However, the role of the founder in the hiring and promotion of his kin members creates a dual system of organization at Poongsan. The chairman not only provides employment opportunity for his kin, but also gives direct financial assistance to his clan organization, including aid for the restoration of the relics of his ancestors. The memorial foundation of the chairman's ancestors is placed in the office of his company's headquarters building. Moreover, Poongsan's special training for middle management takes place at a Confucian academy, sŏwŏn, using the facilities of the former yangban clans located in the chairman's hometown.

Sometimes, the boundaries making Poongsan as a business enterprise distinct from Poongsan as a clan organization can be blurred, even though the chairman uses his personal funds to assist his clan organization, mainly because the foundation office is housed in his corporate headquarters building. This characteristic makes Poongsan distinctly different from the rational bureaucratic organizations of the West, which, according to the Weberian school, emphasize a separation of personal from official property and rights.

Despite young workers' resentment of authoritarian rules, they remain faithful to the Confucian hierarchical order. Routine and mundane matters are initiated at the bottom and go to the top for approval. Yet ultimate decisions on key issues are made by the very

top executive, the chairman. It is widely known in the West that
Japanese decision making is commonly cast as participatory and con-
sensual, with the initiative coming from lower levels and the responsibility for outcomes lying with groups instead of the individual
(Sasaki 1981; Vogel 1975; Yoshino 1968). Others point out that the
circulation of a petition or proposal (ringgi-sho) is just the formal
manifestation of a process of consensus building through informal
networking (Lincoln and McBride 1987). Such a practice also occurs
in China. Serrie (1986) traces its origin there from the Confucian-
based big family with the father-son dominant dyad.

Despite the resentment of a growing number of young workers
toward the emphasis on loyalty and obedience, the New Factory
Movement epitomizes the ideology and belief of Korean management and the government: "Treat the employees like family; do factory work as if it were my own personal work." Because the ideology
asks for workers' loyalty to the company just as they would give it to
their parents, 20 percent of the evaluation points a Poongsan employee can earn is based on a superior's assessment of his or her
dependability, cooperation, and harmony.

Concurrently, Poongsan's wage system includes extensive welfare
benefits that resemble those of the Japanese. Poongsan provides
some free housing (although limited, this is expanding), bonuses, a
position allowance, a work allowance, free meals during working
hours, and free uniforms and security equipment, and it makes an
effort to provide overtime pay equivalent to 23.8 percent of the
monthly wage. It also provides free transportation and scholarships
for the children of the employees.

Because of the prevailing authoritarianism and paternalism, the
recent labor strike challenging the company's authority is too painful
for the executives to accept. It is as if children had not fulfilled their
filial duty to their parents.

As specified in the five basic social relationships in the Doctrine
of the Mean, the husband is superior to his wife, and the wife's role
is supposed to be one of compliance. This tradition has been rein-
forced by the strong patriarchal family system, which allocates authority to the males. The patrilineal rule of descent affiliates an individual with a group of kin, all of whom are related to him or her
through male lines. This system, which condones sexual discrimina-

tion against females within the family, is extended into society and is perpetuated by industry.

As some foreign scholars have observed, Korea has surpassed other countries in its discrimination against female workers (Amsden 1989:203). Among Poongsan's 1,175 female employees (12.5 percent of a total of 9,430 employees), no woman is assigned above rank 3 (3-kŭp) on a ten-point ranking system. And no woman is in a managerial position. The wage gap between male and female employees with the same qualifications is slightly over 80 percent, although the gap is less than the norm in Korea (Amsden 1989:203). Despite legal guarantees of equal work rights and retirement age for males and females, most female workers retire upon their marriage. Nearly 80 percent of Poongsan's 1,175 female employees are twenty-five years old or younger. When the company faces financial difficulty, as Poongsan did in 1981–82, female employees are more vulnerable to termination than are male employees.

Over a three-year period of fieldwork, it was my impression that Poongsan is not managed according to a Taylorist rational model. No systematic study of labor needs has ever been made; no one at Poongsan has an MBA degree. As one managing director commented, "Poongsan plants are over-staffed." By Western standards, Poongsan is loosely organized.

Management, especially the chairman and founder of Poongsan, however, resists maximizing profits at the expense of human feelings or by terminating their employees. In 1981–82, after the impact of the second "oil shock" imposed by OPEC, Poongsan faced a period of financial stringency, and many of the employees were terminated. Poongsan makes an extra effort to avoid terminating its employees. Indeed, just as it is shameful and dishonorable for a father to be unable to support his children, it is disgraceful and ignominious for an employer to terminate his own employees because he cannot support them. This belief warrants a system of semi-lifetime employment in most large Korean firms, including Poongsan, without there being an institutionalized lifetime employment system offered by large Japanese firms. Despite much publicity, by the way, the "Japanese work force covered by permanent employment guarantees are no more than 30–40%" (Lincoln and McBride 1987:291; Hashimoto and Raisian 1985).

During a prolonged strike and at a time of uncertain business prospects in 1988 and 1989, Poongsan temporarily halted the recruitment of new employees to avoid having to terminate any more of the current employees. In another benevolent gesture, Poongsan paid 60 percent of the striking workers' basic wages, including a 100 percent bonus, for the seventy-two days of the strike, despite the government's insistence that companies not pay any wages during a strike. The government's position was based on the principle of "no work, no pay."

Such an emotional human bond between employer and employees as evidenced in Poongsan is enhanced by the Korean word, ŭiri, meaning "a deeply held system of morality, integrity, loyalty, and sense of obligation developed in the context of interpersonal relations" (Y. Chung 1989:154). The concept resembles the Japanese giri described by Benedict (1946:133–76), Dore (1958:258), and Cole (1971:199–213). The ŭiri can assure the job security of Korean workers in the absence of institutionalized lifetime employment, and management can count on the workers' dependability.

Traditionally, on the basis of Confucian teachings, Koreans place commerce and industry beneath the work of the scholar or official, farmer, artisan, and merchant. Koreans traditionally have not had much respect for industrial techniques or for physical or manual work. Though recent Korean industrialization and rapid economic growth have altered this traditional belief somewhat, its impact apparently still lingers in the minds of many Koreans.

Indeed, although blue-collar workers' rewards are higher than those of white-collar employees as far as the position allowance, work allowance, and overtime are concerned, the basic wages are better for white-collar employees. Consequently, the blue-collar worker's average monthly pay at Poongsan is barely 80 percent of the white-collar employee's. If there were no overtime pay, the gap between them would be wider. Even when workers have the same educational qualifications, those who have white-collar jobs are paid better than blue-collar workers.

The traditional preferences are apparent even in the higher echelons. University-educated engineers and technicians are placed in the plants, whereas executives who do not have technical degrees are given positions in the headquarters office. Top management is trained predominantly in law, economics, management, and other

social sciences, not technology or metallurgy, even though Poongsan
is producing and selling copper and copper-related products.

Modern Cultural Traits

Despite the persistence of traditional Korean cultural elements,
Poongsan's organizational culture also reveals the influence of modern cultural elements in the main pillars of industrial relations:
promotion, reward, and security systems.

The dual nature of Poongsan's organization allows its chairman to
be flexible, incorporating his business enterprise with his kin-group
organization. Nevertheless, the fundamental organization of Poongsan matches the characteristics of a formal and rational model as
delineated by the Weberian school. It has a fixed division of labor
among the participants with official titles and job descriptions, a
rigid hierarchical order ranging from rank-and-file workers to the
chairman of the company, and codified rules and regulations governing the company and its personnel. Moreover, each position is filled
with technically qualified personnel (Weber 1946:196–204, 1957:
329–36).

Ouchi (1981:25–32) argues that the Japanese system, in contrast,
favors nonspecialized career paths by rotating workers' job assignments within a single organization. But in the United States and the
West generally, workers pursue specialized career paths, and career
movements between organizations occur within a single speciality.
In this respect, Poongsan more clearly resembles the Western model
than it does the Japanese.

My survey of Poongsan's Bupyung employees indicates that 46.2
percent of the respondents have never changed job assignments since
the time they were first employed; 33.7 percent have changed only
once; 18.3 percent have changed twice; and only 1.9 percent have
changed more than four times. Even for those who have changed more
than four times, the changes were not from one speciality to another,
but within the same speciality in different sections. Such career paths
allow workers to achieve expertise in a speciality in any work setting
and to pursue career plans as specialists. Certainly Poongsan is less
flexible in reallocating its labor than is the Japanese industry with
its system of nonspecialized career paths and lifetime job rotation.

Before 1976 and during the period when Poongsan was small in scale, connection-hiring through the kin network, along with the reliance on recommendation by friends and acquaintances, was the firm's dominant recruiting mechanism. Nearly 93 percent of Poongsan's top executives were hired through their connections. Beginning in 1976, however, Poongsan adopted the *kongch'ae* system in hiring its employees, especially four-year university graduates. This system eliminates personal connections and ties and considers the applicant's qualifications and merit on the basis of school recommendations and an entrance examination score. The company has gradually expanded its use of this system to include non-university graduates. The *kongch'ae* system is considered an ideal system for acquiring employees capable of coping with the rapid industrialization of Korea.

The *kongch'ae* fits a modern social order characterized by universalism (Parsons 1937:550–51; 1951:51–67). Particularism is characteristic of traditional societies, which treat the individual differently from others, whereas universalism treats all people equally and applies the same set of criteria to everyone. Parsons considers universalism to be one of the fundamental characteristics of the modern Western social order that clearly sets it apart from the Confucian ethic.

Although the Poongsan reward structure includes aspects of the Japanese system, including the provision of allowances, free transportation, free meals, and the like, the basic wage rate structure tilts more toward the Western pattern. Poongsan's wage determinants are the type of job (blue-collar or white-collar work) and the employee's gender, level of education, military service, possession of skill, and previous experience. The worker's age, marital status, family obligations, and seniority are less emphasized in Poongsan's wage rate structure than they are in the Japanese *nenkō joretsu* system.

Parsons' concept of universalism is evidenced in Poongsan's evaluation criteria for promotion: 80 percent of the evaluation is based on the employee's length of service and achievement, including awards, training, and foreign-language competence for the university graduates. Although the length of service is important, age is not as important, in contrast to the Japanese *nenkō* system. There are specifications for each of these criteria, and every criterion is quantifiable. The system is as rigid as any evaluation system employed by a Western bureaucracy.

Not only is age grading not formalized, but in Poongsan's promotion system, a prolonged term of service can become a liability. When a prospective candidate for promotion meets the minimum years of service specified in each rank, the candidate earns 60 points; thereafter, the candidate can earn a small number of points each year until five more years have passed. Then points start being deducted if promotion still does not occur. In other words, the longer one stays in the same rank, the less likely it is that one can be promoted.

Some believe that, like the Japanese *nenkō* system, in Korean industries, age grading is based on Confucian respect for the older person. However, this does not appear to be as true as one would expect at Poongsan. In fact, many rank-and-file workers are supervised by younger foremen whose educational and skill qualifications are on the same level as those of the workers. Foremen are selected more on the basis of the performance-ability-leadership formula than on age. One foreman hired three years later than another caught up to the senior and was promoted to the same rank. Even among the top executives just below the chairman, who is oldest of all (he was sixty-five years old in 1989), rank does not follow age. The vice chairman, for instance, is younger than the president, and he in turn, is younger than four of the five vice presidents. Of the thirty-seven supporting executives to the president, twelve are older than the president, and three of the twelve are kin members to the chairman—one brother, one son, and one clan member.

Ouchi (1981:22–25) has pointed out that while the Japanese evaluation system is typically slow, the Western system is marked by more rapid evaluation and promotion. Here, too, the Poongsan system and Korean firms generally are closer to the Western model. In fact, the average age of Korean employees is six years younger than the Japanese in comparable firms and at equivalent ranks.

Despite the Korean government's labor control policy since the birth of the republic in 1948 and the ongoing effort to indoctrinate workers with values centered on dependability and Confucian ideology, the workers' demands and union actions seem unremitting. Poongsan's seventy-two-day strike in 1988–89 has amply demonstrated that Poongsan's workers, despite their Confucian cultural heritage, are no longer cheap, docile, and loyal, as some scholars have portrayed them. Labor's latent dissatisfaction has erupted whenever authoritarian control has loosened its grip. And when they were under intense government oppression, Korean workers resorted to bizarre forms of protest to dramatize the misery of their working conditions. Korean industrial workers have learned quickly the "'rules of the game' of industrialism and . . . committed themselves to organizing labor unions to represent their interest" (Choi 1983: 104). Japanese labor unions are not their frame of reference.

Former farmers who were uprooted have already become militant. Future industrial workers, the sons and daughters of the uprooted farmers who are growing up in industrial settings, will make demands no less than did their parents. Perhaps the labor problems of yesterday's Western industrial sector are to be tomorrow's Korean labor-management tasks. As Deyo (1989) has indicated in his recent work, the Korean labor movement is exceptional among the rest of the East Asian countries, for it closely resembles the labor movements of Western industrial workers.

Tradition and Modernity in Coexistence

The ethnographic study of Poongsan has led me to reconsider the intellectual tradition behind the polar concepts of tradition and modernity in terms of three assumptions Bendix (1967) has identified.

First, regarding the conceptions of tradition and modernity, the ethnographic information on Poongsan reveals that they are not mutually exclusive and exhaustive but dualistic or syncretistic. Most of the organizational cultural traits are logically contradictory, contrasting, and inclusive. Brandt (1971:28) has observed that "contradictory forms of behavior are found in all cultures, but they seem to have been more dramatically expressed in Korea than in some other parts of the world." As a late entrant in industrialization, Korea has borrowed technology and scientific knowledge from the industrialized West. The Korean emphasis on scientific knowledge and machine technology and Korea's intensive training for the skill to operate sophisticated machines almost amount to a religion. Yet, their praying for a supernatural power to secure business prosperity via the shamanistic ritual of the kosa is a clear contradiction. Training on the job for technical knowledge is matched by another contradiction in sŏwŏn training at the Confucian academy for the middle management. Korean business organization is basically bureaucratic, yet management includes as well the principles of Korean kinship and uses the family analogy. The aim of the corporation is to make a profit as an economic enterprise, yet every effort is made to patronize the employees by offering them a package of many fringe benefits. It appears that the management views these benefit packages as manifestations of paternalism. Evaluation criteria seem to be based on the modern ethic of universalism, to use Parsons's term, but dependency and docility for the sake of harmonious relationships are favored over creativity and independence.

The Poongsan employees are determined to voice their demands through organized labor, which is modern and Western, instead of appealing to the Confucian family values, yet some important elements in the agreements won by collective bargaining reflect the traditional heritage of Korean kinship and family. Despite the rise of Western democratic values, especially among the young, Confucian values remain powerfully at work in the minds of many Korean industrial workers. In response to my survey question, "What is an ideal way to bring about prosperity to the company and to the workers?" a large number of Bupyung workers answered that the company has to create a family atmosphere based on Confucian values. The workers' choice of Confucian values over Western democratic values was overwhelming, even among the workers whose religious beliefs were incompatible with Confucianism. For instance, 29 workers (28.2 percent) in the survey identified themselves as Buddhists, yet 17 out of 28 respondents (58.6 percent) believed that the company should be managed on the basis of Confucian values. Such a tendency is also true among Christians.

Some scholars view tradition and modernity as mutually exclusive. A certain model like Tai's affective versus rational might work in the Euro-American cultural tradition where there is one universal cultural norm established under the Christian tradition (Bendix 1967:322) and religious beliefs are exclusive. Perhaps the inclusive characteristic of the organizational culture of Korean industry is analogous to the religious inclusiveness of Koreans, as well as the Japanese and Chinese. Hsu (1970:242) has portrayed such an inclusive nature with an example: one may to go a Buddhist monastery to pray for a male heir but then may proceed to a Taoist shrine to beseech a god to cure him of malaria.

Second, as for the conceptualization of change as intrinsic (Bendix 1967:324–26), Korean industrialization cannot be explained entirely by intrinsic factors. The Japanese colonial impact was profound. Some Western scholars trace the political economy of Korea to the Japanese colonial government, emphasizing the close ties between native Korean business elites and the Japanese colonial government. Others have intimated that Japanese colonial policy laid the infrastructure for recent Korean industrialization (Cumings 1987). Bae (1987:54) has recognized Japanese practices in Korean personnel policy. (Such practices are found in Poongsan's evaluation of its employees.) The authoritarian management of Korean enterprises is another residue of the Japanese influence, according to Bae (1987:55). The fringe benefits package of Poongsan also more closely resembles Japanese practice than it does Western practice.

Korean industry has also been on the receiving end of the diffusion of technology from the West. The process was perhaps the inevitable result of an intensive interaction with the West, particularly with the United States, since World War II; the massive U.S. aid during and immediately after the Korean War was a particularly important contributing factor. The United States figured prominently in Korea's adopting an export-led industrialization strategy in the early 1960s, in its attracting foreign investment to industrialize, and in its sending technocrats to be educated in the West. All these have been important factors in the domestic socioeconomic and cultural mix that has fostered the recent Korean industrialization.

Although it has been largely overlooked, there remains one non-economic variable in the explanation of rapid Korean industrialization and modernization, and that is the experience of the Korean War. Massive numbers of Korean peasants would have had little or no formal training in modern technology without the wartime mobilization through a mandatory military draft system. Not only did they become literate, but they also had opportunities to gain skills and knowledge to handle sophisticated equipment and machinery. The process was most visible in the construction field, where those skills became a major advantage in Korea's ability to bid on jobs for Middle Eastern countries. Moreover, Korean workers and managers existed precariously, hovering between life and death, learning endurance through three wars: World War II, the Korean War, and the Vietnam War. Such experiences help to explain how Korean construction workers have been so successful in undertaking the most difficult tasks in the Arabian desert under the most inhospitable circum-

(3) convergence theory: as long as industry on its way
? no individuation
rationality. bureaucracy

stances. I myself have witnessed hardworking Korean construction workers in Middle Eastern countries; they work as if they are soldiers in the combat zones.

Indeed, not many people on earth have had experiences, good or bad, to match those of the current generation of Korean workers. Cole's (1971:11) remarks on Japan's uniqueness seem applicable to the Korean case: "As an object lesson with specific application to developing countries, the Japanese experience is probably of limited value, for . . . the historical period during which Japan industrialized had unique characteristics which can never be repeated for the benefit of presently industrializing countries." It is important for scholars to remember that generalizing about East Asian industrialization by using models such as Tai's affective versus rational traits might be misleading, for the models may override the local realities and obscure important details.

Third, regarding the tradition-versus-modernity dichotomy, industrialization is understood largely as a uniform process of structural change. As Bendix (1967:325) has pointed out, some intellectuals believe that "once industrialization is underway, it has certain inevitable results. . . . Modernity will drive out tradition and fully industrialized societies will become more and more alike." This view shares the premise of the theory of convergence (Kerr et al. 1960). Influenced by Veblen, who is considered an evolutionist (see Sahlins and Service 1960:102), convergence theorists explain that the technology common to industrializing societies generates increasingly uniform patterns of bureaucracy and rationality and growing individualism; thus, industrial societies become more alike than different with the passage of time.

Several sociologists have advocated the application of convergence theory to the Korean industrial setting. Shepard and her associates (1979) compared Korean and American workers in automobile manufacturing and oil refineries for their alienation responses to technology and found strong support for the theory. Also, Form and Bae (1988; Bae 1987; Bae and Form 1986) have studied the Hyundai Motor Company and have concluded that, despite their socialization in the traditional Korean values of Confucian ethics, Korean auto workers adapted just as quickly to industrial and related social systems. Their assessment was that, as evidenced in the Hyundai Motor workers, the convergence theory is robust.

Others have expressed their doubts about the use of convergence theory in the case of Korea, at least at present. Instead, they have noticed the endurance and preservation of the traditional culture (Kim and Kim 1989:215; Steinberg 1989:195). Choi (1983:35) relates that "generally, industrialization bears some typical social concomitants, such as division of labor, structural and occupational differentiation, urbanization, industrialization, and so on, breaking up traditional society or accelerating its transition toward a more modern one. But distinctive cultural context also does filter, screen out, or mediate social and political effects of industrialization."

Sorensen (1988), in his recent study of rural Korean peasant households and their adaptations to rapid industrialization, has learned that, contrary to the belief that industrialization produces roughly similar social results in all societies, in the village, Korean industrialization has not led to a fundamental change in the structure of rural families. Rather, it has led to strategic allocation and residence "without sacrificing fundamental principles of family continuity, division of labor, and kinship obligation" (Sorensen 1988:231). He further states, "Although both native and foreign observers of the contemporary Korean rural family have often been impressed by the dramatic changes in family organization that have appeared in recent years, preoccupation with this change has led many, in my opinion, to ignore some of the deeper continuities in the response of rural residents of central Korea to the urbanization and industrialization of South Korea since 1960" (Sorensen 1988:231).

Steers and his associates (1989:142) also have observed,

> The emerging Korean management style will resemble somewhat more closely what we are familiar with in the West. However, it would be a mistake to describe this as Western-style management. Instead, the new management will be highly pragmatic, adopting new techniques from different sources and modifying them to meet the unique cultural and environmental demands, and throughout this evolutionary process, the traditional values that have defined Korean culture and business enterprise for centuries will play a central role. The new Korea will not abandon or forget the old.

The ethnographic information I have gathered about Poongsan may allow us to assess the general myths about Korean industry that were summarized in the introduction. My observation at Poongsan indicates that, although some traditional characteristics are declin-

[handwritten annotations: "not convergence, — but contrasting dual ethics. as worker strike. go back to hire clan member."]

ing and modern cultural elements are becoming prominent in Korea, other traditional elements are surviving as they are adapted into an inclusive system. For example, the once-traditional mode of connection-hiring evolved into *kongch'ae*, but then labor unrest has turned the system back toward the more traditional forms of connection-hiring. The situation remains fluid, and there is no clear straight progression from tradition toward modernity in all facets of the industrial system.

Also, this study does not support the myth that Korean industry is merely traditionally Oriental with special emphasis on Confucian ethics. The docility among Korean industrial workers is not necessarily endemic to the culture but may instead be the result of authoritarian political control. As for yet another myth, industrialization may drive out traditional Korean culture, but such a convergence will likely occur on a planetary scale, and it is too early to make an accurate assessment. It is important to remember, though, that some traditional Japanese culture has survived, despite the fact that Japan's is the oldest economic modernization in Asia (Tai 1989:13–14).

In summary, my ethnographic study has led me to conclude that the culture of Poongsan cannot be dichotomized in terms of Tai's and others' polar concepts, as if they were mutually exclusive and exhaustive. Rather, the traditional and modern cultures coexist in Poongsan's organizational culture. For the present, at least, the behavior patterns of Poongsan industrial workers seem to be marked not by convergence but by contrasting dual ethics, the traditional and the modern.

As for the precise balance between tradition and modernity in the organizational culture of Poongsan, it is difficult to discern or assess the ranges of the two cultures for each employee and manager. The balance differs from issue to issue, and from one individual to another. The self-interest of managers and workers leads them to respond to each situation selectively, choosing between two contrasting ethics at each time.

The absence of consistency gives a strong impression to an outsider that the organizational culture of Poongsan is contradictory. Brandt's (1971:19–36) observations about Korean patterns of behavior is perceptive, and his structural model of contrasts is certainly applicable to what I discovered in the organizational behavior of Poongsan and in Korean industry as a whole.

Epilogue

Writing this book has allowed me to review the available literature dealing with Korea's economic growth and recent industrialization. The literature, especially the works by foreign scholars in English-language editions, is predominantly positive about Korea's past accomplishments and prospects for the future. The complimentary adjectives to describe the nation's remarkable progress in a relatively short period include such words as "remarkable," "astonishing," and "miracle." Amsden's (1989) *Asia's Next Giant* is but one of many works praising Korean achievement. Their optimism is based on their assessments of the well-educated and disciplined work force, the well-defined industrial policy of the government and its technocrats, and the discipline of business in following the governmental policy.

In contrast to the optimism of foreign scholars is the greater caution of native scholars, who recognize a growing new challenge that may be a hindrance to future progress. The increasing demand of workers to share the profits of the growing Korean economy through wage increases will make Korea less competitive in the world export market. As Amsden (1989:203) has pointed out, "Korea has set world records with its growth rate in wages." In 1989 the growth rate in the manufacturing sector was 3.7 percent, largely because of the acute labor unrest, and exports were reduced to 4 percent, the first decrease since 1974. The overall economic growth rate in 1989 was only 6.7 percent, the lowest since 1981 (*Hankook Ilbo*, 28 Mar. 1970: 7). Workers' demands for economic justice will increase as the former farm work force is replaced by the urban offspring of the uprooted farmers.

The rising position of women and their claims for equal rights as guaranteed in the Korean Constitution are also a new challenge. As is the case in Japan, the Korean female work force has been a buffer that has allowed management to offer semi-lifetime employment to the regular work force. Women's wages have been lower, and women have been virtually excluded from promotion to managerial positions, thus providing room for male workers. Women's right to work and to pursue new career paths will alter the flexibility that Korean management has enjoyed for so long.

In addition, Korean industry faces a new challenge. In the 1970s and the early 1980s, when Korean business firms were expanding at an unprecedented rate, a university-educated and capable employee could be promoted to *pujang* (division head) within ten years or so. A recent survey shows that it takes almost twice that long today. In the very near future, Korean firms may face the same problem that Japan has faced: many qualified candidates must wait their turn for promotion because of the limited number of openings (*Dong-A Ilbo*, 29 Apr. 1989:7).

Increasing demands for fair trade imposed by the United States are another real challenge, in the short run at least. Somewhat militant farmers may become more militant because of the liberalization of import restrictions on agricultural products. As long as Korea remains a trade surplus nation with the United States, pressure from the United States for Korea to open its markets to U.S. goods and to give the United States the freedom to enter Korea's financial markets to buy into Korean prosperity will be intensified. Native intellectuals express the fear that because most Korean business and industrial sectors enjoyed prosperity under the protection of the government, they are unaccustomed to competing with foreign entrepreneurs.

Korea's competition also extends to its newly emerging late industrializing neighbors, mostly Southeastern Asian countries. Rising Korean wages cannot compete with the low wages of those countries.

A growing number of Korean industrial plants are moving to the countries where industrial workers' wages are lower and labor is abundant. Many native Korean intellectuals express their concern over a possible reduction of manufacturing facilities on Korean soil.

Even the consumption patterns of Koreans pose a challenge. Under the influence of Confucianism, Koreans have proven themselves to be diligent and frugal, maintaining the high savings that are characteristic of most East Asians (Tai 1989:22–24). Some writers have indicated that "the level of savings in traditional Korea was obviously low" (Y. Chung 1989:156), but the level of Korean national savings in 1987 remained at 37.4 percent (National Bureau of Statistics 1988b: 85), about the same as that of Taiwan in 1986 (38 percent), and above that of Japan (33 percent) in 1965 (Tai 1989:23). These figures are higher than those for any other block of nations in the world.

Nonetheless, the self-indulgent consumerism that now prevails among urban Koreans has caught the attention of concerned natives. The Korean media have criticized the casting off of traditional values of security and thrift (*Hankook Ilbo*, 26 Sept. 1989:1; 27 Sept. 1989:5; 29 Sept. 1989:5; 30 Sept. 1989:20; 4 Oct. 1989:1, 25). Some foreign media, including the *Washington Post* (21 Sept. 1989:E1, E10), have reported the consumerism of privileged Seoulites. Such consumption patterns have contributed to industrial workers' feelings of relative deprivation and have prompted them to demand economic justice.

When Korea was backward technologically and economically, self-indulgence might have been viewed as shameful, and frugal workaholics might have been viewed as virtuous. Perhaps such an ethical point of view is a "privilege of backwardness," as theorized by Trotsky (n.d. 405), Gerschenkron (1962, 1968), and Sahlins and Service (1960). And the challenges that worry observers may be the "penalty of taking the lead," as Veblen (1915:ch. 2–4) has pointed out.

In viewing the future of Korean economic growth, I, too, remain optimistic. There may be periods of slow growth for the short run every now and then, as Korean industry weathers the challenges. My optimism is based on two points in particular: one is the confidence, determination, and wisdom of the Koreans themselves, qualities they have demonstrated in the past several decades; and the other is the effort of Koreans to emulate Japanese success. Koreans have shown themselves able to overcome the challenges, as is already manifest in the grass-roots movements of civic organizations such as the Korean Christian Youth Association (KCYA). Recently, more than 8,000 young Christians have launched a nationwide campaign to appeal to "those-who-have" to restrain their affluent consumerism and to resist the rise in rents for "those-who-have-not" (*Hankook Ilbo*, 16 Apr. 1990:1). The civic movement has been received well and is spreading rapidly throughout the nation. Chronic labor unrest has been curtailed significantly in 1990 by cooperation between labor and management to overcome the recent slow growth in the economy. The number of labor disputes in 1990 have been reduced 75 percent from the level reached in 1989 (*Hankook Ilbo*, 26 Feb. 1990:1). The number of labor disputes in 1991 again have been reduced 29.1 percent from the level reached in 1990 (*Hankook Ilbo*, 30 Aug. 1991:14). Although there was a large gap between the association of Korean business organizations and labor organizations concerning wage guidelines for 1990 (*Hankook Ilbo*, 23 Mar. 1990:7), more than 80 percent of the industrial firms settled their rates of wage increase for 1990 under the double-digit level (*Hankook Ilbo*, 22 Mar. 1990:8).

Korea not only has benefited directly from the technological know-how of Japan, as evidenced in POSCO, but Japanese success has become a guiding metaphor for Korean endeavor. As I read Cole's (1971:1–15) description of Japanese industrial workers in the late 1960s, including the remarks made by contemporary foreign journalists, I was struck by the similarity to Korean industrial workers in the late 1980s. Despite the many challenges facing Japan in those years, it has risen to be a world economic superpower, and Japanese per capita GNP surpassed that of Americans in 1990. As Cumings (1987:51) has pointed out, it may be painful for most Korean nationalists to admit that they wish to emulate the Japanese because of the unfortunate historical past. Nonetheless, it is undeniable that the Japanese success is the Koreans' frame of reference as a role model.

When Korea achieves the same level that Japan did in the late 1980s, it may face the same challenges Japan faces now. Today's challenges in Japan are seemingly tomorrow's tasks in Korea. Anthropologists have a role to play: today's industrial ethnography may shed some light on the coming age in industrializing societies such as Korea.

References

Daily and weekly newspapers are not included.

Following the customary practice of Korean and Japanese usage, contrary to American usage, I give the family names of people first in the reference list without placing a comma before their personal names when their publications are in their native language.

Abegglen, James C.
    1958   *The Japanese Factory: Aspects of Its Social Organization.*
            Glencoe, Ill.: Free Press.
Adelman, Irma, ed.
    1969   *Practical Approaches to Development Planning: Korea's Second
            Five-Year Plan.* Baltimore: Johns Hopkins University Press.
Amsden, Alice H.
    1989   *Asia's Next Giant: South Korea and Late Industrialization.* New
            York: Oxford University Press.
    1990   South Korea's Record Wage Rates: Labor in Late
            Industrialization. *Industrial Relations* 29:77–93.
Baba, Marietta L.
    1986   *Business and Industrial Anthropology: An Overview.* NAPA
            Bulletin, no. 2. Washington, D.C.: American Anthropological
            Association.

Bae, Kyuhan
  1987   *Automobile Workers in Korea.* Seoul: Seoul National University
          Press.
Bae, Kyu Han and William Form
  1986   Payment Strategy in South Korea's Advanced Economic Sector.
          American Sociological Review 51:120–31.
Baker, Christopher
  1981   Economic Reorganization and the Slump in South and South-East
          Asia. *Comparative Studies in Society and History* 23:325–49.
Barry, Herbert, III, et al.
  1959   Relation of Child Training to Subsistence Economy. *American
          Anthropologist* 61:51–63.
Befu, Harumi
  1971   *Japan: An Anthropological Introduction.* New York: Thomas Y.
          Crowell.
Bendix, Reinhard
  1967   Tradition and Modernity Reconsidered. *Comparative Studies in
          Society and History* 9:292–346.
Benedict, Ruth
  1946   *The Chrysanthemum and the Sword.* Boston: Houghton Mifflin.
Benjamin, Roger
  1982   The Political Economy of Korea. *Asian Survey* 22:1105–16.
Booth, David
  1984   Marxism and Development Sociology: Interpreting the Impasse.
          World Development 13:761–87.
Brandt, Vincent S. R.
  1971   *A Korean Village: Between Farm and Sea.* Cambridge: Harvard
          University Press.
  1980   Case Studies of Small and Medium Enterprises. In *Government,
          Business, and Entrepreneurship in Economic Development: The
          Korean Case,* Leroy P. Jones and Il Sakong, pp. 313–42.
          Cambridge: Council on East Asian Studies, Harvard University.
Burmeister, Larry L.
  1988   *Research, Realpolitik, and Development in Korea: The State and
          the Green Revolution.* Boulder, Colo.: Westview Press.
Chang, Chan Sup
  1989   Human Resource Management in Korea. In *Korean Managerial
          Dynamics,* ed. Kae H. Chung and Hak Chong Lee, pp. 195–205.
          New York: Praeger.
Chang In-sŏk
  1989   Chaebŏl-Chŏngch'i'indŭl Honmaek Inmaek [Personal and
          Marital Ties between Politicians and *Chaebŏls*]. *Yŏsŏng Dong-A,*
          November 1989:238–45.

Chang, Yunshik
   1989   Peasants Go to Town: The Rise of Commercial Farming in
           Korea. *Human Organization* 48:236–51.
Chen, Yu-hsi
   1981   Dependent Development and Its Sociopolitical Consequences: A
           Case Study of Taiwan. Ph.D. diss., University of Hawaii.
Cho, Dong Sung
   1989   Diversification Strategy of Korean Firms. In *Korean Managerial
           Dynamics*, ed. Kae H. Chung and Hak Chong Lee, pp. 99–112.
           New York: Praeger.
Cho Kang Hi
   1984   Yŏngnam Chibang-ŭi Honban Yŏngu [Marriage Patterns of a
           Yŏngnam *Yangban* Clan]. *Journal of the Institute for Korean
           Culture* 6:79–121.
Cho, Soon-Kyoung
   1989   Beyond Docility: "Unskilled" Women Workers in Export
           Industries in Korea. *Korean and Korean American Studies
           Bulletin* 3:10–16.
Choi, In-hak
   1979   *A Type of Index of Korean Folktales.* Seoul: Myong Ji University
           Press.
Choi, Jang Jip
   1983   Interest Conflict and Political Control in South Korea: A Study
           of the Labor Unions in Manufacturing Industries, 1961–1980.
           Ph.D. diss., University of Chicago.
Choi Sŏk-ch'ae
   1984   Sanŏpsahoe-wa Chŏngnyŏn [Industrial Society and Retirement].
           In *Sanŏpsahoe-wa Chŏngnyŏn [Industrializing Society and
           Retirement]*, ed. Chŏng Chu-yŏng, pp. 19–30. Seoul: Ansanpokji
           Saŏpjaedan.
Chŏn Ki-ho
   1989   *Han'guk Nodong Kyŏngjae-ron [Discussions on the Korean
           Labor Economy]*. Seoul: Hangil-sa.
Chung, Kae H.
   1989   An Overview of Korean Management. In *Korean Managerial
           Dynamics*, ed. Kae H. Chung and Hak Chong Lee, pp. 1–8. New
           York: Praeger.
Chung, Kae H., and Hak Chong Lee
   1989   National Differences in Managerial Practices. In *Korean
           Managerial Dynamics*, ed. Kae H. Chung and Hak Chong Lee,
           pp. 163–80. New York: Praeger.
Chung, Kae H., and Harry K. Lie
   1989   Labor-Management Relations in Korea. In *Korean Managerial*

Dynamics, ed. Kae H. Chung and Hak Chong Lee, pp. 217–31. New York: Praeger.

Chung, Young-iob
  1989 The Impact of Chinese Culture on Korea's Economic Development. In *Confucianism and Economic Development: An Oriental Alternative?* ed. Hung-chao Tai, pp. 149–65. Washington, D.C.: The Washington Institute for Values in Public Policy.

Cole, Robert E.
  1971 *Japanese Blue Collar: The Changing Tradition.* Berkeley: University of California Press.

Covell, Alan Carter
  1983 *Ecstasy: Shamanism in Korea.* Seoul: Hollym International Corporation.

Cumings, Bruce
  1981 *The Origins of the Korean War: Liberation and the Emergence of Separate Regimes, 1945–1947.* Princeton: Princeton University Press.
  1984 *The Two Koreas.* Headline Series, no. 269. New York: Foreign Policy Association.
  1987 The Origins and Development of the Northeast Asian Political Economy: Industrial Sectors, Product Cycles, and Political Consequences. In *The Political Economy of the New Asian Industrialism,* ed. Frederic C. Deyo, pp. 44–83. Ithaca, N.Y.: Cornell University Press.

Deyo, Frederic C.
  1989 *Beneath the Miracle: Labor Subordination in the New Asian Industrialism.* Berkeley: University of California Press.

Dore, Ronald
  1958 *City Life in Japan.* Berkeley: University of California Press.

Durkheim, Emile
  1947 *The Division of Labor in Society.* Glencoe, Ill.: Free Press.

Eckert, Carter Joel
  1986 The Colonial Origins of Korean Capitalism: The Koch'ang Kims and the Kyongsong Spinning and Weaving Company, 1876–1945. Ph.D. diss. University of Washington.
  1990 The South Korean Bourgeoisie: A Class in Search of Hegemony. *Journal of Korean Studies* 7:115–48.
  1991 *Offspring of Empire: The Koch'ang Kims and the Colonial Origins of Korean Capitalism, 1876–1945.* Seattle: University of Washington Press.

Eckert, Carter, et al.
  1990 *Korea Old and New: A History.* Cambridge: Korean Institute, Harvard University.

Eisenstadt, S. N.
  1966   *Modernization: Protest and Change.* Englewood Cliffs, N.J.:
          Prentice-Hall.
Erikson, Erik
  1968   *Identity: Youth and Crisis.* New York: W. W. Norton.
Fei, John, et al.
  1979   *Growth with Equity: The Taiwanese Case.* New York: Oxford
          University Press.
Form, William, and Kyu Han Bae
  1988   Convergence Theory and the Korean Connection. *Social Forces*
          66:618–44.
Gallin, Barnard, and Rita Gallin
  1982   Socioeconomic Life in Rural Taiwan: Twenty Years of
          Development and Change. *Modern China* 8:205–45.
Geertz, Clifford
  1965   *Peddlers and Princes.* Chicago: University of Chicago Press.
Gerschenkron, Alexander
  1962   *Economic Backwardness in Historical Perspective.* Cambridge:
          Harvard University Press.
  1968   *Continuity in History and Other Essays.* Cambridge: Harvard
          University Press.
Grajdanzev, Andrew J.
  1978   *Modern Korea.* New York: John Day.
Greenhouse, Carol J.
  1985   Anthropology at Home: Whose Home? *Human Organization*
          44:261–64.
Gusfield, Joseph
  1967   Tradition and Modernity: Misplaced Polarities in the Society of
          Social Change. *American Journal of Sociology* 72:351–62.
Hahm Pyong-choon, Yang Seung Doo, and Kim Choong Soon
  1964   Han'guk Nodongjohap-ŭi Hyŏnsil-gwa Nodongbŏp [Labor Law
          and the Reality of the Trade Unionism in Korea]. *Yonsei Non-
          Chong* 3:213–50.
Hamabata, Matthews Masayuki
  1990   *Crested Kimono: Power and Love in the Japanese Business
          Family.* Ithaca: Cornell University Press.
Hamilton, Gary G., and Narco Orru
  1989   Organizational Structure of East Asian Companies. In *Korean
          Managerial Dynamics*, ed. Kae H. Chung and Hak Chong Lee,
          pp. 39–47. New York: Praeger.
Hamilton, Richard F.
  1967   *Affluence and the French Worker in the Fourth Republic.*
          Princeton: Princeton University Press.

Handlin, Oscar
  1952   *The Uprooted.* Boston: Little, Brown.
Harvey, Youngsook Kim
  1976   The Korean *Mudang* as a Household Therapist. In *Culture-Bound Syndromes, Ethnopsychiatry, and Alternate Therapies,* ed. W. P. Lebra, pp. 189–98. Honolulu: University of Hawaii Press.
  1979   *Six Korean Women: The Socialization of Shamans.* St. Paul: West Publishing.
  1980   Possession Sickness and Women Shamans in Korea. In *Unspoken Worlds: Women's Religious Lives in Non-Western Cultures,* ed. N. Falk and R. Gross, pp. 41–52. New York: Harper and Row.
Hasan, Parvez
  1976   *Korea: Problems and Issues in a Rapidly Growing Economy.* Baltimore: Johns Hopkins University Press.
Hasan, Parvez, and D. C. Rao
  1979   *Korea, Policy Issues for Long-Term Development: Report of a Mission Sent to the Republic of Korea by the World Bank.* Baltimore: Johns Hopkins University Press.
Hashimoto, M., and J. Raisian
  1985   Employment Tenure and Earnings Profiles in Japan and the United States. *American Economic Review* 75:721–35.
Hatada, Takashi
  1969   *A History of Korea,* ed. and trans. W. W. Smith, Jr., and B. H. Hazard. Santa Barbara: American Bibliographic Center.
Hattori Tamio
  1986   Han'guk-gwa Ilbon-ŭi Taekiŏp-group Pikyo: Soyu-wa Kyŏngyŏng-ŭl Chungsimŭro [Comparison Between the Large Korean and Japanese Enterprises]. In *Han'guk Kiŏp-ŭi Kujo-wa Chŏnryak* [*Structure and Strategy of Korean Enterprises*], ed. Lee Hakchong and Jung Ku Hyun, pp. 149–203. Seoul: Pŏmun-sa.
  1989   Japanese Zaibatsu and Korean Chaebol. In *Korean Managerial Dynamics,* ed. Kae H. Chung and Hak Chong Lee, pp. 79–95. New York: Praeger.
Henderson, Gregory
  1968   *Korea: The Politics of the Vortex.* Cambridge: Harvard University Press.
Ho, Samuel P. S.
  1978   *Economic Development of Taiwan, 1860–1970.* New Haven, Conn.: Yale University Press.
Hofheinz, Roy, Jr., and Kent E. Calder
  1982   *The Eastasia Edge.* New York: Basic Books.
Hofstede, Geert, and Michael Harris Bond
  1988   The Confucius Connection: From Cultural Roots to Economic Growth. *Organizational Dynamics* Spring:5–21.

Holzberg, Carol S., and Maureen J. Giovannini
  1981   Anthropology and Industry: Reappraisal and New Directions.
          Annual Review of Anthropology 10:317–60.
Homma-True, Reiko
  1976   Characteristics of Contrasting Chinatowns: 2 Oakland,
          California. *Social Casework: The Journal of Contemporary
          Social Work* 57:155–59.
Hsu, Francis L. K.
  1965   The Effect of Dominant Kinship Relationships on Kin and Non-
          Kin Behavior: A Hypothesis. *American Anthropologist* 67:638–
          61.
  1970   *Americans and Chinese: Purpose and Fulfillment in Great
          Civilizations.* Garden City, N.Y.: The Natural History Press.
  1971   *Kinship and Culture.* Chicago: Aldine.
  1975   *Iemoto: The Heart of Japan.* Cambridge, Mass.: Schenkman.
  1983   *Rugged Individualism Reconsidered: Essays in Psychological
          Anthropology.* Knoxville, Tenn.: University of Tennessee Press.
Huhm, Halla Pai
  1980   *Kut: Korean Shamanist Ritual.* Seoul: Hollym International
          Corporation.
Hwang, In-Joung
  1981   *Management of Rural Change in Korea: The Saemaul Undong.*
          Seoul: Seoul National University Press.
Jackall, Robert
  1988   *Moral Mazes: The World of Corporate Managers.* New York:
          Oxford University Press.
Jacobs, Norman
  1985   *The Korean Road to Modernization and Development.* Urbana:
          University of Illinois Press.
Janelli, Roger L., and Dawnhee Yim Janelli
  1982   *Ancestor Worship and Korean Society.* Stanford, Calif.: Stanford
          University Press.
Jones, Leroy P., and Il Sakong
  1980   *Government, Business, and Entrepreneurship in Economic
          Development: The Korean Case.* Cambridge: Council on East
          Asian Studies, Harvard University.
Jung Ku Hyun
  1987   *Han'guk Kiŏp-ŭi Sŏngjangjŏnryak-gwa Kyŏngyŏng Kujo* [Growth
          Strategy and Management Structure of Korean Business
          Enterprise]. Seoul: Taehan Sang'gong Hoeŭiso [Korean Chamber
          of Commerce].
Kendall, Laurel
  1985   *Shamans, Housewives, and Other Restless Spirits: Women in
          Korean Ritual Life.* Honolulu: University of Hawaii Press.

1988   *The Life and Hard Times of a Korean Shaman: Of Tales and the Telling of Tales.* Honolulu: University of Hawaii Press.

Kerr, Clark, et al.

1960   *Industrialism and Industrial Man.* Cambridge: Harvard University Press.

Keyes, Charles F.

1983   Peasant Strategies in Asian Societies: Moral and Rational Economic Approaches—A Symposium. *Journal of Asian Studies* 42:753–68.

Kim, Chan-Jin

1982   Legal Aspects of Private Foreign Investment in Korea. In *Business Laws in Korea: Investment, Taxation and Industrial Property,* ed. Chan-Jin Kim, pp. 141–204. Seoul: Panmun Book.

Kim, Choong Soon

1972   Life Patterns of Pulpwood Workers in a South Georgia Community. Ph.D. diss., University of Georgia.

1974   The Yon'jul-hon or Chain-String Form of Marriage Arrangement in Korea. *Journal of Marriage and the Family* 36:575–79.

1977   *An Asian Anthropologist in the South: Field Experiences with Blacks, Indians, and Whites.* Knoxville, Tenn.: University of Tennessee Press.

1987   Can an Anthropologist Go Home Again? *American Anthropologist* 89:943–45.

1988a   *Faithful Endurance: An Ethnography of Korean Family Dispersal.* Tucson: University of Arizona Press.

1988b   An Anthropological Perspective on Filial Piety Versus Social Security. In *Between Kinship and the State: Social Security and Law in Developing Countries,* ed. Von Benda-Beckmann et al., pp. 125–35. Dordrecht, Holland: Foris Publications.

1989   Attribute of "Asexuality" in Korean Kinship and Sundered Koreans during the Korean War. *Journal of Comparative Family Studies* 20:309–25.

1990   The Role of the Non-Western Anthropologist Reconsidered: Illusion versus Reality. *Current Anthropology* 31:196–201.

Kim, Choong Soon, and Wilfrid C. Bailey

1971   *Community Factors in Productivity of Pulpwood Harvesting Operations.* Atlanta: American Pulpwood Association Harvesting Research Project.

Kim, Dong Ki, and Chong W. Kim

1989   Korean Value Systems and Managerial Practices. In *Korean Managerial Dynamics,* ed. Kae H. Chung and Hak Chong Lee, pp. 207–16. New York: Praeger.

Kim, Duk Choong

1986   Role of Entrepreneurs in Korea. In *Toward Higher Productivity,* ed. D. K. Kim, pp. 51–64. Tokyo: Asian Productivity Center.

Kim, Jay S., and Chan K. Hahn
1989   The Korean Chaebol as an Organizational Form. In *Korean Managerial Dynamics*, ed. Kae H. Chung and Hak Chong Lee, pp. 51–64. New York: Praeger.

Kim, Kwang Suk, and Michael Roemer
1979   *Growth and Structural Transformation*. Cambridge: Council on East Asian Studies, Harvard University.

Kim Kyong-Dong
1988   *Nosagwangae-ŭi Sahoehak [The Sociology of Labor-Management]*. Seoul: Kyŏngmun-sa.

Kim, Linsu
1989   Technological Transformation of Korean Firms. In *Korean Managerial Dynamics*, ed. Kae H. Chung and Hak Chong Lee, pp. 113–29. New York: Praeger.

Kim Man-hum
1989   Yuk'gong, Tŏuk Kip'ŏjin Chiyŏk Kamjŏng [The Sixth Republic, the Deepened Regional Sentiment]. *Shin Don-A* 336:288–97.

Kim, Seung-Kyung
1989   The Catholic Church and the Labor Movement in Masan, Korea. Paper presented at the 88th Annual Meeting of the American Anthropological Association, Washington, D.C., 15–19 November 1989.

Kim Taik-kyoo
1964   *Tongjokburak-ŭi Saengwhalgujo Yŏngu [The Cultural Structure of a Consanguineous Village]*. Taegu: Ch'ŏnggu University Press.
1979   *Ssijokburak-ŭi Kujo Yŏngu [The Structure of a Korean Clan Village]*. Seoul: Iljogak.

Kim, Yŏl-kyu
1981   *Han'maekwŏnru [The Roots of Han]*. Seoul: Chu'u.

Kim, Yung-chung, ed. and trans.
1979   *Women of Korea: A History from Ancient Times to 1945*. Seoul: Ewha Womans University Press.

Koh, Yang Kon
1983   An Exploratory Study on Filial Support and the Use of Formal Services among the Korean Aged in New York. Ph.D. diss., Florida State University.

Koo, Hagen
1987   The Interplay of State, Social Class, and World System in East Asian Development: The Cases of South Korea and Taiwan. In *The Political Economy of the New Asian Industrialism*, ed. Frederic C. Deyo, pp. 165–81. Ithaca: Cornell University Press.
1990   From Farm to Factory: Proletarianization in Korea. *American Sociological Review* 55:669–81.

Krueger, Anne O.
   1979   *The Developmental Role of the Foreign Sector and Aid.*
           Cambridge: Council on East Asian Studies, Harvard University.
Lee Hak Chong
   1989a   *Kiŏp Munhwa-ron [Corporate Culture].* Seoul: Pŏmun-sa.
   1989b   Managerial Characteristics of Korean Firms. In *Korean
           Managerial Dynamics,* ed. Kae H. Chung and Hak Chong Lee,
           pp. 147–62. New York: Praeger.
Lee, Jeong-Taik
   1987   Economic Development and Industrial Order in South Korea.
           Ph.D. diss., University of Hawaii.
Lee, Ki-baik
   1984   *A New History of Korea,* trans. Edward W. Wagner and Edward J.
           Shultz. Cambridge: Harvard University Press.
Lee Kwang-kyu
   1983   *Han'guk Kajok-ŭi Sajŏk Yŏngu [A Historical Study of the Korean
           Family].* Seoul: Ilchi-sa.
Lee, Sang M.
   1989   Management Styles of Korean Chaebols. In *Korean Managerial
           Dynamics,* ed. Kae H. Chung and Hak Chong Lee, pp. 181–92.
           New York: Praeger.
Lee Wŏn Tŏk
   1988   Han'guk-ŭi Imgŭmgujo Punsŏk [Analysis of Korean Wage
           Structure]. *Sasang-gwa Chŏngch'aek [Ideology and Policy]*
           Summer:71–72.
Leggrett, John C.
   1963   Uprootedness and Working-Class Consciousness. *American
           Journal of Sociology* 68:682–92.
Lenski, Gerhard
   1966   *Power and Privilege.* New York: McGraw-Hill.
Levy, Marion J., Jr.
   1966   *Modernization and the Structure of Society.* Princeton:
           Princeton University Press.
Lewis, W. Arthur
   1966   *Development Planning: The Essentials of Economic Policy.* New
           York: Harper and Row.
Lim, Youngil
   1981   *Government Policy and Private Enterprise: Korean Experience in
           Industrialization.* Berkeley: Institute of East Asian Studies,
           University of California.
Lincoln, James R., and Kerry McBride
   1987   Japanese Organization in Contemporary Perspective. *Annual
           Review of Sociology* 13:289–312.

Luthans, F., et al.
  1985   Organizational Commitment: A Comparison of American, Japanese, and Korean Employees. *Academy of Management Journal* 28:213–19.

McNamara, Dennis
  1988   Entrepreneurship in Colonial Korea: Kim Youn-su. *Modern Asian Studies* 22:165–77.
  1989   The Keisho and the Korean Business Elite. *Journal of Asian Studies* 48:310–23.
  1990   *The Colonial Origins of Korean Enterprise, 1910–1945.* New York: Cambridge University Press.

Maine, Henry Sumner
  1965   *Ancient Law.* New York: Dutton.

Marsh, Robert M., and Hiroshi Mannari
  1976   *Modernization and the Japanese Factory.* Princeton: Princeton University Press.

Maruyama, Magoroh
  1969   Epistemology of Social Science Research: Explorations Inculture Researchers. *Dialectica* 23:229–80.

Mason, Edward S., et al.
  1980   *The Economic and Social Modernization of the Republic of Korea.* Cambridge: Council on East Asian Studies, Harvard University.

Ministry of Agriculture and Fisheries
  1988   *Basic Statistics on Agriculture, 1988.* Seoul: Ministry of Agriculture and Fisheries, Republic of Korea.

Nakane, Chie
  1970   *Japanese Society.* Berkeley: University of California Press.

National Bureau of Statistics
  1988a   *Korea Statistical Year Book, 1988.* Seoul: Economic Planning Board, Republic of Korea.
  1988b   *Social Indicators in Korea, 1988.* Seoul: Economic Planning Board, Republic of Korea.
  1989   *Monthly Statistics of Korea, 1989.* Seoul: Economic Planning Board, Republic of Korea.

Ohnuki-Tierney, Emiko
  1984a   Native Anthropologists. *American Ethnologist* 11:584–86.
  1984b   *Illness and Culture in Contemporary Japan.* New York: Cambridge University Press.

Osgood, Cornelius
  1951   *The Koreans and Their Culture.* New York: Ronald Press.

Ouchi, William G.
  1981   *Theory Z.* Reading, Mass.: Addison-Wesley.

Park Kee Dong
  1978   Kiŏp Kyŏngyŏng-ae Ittŏsŏ Nepotism-ae Kwanhan Yŏngu
          [Nepotism and Business Management]. *Sahoe Munhwa
          Non'ch'ong [Journal of Culture and Society]* 1:53–83.
Park Pong-hyŏn
  1989   Nojo-ŭi Makhu Saerŏk-ŭl Pŏtginda [Behind the Force of the
          Labor Union]. *Chosun*, March 1989:346–61.
Parsons, Talcott
  1937   *The Structure of Social Action*. New York: Free Press.
  1951   *The Social System*. New York: Free Press.
Peacock, James L.
  1986   *The Anthropological Lens: Harsh Light, Soft Focus*. New York:
          Cambridge University Press.
Perkins, Dwight H.
  1986   *China: Asia's Next Economic Giant?* Seattle: University of
          Washington Press.
Peterson, Mark
  1974   Adoption in Korean Genealogies: Continuation of Lineage. *Korea
          Journal* 14:28–35.
Powdermaker, Hortense
  1966   *Stranger and Friend: The Way of an Anthropologist*. New York:
          Norton.
Redfield, Robert
  1947   The Folk Society. *American Journal of Sociology* 52:293–308.
Reischauer, Edwin O., and John K. Fairbank
  1960   *East Asia: The Great Tradition*. Boston: Houghton Mifflin.
Reynolds, Lloyd
  1951   *The Structure of Labor Markets*. New York: Harper.
Robinson, Michael Edison
  1988   *Cultural Nationalism in Colonial Korea, 1920–1925*. Seattle:
          University of Washington Press.
Rohlen, Thomas P.
  1973   "Spiritual Education" in a Japanese Bank. *American
          Anthropologist* 75:1542–62.
  1974   *For Harmony and Strength: Japanese White-Collar Organization
          in Anthropological Perspective*. Berkeley: University of
          California Press.
Ryan, Angela Shen
  1965   Cultural Factors in Casework with Chinese-Americans. *Social
          Casework: The Journal of Contemporary Social Work* 66:333–40.
Sahlins, Marshall D., and Elman R. Service
  1960   *Evolution and Culture*. Ann Arbor: University of Michigan
          Press.

Sasaki, N.
  1981   *Management and Industrial Structure in Japan.* New York:
          Pergamon.
Sayigh, Y. A.
  1962   *Entrepreneurs of Lebanon.* Cambridge: Harvard University Press.
Sayles, Myrna
  1978   Behind Locked Doors. In *Applied Anthropology in America,* ed.
          E. Eddy and W. L. Partridge, pp. 201–28. New York: Columbia
          University Press.
Serrie, Hendrick
  1976   Constancy and Variation in Chinese Culture: An Analysis of
          Fourteen Mainland, Offshore, and Overseas Communities in
          Terms of the Hsu Attributes. Ph.D. diss., Northwestern
          University.
  1986   Chinese Business Management Behavior and the Hsu Attributes:
          A Preliminary Inquiry. In *Anthropology and International
          Business,* ed. H. Serrie, pp. 59–71. Studies in Third World
          Societies, Publication No. 28. Williamsburg, Va.: Department of
          Anthropology, College of William and Mary.
Shepard, Jon M., et al.
  1979   Effects of Technology in Industrialized and Industrializing
          Societies. *Sociology of Work and Occupations* 6:457–81.
Shin Yoo Keun
  1986   *Han'guk Kiŏpŭi T'ŭksŏng-gwa Kwajae [Characteristics and
          Tasks of Korean Business Enterprises].* Seoul: Seoul National
          University Press.
Shin Young Ja et al.
  1988   *Yŏsŏng Kŭnroja-ŭi Chŏngnyŏn-ae Kwanhan Yŏngu [A Study on
          the Retirement System for Female Workers].* Seoul: Han'guk
          Yŏsŏng Kaebal Won [The Center for the Development of Korean
          Women].
Silin, Robert H.
  1976   *Leadership and Values: The Organization of Large-Scale
          Taiwanese Enterprises.* Cambridge: East Asian Research Center,
          Harvard University.
Son Chong-sok
  1984   Chŏngnyŏn Chŏng'ch'aek-gwa Kwanyŏnjaedo [Policies on
          Retirement System]. In *Sanŏpsahoe-wa Chŏngnyŏn
          [Industrializing Society and Retirement],* ed. Chŏng Chu-yŏng,
          pp. 374–85. Seoul: Asanpokji Saŏpjaedan.
Song, Byung-Nak
  1977   The Production Structure of Korean Economy: International and
          Historical Comparison. *Econometrica* 45:147–62.

1988   Han'guk Kyŏngjae-ron [Korean Economy]. Seoul: Paekyŏng-sa.

Sorensen, Clark W.
1985   Patterns of Misinformation in South Korean Fieldwork. Paper
        presented at the Eighty-fourth Annual Meeting of the American
        Anthropological Association, Washington, D.C., 4–8 December.
1988   *Over the Mountains Are Mountains: Korean Peasant
        Households During Rapid Industrialization.* Seattle: University
        of Washington Press.

Spencer, Barbara G., et al.
1975   *Choctaw Demographic Survey.* Philadelphia, Miss.: Mississippi
        Band of Choctaw Indians.

Spencer, Robert F.
1988   *Yokong: Factory Girl.* Seoul: Royal Asiatic Society, Korean
        Branch.

Steers, Richard M., et al.
1989   *The Chaebol: Korea's New Industrial Might.* New York: Harper
        & Row, Publisher.

Steinberg, David I.
1989   *The Republic of Korea: Economic Transformation and Social
        Change.* Boulder, Colo.: Westview Press.

Strathern, Andrew
1983   Research in Papua New Guinea: Cross-Currents of Conflict.
        Royal Anthropological Institute News 58:4–10.

Sumiya, Mikio
1991   Japan: Model Society of the Future? *The Annals of the American
        Academy of Political and Social Science* 513:139–50.

Tai, Hung-chao
1989   The Oriental Alternative: A Hypothesis on Culture and
        Economy. In *Confucianism and Economic Development: An
        Oriental Alternative?* ed. Hung-chao Tai, pp. 6–37. Washington,
        D.C.: Washington Institute for Values in Public Policy.

Taira, Koji
1962   Characteristics of Japanese Labor Markets. *Economic
        Development and Cultural Change* 10:150–68.

T'ak Hŭi-jun
1984   Chŏngnyŏnjaedo-ŭi Hyŏnhwang-gwa Munjaejŏm [Current
        Practice and Problems of the Retirement System]. In
        *Sanŏpsahoe-wa Chŏngnyŏn [Industrializing Society and
        Retirement]*, ed. Chŏng Chu-yŏng, pp. 31–41. Seoul: Asanpokji
        Saŏpjaedan.

Tönnies, Ferdinand
1963   *Community and Society,* ed. and trans. Charles P. Loomis. New
        York: Harper Torchbooks.

Trotsky, Leon
  n.d.   *The History of the Russian Revolution.* Ann Arbor: University of
          Michigan Press.
Tu, Wei-ming
  1976   *Neo-Confucian Thoughts in Action: Wang Yang-ming's Youth
          (1472–1509).* Berkeley: University of California Press.
  1984   *Confucian Ethics Today: The Singapore Challenge.* Singapore:
          Federal Publications.
Veblen, Thorstein
  1915   *Imperial Germany and the Industrial Revolution.* New York:
          Macmillan.
Vogel, Ezra F.
  1975   *Modern Japanese Organization and Decision-Making.* Berkeley:
          University of California Press.
von Glinow, Mary Ann, and Byung Jae Chung
  1989   Korean Chaebols and the Changing Business Environment. In
          Korean Managerial Dynamics, ed. Kae H. Chung and Hak Chong
          Lee, pp. 27–38. New York: Praeger.
Wade, Larry L., and Bong-Sik Kim
  1978   *Economic Development of South Korea: The Political Economy
          of Success.* New York: Praeger.
Weber, Max
  1946   *From Max Weber: Essays in Sociology,* ed. and trans. Hans H.
          Gerth and C. Wright Mills. New York: Oxford University Press.
  1951   *The Religion of China.* New York: The Free Press.
  1957   *The Theory of Social and Economic Organization,* trans. A. H.
          Henderson and Talcott Parsons. New York: Free Press of
          Glencoe.
Westphal, Larry E.
  1978   The Republic of Korea's Experience with Export-Led Industrial
          Development. *World Development* 6:347–82.
Willigen, John, and Richard Soffle
  1986   The Americanization of Shoyu: American Workers and a
          Japanese Employment System. In *Anthropology and
          International Business,* ed. H. Serrie, pp. 125–62. Studies in
          Third World Societies, Publication No. 28. Williamsburg, Va.:
          Department of Anthropology, College of William and Mary.
Winckler, Edwin
  1984   Industrialization and Participation for Taiwan: From Hard to Soft
          Authoritarianism? *China Quarterly* 99:481–99.
World Bank
  1989   *World Development Report 1989.* New York: Oxford University
          Press.

Woronoff, Jon
  1983   *Korea's Economy: Man-Made Miracle.* Seoul: The Si-sa-yong-
          o-sa.
Yang, Key P., and Gregory Henderson
  1958   An Outline of Korean Confucianism. *Journal of Asian Studies*
          18:81–101.
Yoo, Sangjin, and Sang M. Lee
  1987   Management Style and Practice of Korean Chaebols. *California
          Management Review.* Summer:95–110.
Yoshino, M. Y.
  1968   *Japan's Managerial System: Tradition and Innovation.*
          Cambridge, Mass.: MIT Press.

Index

Abegglen, James C., 133
Adelman, Irma, 6
Affective model, 213, 215; of the Orient, 200
Age: attitude of workers by, 168, 183; in determining wage, 101; hierarchical order by, 169; of management, 74; of marriage for females, 146; in promotion, 109, 210–11; of retirement, 118, 140–41, 147, 184; social relations of workers by, 166, 168; of union organizers, 180
Amsden, Alice H., 7, 18–20, 99–100, 174, 183, 196, 207, 218
Ancestor's shadow, 41, 43–44, 50
Ancestor worship (*chaesa*), 203
Antigovernment demonstration(s), 12, 24, 59, 178
Authoritarianism: of *chaebŏl*, 65; in management, 214; resentment of, 205

Baba, Marietta L., 21, 27
Backwardness, 6, 220
Bacon, Margaret K., 170, 191
Bae, Kyuhan, 14, 23, 92, 108, 164, 170, 177, 194, 214–15
Bank of Korea, 11
Barry, Herbert, III, 170, 191
Befu, Harumi, 203
Bendix, Reinhard, 200, 212–13, 215
Benedict, Ruth, 208
Benjamin, Roger, 171, 197
Blue-collar workers: activities in work setting of, 149, 155; attitude toward union, 183; attitude toward white-collar workers, 167; characteristics of, 69; comradeship among, 164; filial support of, 141; interaction among, 157; Japanese, 96, 103, 200; midnight shift of, 168; negative

image of, 167; number of, 23;
promotion of, 111, 115, 168;
recruitment of, 89; retirement
age of, 141; shortage of, 83, 85–
86; social stigma attached to,
167; training of, 119, 131; wage
of, 103–4, 107, 208; working
hours of, 155
Boas, Franz, 21
Bond, Michael Harris, 4
Brandt, Vincent S. R., 22, 26–27,
30, 33, 139, 212, 217
Burmeister, Larry L., 176

Cafeteria, seating in, 153
Calder, Kent E., 171, 197
Calvinism, 15
Chaebŏl (business conglomerate),
49, 58–59, 62–63, 68, 73, 86–
88, 116, 130–31, 186, 193, 196;
affiliation(s) of, 53; authoritarian rule of, 65; business
ethics of, 54, 194–96;
categorical treatment of, 195;
characteristics of, 52–53, 65;
criticism against, 53, 194;
definition of, 52–53; diversified
business operations of, 52, 58,
194–95; founding of, 49, 65;
governmental favors for, 194;
growth of, 83; informal organizations of, 160; managerial
behavior of, 65; marriage
patterns of, 77
Chang, Chan Sup, 151
Chang In-sŏk, 77
Chang Myŏn, 11, 19, 174
Chang, Yunshik, 81–82
Chen, Yu-hsi, 171, 197
Child, Irvin L., 170, 191
Cho, Dong Sung, 53
Cho Kang Hi, 76
Cho, Soon-Kyoung, 133, 197
Choi, In-hak, 13, 78
Choi, Jang Jip, 6, 173–74, 176–77,
179, 197, 212, 216

Choi Kyu Ha, 12
Choi Sŏk-ch'ae, 141
Chŏn Ki-ho, 172–75, 178
Chŏn'nohyŏp, 196
Chosŏn dynasty, 5. See also Yi
dynasty
Chosŏn Nodongjohap Chŏnguk
P'yŏngŭihoe (Chŏn'p'yŏng), 173
Chun Doo Hwan, 12, 36, 45, 58–
59, 177
Chung, Byung Jae, 21
Chung, Kae H., 6, 22, 172
Chung, Young-iob, 14, 208, 220
Ch'usŏk (harvest festival), 78
Class endogamy, 76
Cold War, 10, 173
Cole, Robert E., 92, 96, 101, 103–4,
106, 118, 132–33, 135–37, 146,
160, 169–70, 200, 208, 215,
221
Collective bargaining, 96, 173,
181, 183–85, 204, 213
Company housing. See Housing,
company
Company motto, 64, 89, 112, 120,
166
Confucianism, 13, 25, 35, 57, 86,
117, 129–30, 167, 199, 206,
213; age grade in, 211; critics
of, 14, 34; economic
development and, 5, 13; ethics
of, 14, 22, 27, 57–58, 64, 177,
193, 210, 215, 217; family in,
15, 213; heritage of, 4, 57, 171–
72, 192, 197–98, 211; hidden,
unconscious Confucian, 58, 62;
impact of, 5, 13–15, 108, 204–
5, 220; indoctrination into, 57,
131; philosophy of, 13, 56;
politicized, 58, 64; positive
aspects of, 5, 14, 64, 128; status
in, 85, 205; teachings of, 4, 13,
75, 125, 208, 211; two faces of,
14; values of, 5, 14–15, 103,
108, 131, 213; virtues of, 55, 57,
64, 128; workers and, 108, 213;

worthies of, 57, 124. *See also* Neo-Confucianism
Connection-hiring, 75, 88, 91, 93–98; kin network for, 87, 210; traditional form of, 217. *See also* Employment; Hiring
Constitution, 145, 173, 183, 219
Consumption patterns, 193, 220
Contingency theory, 22
Convergence theory, 22–23, 215–16
Corporate culture, 62–64
Covell, Alan Carter, 201
Cultural nationalism, 16, 19, 52
Cultural nationalists, 16–17, 19, 21, 32, 130
Cumings, Bruce, 6, 10, 17, 173, 214, 221

Demilitarized Zone (DMZ), 11
Deyo, Frederic C., 172, 192, 197, 212
Dismissal of employees, 137, 140. *See also* Termination
Diversification of business, 51–53, 195; ethics of, 54; octopus tentacles (*mun'ŏbal*) of, 54, 58, 60, 194
Divorce, 75
Docility of workers, 111, 132, 171, 191; cultural heritage of, 171, 197; demographic patterns of, 168–69, 170, 197; political control and, 197–98, 211, 217; reasons for, 111–12, 213
Dodd, N. G., 70
Dore, Ronald, 208
Dual economic structure: in Japan, 96, 133; in Korea, 96
Durkheim, Emile, 199

Eckert, Carter Joel, 4–5, 15–20, 41, 58, 130, 184, 194
Education, level of, 70, 72, 88, 92, 101–6, 108–9, 112, 182; attitude toward union and, 183;

colonial rule and, 18; of entrepreneurs, 62–64; of management, 73; for promotion, 112; in social interaction, 164; of union organizers, 180; wages and, 106, 108, 180
Eisenstadt, S. N., 200
Employment, 22, 98, 117, 138; connections and, 93, 95; by examination, 85, 88, 95; manner of, 93, 95; marriage and, 146–47; nationally, 83, 85, 133; policy of, 96; of retirees, 142. *See also* Connection-hiring; Hiring; *Kongch'ae*
Employment security, 118. *See also* Job security
Entrepreneurs: background of, 19, 22, 32, 60–62, 64, 87; criticism of, 58, 195; ethics of, 28, 31, 51, 60; first generation of, 32, 65; governmental support for, 194; in Korea, 50, 87; managerial philosophy of, 19, 22, 28, 51; origin of, 42, 62, 64, 82; patriotism of, 52
Equal Employment Opportunity Act (EEOA), 145
Erikson, Erik, 169

Fairbank, John K., 13
Family: analogy in management, 117, 137, 213; collective bargaining and, 213; inheritance of business, 66; participation in business, 112; sexual discrimination in, 207; workers' view of, 193
Fei, John, 192
Female employees: in company cafeteria, 153; discrimination against, 105, 108, 146, 197, 207; in labor movement, 197; in managerial positions, 72, 207; in manufacturing, 146; retirement of, 145–46, 165,

207; rural development of, 81;
semi-lifetime employment and,
219; social interaction of, 153,
159, 164–65; training of, 120–23.
See also Women, as employees
Fictional kin, 50
Fieldwork, anthropological, 3–4,
    23–24, 55, 62, 70, 82, 90, 100,
    112, 117, 123, 137, 157, 160,
    171, 186, 207; at home, 26–27;
    identity of fieldworker, 24–25,
    27
Filial piety, 13, 56, 78, 176
Filial support by workers, 70, 141,
    143, 145, 147, 206
Five-year economic development
    plan(s), 12, 19, 23, 27, 38, 42,
    45, 174
Foreign Capital Inducement Act
    (FCIA), 38
Foreman: appointment of, 156,
    211; role of, 157
Form, William, 23, 108, 215
Fringe benefit(s), 15, 86, 88, 97,
    163, 213–14

Gallin, Barnard, 192
Gallin, Rita, 192
Geertz, Clifford, 62
Gerschenkron, Alexander, 6, 220
Giovannini, Maureen, J., 21
Grajdanzev, Andrew J., 173
Greenhouse, Carol J., 25
Gusfield, Joseph, 199

Hahm Pyong-choon, 174
Hahn, Chan K., 52
Hahoe, village of, 30–37, 43, 55–
    57, 60, 68, 76, 124, 129
Hamabata, Matthews Masayuki,
    26
Hamilton, Richard F., 170, 192
Han (bitterness and anger), 4–5,
    15–16, 18, 31, 36, 69, 143, 172
Handlin, Oscar, 192

Harmony (*inhwa*), 4–5, 206; goals
    of, 132; between labor and
    management, 176; stress on, 4,
    166; theme of, in training, 131,
    166
Harvey, Youngsook Kim, 201
Hasan, Parvez, 6
Hashimoto, M., 207
Hatada, Takashi, 30
Hattori Tamio, 27, 65, 88, 114
Henderson, Gregory, 10, 13
Hideyoshi, Toyotomi: invasion of
    Korea by, 10, 31, 43
Hiring: of blue-collar workers, 89;
    by connections, 87–88, 92–93,
    98; falsified credentials in, 136;
    of kin member, 205; by
    kongch'ae, 87, 90, 120, 140;
    labor instigators and, 89; role of
    the founder in, 205. *See also*
    Connection-hiring; Employ-
    ment; *Kongch'ae*
Historical particularism, 8, 21
Ho, Samuel P. S., 6
Hobby club(s), 164–65. *See also*
    Informal organization(s)
Hofheinz, Roy, Jr., 171, 197
Hofstede, Geert, 4
Holzberg, Carol S., 21
Homma-True, Reiko, 143
Houghland, James G., Jr., 23
Housing, company, 70, 79, 102–3,
    180, 206: for blue- and white-
    collar workers, 162–63;
    demand for, 163
Hsu, Francis L. K., 13, 65, 203, 213
Huhm, Halla Pai, 201
Hwang, In-Joung, 176

Industrial accident(s), 44–45, 184,
    202; cost of, 119
Industrial anthropology, 27
Industrial ethnography, 21, 221
Industrial culture, 21; of Korea,
    28; of Poongsan, 23, 199

Industrial relations, 15, 28, 117; Confucian ethics and, 57; pillar of, 99, 209; rules for, 4–5, 148
Informal organization(s), 158–61, 164–65, 199
Inheritance of business, 65–66
Innovation: definition of, 7; indigenous sources of, 8, 39
Inside anthropologist, 24, 26, 27
Invention, Korean, 7, 39
Interaction, social: among blue-collar employees, 157; between blue- and white-collar employees, 164; patterns of, 166; between superiors and subordinates, 153; among white-collar employees, 152, 155

Jackall, Robert, 25
Jacobs, Norman, 200
Janelli, Dawnhee Yim, 13, 78
Janelli, Roger L., 13, 26, 78
Japanese influence: on authoritarian management, 214; in colonial era, 6, 10–11, 16, 104, 214; on infrastructure of industrialization, 6; by invasion and annexation, 7–8, 10; as role model, 220–21; of *sŏwŏn* training, 128; through technology, 7, 221
Jeunesse Ouvrière Chrétienne (JOC), 177
Job categories, 71
Job opening(s), 83; applicants and, 83; for manual labor, 85; number of, 97
Job rotation, 209
Job security, 28, 96, 132–33, 209; feelings toward, 117; in large enterprises, 97
Jones, Leroy P., 6, 19, 41–43, 52, 60–63, 73, 103, 165
June 29 Proclamation, 12, 24, 82, 172, 178–79

Jung Ku Hyun, 23, 87

Kendall, Laurel, 4, 26, 201–3
Kerr, Clark, 22, 215
Kim, Bong-Sik, 6
Kim, Chan-Jin, 38
Kim, Chong W., 14, 216
Kim, Choong Soon, 11, 13, 15, 24–25, 65, 75, 143, 147, 174
Kim, Dong I., 23
Kim, Dong Ki, 14, 216
Kim, Duk Choong, 6
Kim, Jay S., 52
Kim, Kwang Suk, 6, 11, 18
Kim Kyong-Dong, 172–73
Kim, Linsu, 7–8, 18
Kim Man-hum, 42
Kim, Seung-Kyung, 178
Kim Taik-kyoo, 32–33
Kim, Yŏl-kyu, 4
Kim, Yung-chung, 75
Kinship: analogy of, 213; in business setting, 22–23, 65, 68, 88, 92, 114; collective bargaining and, 213; informal relations and, 51; power groups and, 51; promotion and, 113–14
Koh, Yang Kon, 143
Kongch'ae (standard hiring), 75, 86–92, 94–98, 120, 140, 217; history of, 86; interviews and, 88–89; turnover rate of, 87; university graduates and, 210. *See also* Employment; Hiring
Koo, Hagen, 6, 192
Korean Central Intelligence Agency (KCIA), 11, 45, 174, 176
Korean Christian Youth Association (KCYA), 221
Korean Development Institute (KDI), 120, 122; facilities of, 132; training center of, 123
Korean Institute of Science and Technology (KIST), 41–42

Korean War, 11, 13, 19–20, 38, 53,
    112, 169, 173, 214
Koryŏ dynasty, 32–33
Kosa (shamanistic ritual), of
    company, 200–204, 212
Krueger, Anne O., 6
Kuo, W. Y., 192
Kut (shamanistic ritual), 202. See
    also Kosa
Kyae (revolving credit society), 143
Kyŏngsang province, favoritism
    for, 42. See also Regional
    favoritism
Kyowŏn Nojo (Teachers' League),
    174

Labor aristocracy, 183, 195
Labor contract, 205. See also
    Collective bargaining
Labor Disputes Adjustment Act,
    183
Labor laws: in defense industries,
    184; revision of, 177–78;
    workers and, 183, 184
Labor-Management Council
    (Nosahyŏpŭihoe), 15, 177; aim
    of, 179; composition of, 179; as
    mechanism for communica-
    tion, 179; as substitute for labor
    union, 175
Labor-Management Council Law
    (Nosahyŏpŭihoe-bŏp), 175
Labor-management relations, 28,
    172, 180
Labor movement, 138–39, 171–
    73, 176, 183, 212
Labor shortage, 133; in
    manufacturing sectors, 96–97,
    146; in small and medium-
    sized firms, 96, 146
Labor strike(s), 50, 89, 95, 98, 132,
    161, 186, 206, 208; crackdown
    on, 195; in defense industries,
    188–89; instigators in, 92, 184,
    192; organizers of, 180, 184,
    190; at Poongsan, 179, 184–85,

    189, 211; prohibition of, 174;
    statistics on, 174; supporters of,
    184, 189
Labor turnover, 96, 134
Labor union(s), 24, 69, 91–92, 96,
    106, 138–39, 154, 160–62, 171,
    204; attitudes toward, 80, 158,
    182–84; government-patronized
    (ŏyong), 174; in Korea, 172, 198;
    leadership of, 183; membership
    of, 70, 80, 181; as political
    instrument, 173–75, 197;
    promotion and, 115; structure
    of, at Poongsan, 158, 179–82; of
    white-collar employees, 174;
    women and, 147
Land reform, 33
Late industrialization, 7, 99
Lateral movement, 137–39, 140
Lee Hak Chong, 22, 51, 63
Lee, Jeong-Taik, 192
Lee, Ki-baik, 10, 16, 35
Lee Kwang-kyu, 75
Lee, Man-Gap, 60, 61
Lee, Sang M., 52
Lee Wŏn Tŏk, 104
Leggrett, John C., 170, 192
Length of service, 70, 164–65,
    182; attitude toward union by,
    183; for bonus, 167; for
    promotion, 109–11, 115; wage
    and, 101; of women, 74
Lenski, Gerhard, 169
Levy, Marion J., Jr., 199
Lie, Harry K., 172
Lifetime employment, 132–36,
    207–8, 219; definition of, 118,
    132; guarantee of, 133; Japanese
    practice of, 118, 133, 207;
    partial, 134, 135
Lim, Youngil, 6, 41, 53
Lincoln, James R., 206–7
Luthans, F., 70

McBride, Kerry, 206–7
McCaul, H. S., 70

McNamara, Dennis, 41
Maine, Henry Sumner, 199
Managerial worldview, 28, 30, 55, 57, 63, 64; Confucian ethics and, 58
March First Movement (Samil Undong), 16
Marital status, 70, 75, 108, 165, 182, 183
Marriage, arranged, 76–77
Maruyama, Magoroh, 25
Mask dancing, 33, 124–26, 130–31
Mason, Edward S., 6, 11, 41
Migration, rural to urban, 80–81, 133
Military coup in 1961, 11, 19, 174
Military service: age and, 74; exemption from, 74, 80, 96; role of, 214; of union organizers, 180
Mint of Korea, 40
Motto, company, 64, 89, 112, 120, 166

Nakane, Chie, 162
National General Mobilization Law of Japan, 37
National Manpower Mobilization of Japan, 36
Native anthropologist, 24, 26, 27
Nenkō joretsu chingin (length-of-service wage and promotion), 99, 101, 108–9, 132
Neo-Confucianism, 5, 13, 50, 56–57, 113–14, 124. See also Confucianism
Neo-elite endogamy, 77
New Factory Movement (Kongjang Saemaŭl Undong), 15, 176–77, 206
New Village Movement (Saemaŭl Undong), 19, 176
Noch'ong, 174
Nohyŏp, 174

Ohnuki-Tierney, Emiko, 24
Organizational culture of Poongsan, 22, 57, 200, 204, 209, 212, 217; impact of Confucianism in, 204–5
Organizational structure of Poongsan, 46, 48
Organization of Petroleum Exporting Countries (OPEC), 89, 136, 207
Origins: of employees (ponjŏk), 74, 80, 90, 182; of union organizers, 180
Osgood, Cornelius, 13, 30
Ouchi, William G., 170, 191, 209, 211
Overtime, 56, 155
Oyabun-kobun, of Japanese, 92

Pacific Rim, 21, 28
Park Chung Hee, 11–12, 18–19, 32, 42–45, 52, 59, 61, 67, 174, 176–77, 179, 195
Park Kee Dong, 113
Park Pong-hyŏn, 176
Parsons, Talcott, 210, 213
Partial lifetime employment, 134, 135. See also Lifetime employment
Paternalism, 15, 206, 213
Peacock, James L., 22
Penalty of taking the lead, 28, 220
Pension system, 141
Perkins, Dwight H., 14
Permanent employment, 132–33, 136. See also Lifetime employment
Peterson, Mark, 13
Pohang Iron and Steel Company, Ltd. (POSCO), 7–8, 39, 118, 221
Political economy, 23; colonial origin of, 214; government and business in, 23, 41, 58
Population of Korea, 62, 79, 142
Powdermaker, Hortense, 26
Privilege of backwardness, 6, 220

Promotion, 22, 28–29, 117, 120,
     133, 138, 209; for blue-collar
     workers, 110–11, 114–15, 168;
     connections and, 113–14, 205;
     determinants of, 109–12;
     influence of executives on, 114,
     205; of Japanese workers, 109;
     of management, 113; new
     challenges for, 115, 219; of non-
     university graduates, 112–13;
     organizational factors for, 109;
     penalty for, 111; procedure for,
     75, 115; for white-collar
     employees, 110–11, 114–16, 168
Provincial favoritism, 42. *See also*
     Regional favoritism
Puritan ethic, 15
Pyŏngsan Sŏwŏn (Confucian
     academy), 55, 57, 120, 124, 128

Quality control, 70

Raise, 106, 108
Raisian, J., 207
Ranis, Gustav, 192
Rao, D. C., 6
Rational model, 213, 215; of the
     West, 200
Recreation program of company,
     155
Recruitment: connections in, 68,
     98, 210; of executives, 67, 210;
     kin network and, 68–69;
     kongch'ae and, 88; nationally,
     68, 83; scholarships in, 85
Redfield, Robert, 199
Regional favoritism, 42, 43, 61, 75,
     91
Regional tie (*chiyŏn*), 50, 51
Reischauer, Edwin O., 13
Religious preference, 61–62, 70,
     79–80, 91, 165, 203; workers
     and Confucian values, 213
Research and development, 54, 70,
     88; investing in, 54, 194

Retention rate(s), 96; of *kongch'ae*
     employees, 97
Retirement, 28; age of, 73, 118,
     140–43, 145–47, 180–81, 207;
     marriage and, 146, 165; pension
     for, 141, 143–44; preparation
     for, 40; of women, 74, 146
Reverse engineering, 8
Reynolds, Lloyd, 92
Rhee, Syngman, 11, 19, 173–74
Robinson, Michael Edison, 15–17,
     19
Roemer, Michael, 6, 11, 18
Rohlen, Thomas P., 57, 83, 85,
     121–23, 126, 137, 146, 151,
     169–70, 191
Roh Tae Woo, 12, 36, 58, 61, 178,
     196
Rotō, of Japanese, 122, 126
Russo-Japanese War, 10
Ryan, Angela Shen, 143
Ryu clan, 32, 37, 55–56, 68–69,
     76, 87; financial assistance to,
     205; involvement in business
     of, 56, 65; reputation of, 130
Ryu Sŏng-nyong (Sŏae), 31–32,
     43–44, 55, 56, 69, 125

Sadae (serving the great), 34–35
Safety, 119. *See also* Industrial
     accident(s)
Sahlins, Marshall D., 6, 215, 220
Sakong, Il, 6, 19, 41–43, 52, 60–
     63, 73, 103, 165
Salary, 141. *See also* Wage rate
Sasaki, N., 206
Savings, 143, 220
Sayigh, Y. A., 62
Sayles, Myrna, 26
School tie (*hakyŏn*), 50–51, 59
Semi-lifetime employment, 207,
     219. *See also* Lifetime
     employment
Senpai-kohai (senior-junior), of
     Japanese, 50, 92

Serrie, Hendrick, 65, 206
Service, Elman R., 6, 215, 220
Shamanism, 200–204, 212
Shepard, Jon M., 23, 215
Shift system, 78, 156–57, 162;
    of blue-collar workers, 155,
    168
Shin Yoo Keun, 6–7, 38, 53, 66, 74,
    99, 169
Shin Young Ja, 146
Silin, Robert H., 152
Silla, dynasty of, 57
Sino-Japanese War, 173
Sŏae Memorial Foundation, 55
Sŏae Yongu (study of Sŏae), 55
Social interaction(s), 28, 148
Social relations, 28; factors of,
    166; between superiors and
    subordinates, 151
Sŏdang (private school for
    yangban youth), 36, 63
Soffle, Richard, 170, 191
Sŏnbae-hubae (senior-junior), 50–
    51
Son Chong-sok, 145
Song, Byung-Nak, 18, 192
Sorensen, Clark W., 25–26, 216
Sŏwŏn (Confucian academy), 57,
    126–27, 130–31; facilities of,
    127; function of, 124; origin of,
    57
Sŏwŏn training, 15, 25, 57, 120,
    122–23, 125–27, 130, 132;
    concept of, 131; curriculum of,
    126–27, 129; for middle
    management, 123, 205, 212;
    Japanese influence on, 128. *See
    also* Training
Spencer, Robert E., 27, 69
Steers, Richard M., 5–7, 14, 53, 99,
    216
Steinberg, David I., 6, 216
Strathern, Andrew, 26
Student revolution of 1960, 11
Sumiya, Mikio, 5

Ta Ming Lü, 75
Taehan Tongrip Ch'oksŏng Nodong
    Yŏnmaeng (Noch'ong), 173
Tai, Hung-chao, 57, 200, 213, 215,
    217, 220
Taira, Koji, 133
T'ak, Hŭi-jun, 141
Termination of employment, 89;
    avoidance of, 117, 136;
    conditions for, 135; of female
    employees, 207; financial
    exigency of, 135, 137; of
    temporary workers, 118
Test of English for International
    Communication (TOEIC), 111,
    119; for promotion, 111, 120
Three Kingdom period, 13
Tönnies, Ferdinand, 199
Training, 22, 24, 28, 118, 120,
    122–23, 128; for blue-collar
    workers, 119–20, 131; budget
    for, 122; categories of, 119–20;
    for female employees, 120–23;
    for foremen, 120; in Japanese
    firms, 121–22; in KDI, 120–21;
    for *kongch'ae* employees, 120;
    off the job, 120; on the job, 119,
    212, 131; promotion and, 111;
    for university graduates, 121;
    for white-collar employees,
    119, 131. *See also Sŏwŏn*
    training
Transfer of employees, 137–39,
    140
Trotsky, Leon, 6, 220
Tu, Wei-ming, 4, 13–15, 58, 62, 64,
    130–31

Ungson, Gerardo R, 6–7, 14, 53,
    99
Uniform, 71, 154; for production-
    line workers, 152
United States Army Military
    Government in Korea
    (USAMGIK), 10–11, 173

Uprootedness: from farm, 69, 170,
  191–92, 219; in industrial
  setting, 212
Urban Industrial Mission (UIM),
  177

Veblen, Thorstein, 215
Vietnam War, 20, 38, 214
Village festival (purak chae), 203
Village Self-Rule (nongch'on
  chach'i), 19
Vogel, Ezra F., 206
von Glinow, Mary Ann, 21

Wade, Larry L., 6
Wage hike, 99–101, 171, 181, 183–
  84, 195, 218, 221
Wage rate, 28, 100–102, 104, 140,
  143, 193–95, 206, 210, 220–21;
  of blue-collar workers, 100, 101,
  103–4, 107, 167–68;
  determining factors of, 101,
  103, 108, 210; by educational
  level, 101, 104–6, 108, 180;
  freeze of, 174; by gender, 105,
  108, 207; by job title and
  assignment, 105, 107; labor
  strikes and, 189, 208; protest
  against, 175; by rank (hobong),
  105–6; by size of firms, 104;
  standard wage, 101–3, 105–6,
  141; structure of, 102–3, 108–
  9; supplementary wage, 101–4;
  during training, 121; union
  negotiation of, 158; of white-
  collar employees, 100, 107
Weber, Max, 13–14, 199, 209
Westphal, Larry E., 6
White-collar employees: midnight
  shift of, 168; number of, 23;
promotion for, 111, 116, 168;
  rewards of, 103–4, 107, 208;
  supply of, 83–84, 86; union
  and, 183; in work setting, 149,
  154–55, 157
Wijang ch'wiŏp (employment
  under false credentials), 176,
  180
Willigen, John, 170, 191
Winckler, Edwin, 171, 197
Women, as employees: claims for
  equal rights for, 219; docility
  of, 197; promotion of, 219;
  rising position of, 219; termination of, 118; wage of, 219.
  See also Female employees
Working hours, 151
World War I, 133
World War II, 11, 15, 37, 112, 133,
  143, 173, 214
Woronoff, Jon, 12, 45

Yang, Key P., 13
Yang Seung Doo, 174
Yangban (nobility), 14, 30, 32–33,
  35, 57, 60–61, 63–64, 76–78,
  124–25, 130–31, 205; deprived
  yangban, 60; traditions of, 33
Yi dynasty, 10, 13, 15, 19, 23, 31–
  33, 35, 57, 75–76, 124, 130,
  167, 199
Yi Ha-ung (Taewŏn'gun), 10
Yi Hwang (T'oegye), 56, 76
Yŏngnam School, 56, 76;
  descendants of, 77
Yoo, Sangjin, 52
Yoshino, M. Y., 206

Zaibatsu, of the Japanese, 52, 87–
  88

About the Author

PROFESSOR CHOONG SOON KIM, born and reared in Korea, came to the United States in 1965. He received degrees in law (L.L.B. & L.L.M.) from Yonsei University, Seoul, Korea; an M.A. in sociology from Emory University; and a Ph.D. in anthropology from the University of Georgia.

In 1971, he joined the faculty of the Department of Sociology and Anthropology at The University of Tennessee at Martin. From 1981 to 1991, he has been the chair of the department. He was Visiting Professor at the Institute of Foreign Affairs and National Security, Ministry of Foreign Affairs, Republic of Korea (1981); Fulbright Professor at Seoul National University, Seoul, Korea (1988–89); and Hirosaki University Visiting Professor, Hirosaki, Japan (1990).

Besides monographs, chapters of books, and articles in professional journals, he authored *An Asian Anthropologist in the South: Field Experiences with Blacks, Indians, and Whites* (Knoxville: University of Tennessee Press, 1977, 1984 paper) and *Faithful Endurance: An Ethnography of Korean Family Dispersal* (Tucson, University of Arizona Press, 1988).

Currently, he is doing fieldwork on Japanese industry in Tennessee to examine the role of culture.